450

GOD AND THE COMMON LIFE

by

ROBERT LOWRY CALHOUN
Yale University

The Shoe String Press

51 Caroline Street   Hamden 17, Connecticut

TO

EDWARD THOMAS CALHOUN, M.D.
1900–1927

AND

ALFRED MAURICE WAKEMAN, M.D.
1897–1929

Foreword to the second printing, 1954.

Reissue of <u>God and the Common Life</u>, now twenty years old, calls for some brief comment on its relation to current theology and to my own thinking, past and present. The mood of current theology, especially in Europe but also in North America, is now far more strongly colored by the influences of Kierkegaard and Barth, of Schweitzer and Bultmann, of Buber and Heidegger than when the book was written. Concern with the natural and social sciences and with philosophy not merely as rivals but as contributors to theological insight runs counter to much present-day thinking. Indeed, it represents a kind of liberal Protestant thought now widely held to be outmoded, if not positively unchristian. My argument was developed, moreover, in a way that has led very friendly critics to read it as an essay in the kind of "natural theology" that seeks to substitute sense experience and speculative reason for revelation and faith as the proper ground of theology.

If I were able to rewrite the book today, I should certainly try to make its perspective and presuppositions stand out more clearly. These were referred to more than once, but evidently without sufficient emphasis (e. g. , pp. viii on "the deep roots," 3 on "My own belief in God," 147-8, 236-40, 243). The argument was meant not to dispense with revelation and faith, but to suggest some interrelations, practical and theoretic, between what is affirmed in Christian faith and what goes on in homes, workshops, laboratories, and classrooms throughout the working world. This basic intention still seems to me valid, and the exploratory temper,and most of the conclusions of the argument I should still affirm and defend. More generally, I should hold that there is just now especial need to re-emphasize many distinctive insights of liberal Protestant thought, which cannot be discarded without serious damage to the Church's effort to speak to the world of our day.

At the same time, my understanding of some major doctrines presupposed but not examined in the book has changed substantially. The revelation of God in Jesus Christ, the significance of the Bible and of Christian tradition for theology, the doctrine of radical creation, and the Church as living matrix of Christian life and thought have appeared in new dimensions and established new perspectives in my thinking. Some of these changes are discernible in part in later published statements: for example, in chapter 4 of The Meaning of the Humanities (ed. T. M. Greene, 1939), in chapter 3 of Making the Gospel Effective (ed. W. K. Anderson, 1945), in the opening chapters of Lectures on the History of Christian Doctrine (privately printed, 1948), and in Work and Vocation (ed. J. O. Nelson, 1954). The last of these volumes develops in a more strictly theological context the theme of vocation in daily work, with which the present book opens.

That theme, along with the whole problem of the place of Christian laymen in the Church and the world, is being explored today with new vigor, in ecumenical discussion. There is good reason to hope that far more adequate statements than any thus far achieved will result. The issue is full of controversial aspects, and much work remains to be done by spokesmen for diverse traditions in Christian thought.

Meanwhile, my thanks go to my colleagues, Prof. Raymond Morris and Mr. John Ottemiller, for undertaking this reprint of one contribution to the debate, and to Mr. William Savage and Charles Scribner's Sons for helping to make it possible.

R. L. Calhoun

New Haven
May, 1954

PREFACE

There are many who wonder why folk should spend time and energy in theological speculation. The answer appears to be partly that many of us, for one cause or another, cannot help doing it; and partly that it seems worth doing. The problems of theology are the obscure but practically inescapable problems bound up with human duty and destiny, and whoever permits his attention (as who does not, now and then) to dwell upon these and to venture trial answers to them is engaged in quasi-theological speculation of some sort, however undeveloped. Moreover, this seems worth doing, for the sake of poise, perspective, and a general heightening of one's total response to the universe in which, willy-nilly, one has to live. Theology so conceived may properly have much in common with the sciences and the more exact philosophical disciplines on one side, and with poetry and music on the other, without being simply identical with either. It may seek to combine something of the intellectual scrupulousness and precision of the one with something of the emotional verve of the other; and thus seek to help men recover, from time to time, that sense of direction and zest for living which in the rapid, confusing flux of events continually tends to be lost.

The present book should be read as a minor study in this major field. The somewhat wide title announces, fairly enough I think, the area to which it is meant to give attention. But the treatment is sharply restricted in a number of ways. First, the discussion is held by intent almost entirely to what may be called a broadly behavioristic line. This does not mean that conscious processes and introspectively discovered data are ruled out. Far from it. They are much too evident a part of human behavior to be excluded by any but a narrow behaviorism. It does mean that everyday human behavior and its total objective setting, rather than the subtle nuances of "inner experience," occupy most of the argument; the visible trunk and branches of religious living and thinking, rather than their roots or their final fruit. It means that attention is given mainly to what can be spoken of in fairly articulate prose, and that only now and again is the argument permitted to lapse into something like half-fledged hymnody. It means in particular that the deep roots of all religion and theology and everyday living, in faith and in insight of various sorts, are everywhere presupposed, occasionally referred to, but nowhere closely examined. This is not (as with more exclusive behaviorisms, religious or secular) because these partly buried roots seem to me unessential; but, on the contrary, because I need to spend much more time in trying to make out what they do and do not involve.

Secondly, this study (like most other current theological writings, but more blatantly than some) betrays from beginning to end a western-masculine point of view, and the prejudices that go with it. This is said not by way of apology, but merely as a statement of fact and a general caution. I have tried to set down here as clearly as I can some account of that approach to the central problems of living which has seemed to me most valid: an approach in which everyday work has a basic place. Whether or not the central point is well made in this essay, I think it likely that to most westerners—at any rate to most men and to some women—it would appeal, if properly presented, as more or less sound and relevant. But I suspect also that to many—perhaps especially to many women —it would seem even at best to miss the most important things in religion altogether. And perhaps it does. If true religion be, for example, pre-eminently a matter of feeling, or of purely personal communion, of quiescent insight, or of unquestioning surrender, then certainly it does. For though this view by no means ignores nor belittles these factors, it does not give them first place. It is quite clear to me that such factors, as I now conceive them and as most writers known to me have described them, should not have first place. But the point is that our whole western-masculine theological perspective may in due course be drastically modified, by more effective pressing upon us of other modes of life and thought than those we have hitherto had presented and described, as "live options." However that be, if the present view points as I hope to a significant part of the truth, it cannot be more than a small part, at best.

Thirdly, the work is restricted not only by the author's intent, and by his inbred perspective, but by his lack of competence in many directions. Special students will quickly discover, and other readers should in fairness be warned, that of the dozen-and-one technical fields into which this account ventures, I have for the most part only such knowledge as a layman may gather from a few books and articles twice or thrice removed from the laboratories and original papers of the specialists. I am painfully aware of shallowness, crudities, and probable errors in my understanding of both the natural sciences and the more concrete social studies; and no part of the essay which deals primarily with these matters should be regarded as in any sense authoritative.

Preface

Within its limits, however, I hope the book may seem to have been worth writing. For the reader who is immersed in the multiple problems of living in a "power age," I hope it may serve as a kind of swift reconnoitring of familiar ground from a perhaps unfamiliar angle; and a pointing of a possible way to approach the reunion of practical and speculative thought which, by common consent, we badly need. For the most part our practical thinking shies away from inclusive theory, and our speculative theory seldom bothers about the problems of everyday living. It is my firm conviction that, whatever be true of abstract philosophy or of secular shrewdness, it is indispensable that theology concern itself boldly with both the homeliest, oldest practice and the newest far-flung theory. Unless the organic connection of these can be kept tolerably plain, there is little hope of maintaining effective unity of life and thought. I have tried to write in the strength of that conviction, hoping the reader may find some profit in what is said here, and more in what others, better informed, may be moved to say further.

To acknowledge even a fair part of one's accumulating indebtedness to persons and groups, for such an argument as this, is manifestly impossible; and in setting down here the names of some, I find myself hoping that neither omission nor inclusion may seem to any of these good friends ground for complaint. Of my teachers, Dean L. A. Weigle and Prof. J. E. Boodin, who introduced me as an undergraduate to philosophy, and later Profs. A. K. Rogers and C. A. A. Bennett in philosophy, and D. C. Macintosh in theology, contributed most directly to giving me some insight into these modes of thought. For glimpses of scientific method and spirit, and of the subject matter of various natural sciences, I am in debt to

Profs. F. F. Exner, L. A. Headley, R. S. Lull, Raymond Hussey (chiefly through my brother), and Clark Hull, and Dr. A. J. Wakeman; though none of them should be held accountable for my present notions. From the two young medical men to whom the book is inscribed, I seem to have learned, in these matters, most of all. Among others of my contemporaries, colleagues, students, and friends, I have learned from very many: perhaps most from conversations, in season and out of season, with Profs. Roland Bainton, Richard and Reinhold Niebuhr, Cornelius Krusé, Filmer Northrop, Edwin Aubrey, John Bennett, Herman Brautigam, and John K. Benton.

To groups no less than to individuals I am directly and heavily obliged for basic conceptions in this book. The school in which I have worked, year in, year out, with fellow-teachers and fellow-students, has given me some notion of what contributive work at a common task might become. Less formal groups—a small ungloved, tough-minded circle called "the club"; a series of Hazen Conferences; an anonymous theological discussion group of twenty-six assorted and strenuous companions—have broken up premature habit-patterns and kept my thoughts moving. The household in which Ella Wakeman Calhoun, and David, Ted, Robert Maurice, Harriet and I have lived together at close range has done more to my thinking than any of them suspects. It is these, with my mother while she lived, and with friends too close or too numerous to name here, who have made it seem to me intolerable to think and write theology without continual reference to everyday needs and facts.

So obvious is my dependence, at every step, upon what others have written, and upon the actual unwritten tradition of Christian thinking and living, that detailed acknowledgments of such debts would be absurd. I cannot omit, however, a word of gratitude to Prof. A. N. Whitehead, whose later writings came to me as a kind of revelation.

The argument of this book was first prepared for delivery as the Nathaniel W. Taylor Lectures at Yale University, in April, 1934. Since then the text has been appreciably expanded, and completely revised more than once, into what I trust is a more effective form. Parts of the manuscript have been read by Profs. R. H. Bainton, E. E. Aubrey, and Norman Torrey, Dr. C. F. Virtue, and Messrs. W. H. Wulfeck and R. M. Fagley, and discussed informally by other friendly critics; and the text has been improved in response to their comments. The opening paragraphs of chapter one were written in their present form before the delivery of Prof. Dewey's Terry Lectures, since published under the title *A Common Faith*. The unobtrusive and competent help of Mr. W. L. Savage and other members of the publisher's staff has made the task of getting the book into print a pleasant part of the whole job of work. I am grateful also to Dr. Amos B. Hulen and to Mr. and Mrs. Donald F. West for needed help with the copy and proofs.

R. L. C.

New Haven, Connecticut,
March, 1935.

CONTENTS

xiii

Contents

Contents

Contents

Contents

Contents

Contents

Contents

Contents

Such Mind as Doer may be thought of as having "natural predilection" and conscious preference for the actualization, at each new juncture, of some possibilities and the exclusion of others: hence, as purposive and good. So acting, God may be thought free from ignorance, inner conflict, restrictions in space-time, and inferiority to particular finite forces: hence, *omnipotent*. But His omnipotence is not absolute, any more than His omniscience: being limited by the very perfection of His own goodness, and by "rigidities" and by waywardness in the world, 189–196.

A second analogy: an "inspiring" leader, in relation with his followers, 196–197.

God is *transcendent* with respect to all human persons: both as Subject (absolutely), and as regards each and all of His attributes (relatively), 197–198.

God also is related to men in the way of *"communicative immanence,"* through revelation and inspiration—or calling, 199–200.

C. THE WORKING OF GOD: A MYTHOS OF REDEMPTIVE WORLD-MAKING.

First stage: establishment and maintenance of conditions suitable for the emergence, growth, and activity of creatures capable of appreciating and achieving good. Upon such creative effort, even for God, inescapable difficulties press, 201–203.

Second stage: calling into existence finite minds, as individuals in social groups. New difficulties arise and persist, 203.

Third stage: quickening such finite selves into conscious devotion to good and co-working with God. The redemptive task of overcoming evil with good, 203–204.

xxii

Contents

Contents

GOD AND THE COMMON LIFE

INTRODUCTION

It seems right to begin these chapters about God and our common life with a rough estimate of what we are concerned to do. Two questions are basic to everything that will be said: Are there in everyday life now intimations of the presence of the Living God? And if such there be, how shall we align our thinking and living with their demands? We shall make no attempt by argument to prove that God exists, nor shall we presuppose it as self-evident, nor assure ourselves of it by definition. It seems to me not in any such wise assured. My own belief in God, and I suspect that of many others who believe, has been generated painfully enough, not by argument but by the concrete ebb and flow of living, in ways that I do not fully understand and cannot control. What may better be attempted, I judge, in such argumentative discussion as this, is not the genesis of such belief, but an inquiry whether and on what terms at this present juncture it may suitably be held, and how it bears on other matters of current anxiety.

No one here need be told that we are in·a time of exaggerated haste, when thinking no less than action swings from extreme to extreme. The Renaissance itself was not, I suspect, a more breathless time. We have outgrown a familiar world-view, compacted of Newtonian physics and evolutionary optimism, which until recently had served us much as Aristotelian physics and scholastic faith had served the men of the later Middle Age; and the confusions of a burgeoning new era are once more upon us. Our fundamentally sober natural sciences have tasted the mixed wine of exciting discovery and popular acclaim, and show noticeable elevation of voice and manner. A more varied array than Medici and Borgias knew of social and political theorists and practitioners, men of vision, men of shrewdness, and men of violence, offer us contradictory advice and leadership. And now as then, preachers and theologians also are trying to make themselves heard in behalf of irreconcilable modes of thought. Neo-pagans within and without the Churches contend against devotees, radical and reactionary. The old social passion of prophets and sectaries reappears alike among staunch theists and militant atheists. Liberals of various milder hues, trying to understand and to be understood by everybody, find themselves manœuvred into alliance with pious naturalism and humanism on the one side, and with cultured mysticism and pietism on the other. An older sort of theological realism, in which faith and reason alike have place, sturdily holds its ground under heavy fire. And against all these arises once more the voice of disillusioned dogmatic faith, uplifted as in Luther's day out of philosophic skepticism, and crying woe on all human reason and human pride.

If one could observe now this turmoil with a god's or an historian's detachment, one might find ours a virile and promising epoch, as human epochs go. But we are less than gods and more than historians. We are live creatures caught, for better, for worse, in the flux of a very baffling present. We stagger about in the conflicting rip tides that always swirl between a cultural phase on the ebb and its yet unrisen successor, fending off wreckage here and marauders there, hardly able to distinguish between friend and foe, and prevented from seeing clearly so much as a cable's length ahead. Some of us, blessed with strong stomachs and limited imaginations, can take sides hardily, plunge about at full cry, and revel in the uproar. Blessed is he whose eye is single! But others of us, not wholly lacking the joy of combat and rough weather, desire intensely a sense of direction which many temporarily have lost. Without it we feel neither virility nor promise in our dizzy locomotion. We can of course, if worse comes to worst, blindly and grimly hang on. Few live things, I suppose, lack that sort of ultimate obstinacy. But, for us, significant living must be more or less coherent and directed living. We must needs try to take bearings from time to time, and lay a course as well as we can, even in the midst of drifting fog and running sea.

In clear weather, the more expert navigators among us perhaps would chart us a truer course by the stars. But for now, with the experts having their own difficulties, we plain mariners seem called on to find our way more simply by compass and dead reckoning, which is to say "without celestial observations." The stars covered, the horizon obscured, where now shall we find a base line from which to reckon? In the mind of man? But how widely just now the minds of men seem to diverge. In Nature? Perhaps. But Nature has little directly to say about good and bad, right and wrong, better and worse—the values that concern us all so vitally. And even as to matters of fact, Nature of late has dazzled us with new problems rather than vouchsafed us final answers to the old ones. Within our own generation she has ceased to talk in the plain, downright, British manner of Newton and Darwin, just as 500 years ago she began to abandon the dry, lucid, Latinized prose of Aristotle. As she prompted Nicolaus Cusanus then, she is prompting our keenest scientists now to mistrust the premature findings of confident common sense in these matters, and to cultivate instead the more exact but much less simple language of what Cusanus called *docta ignorantia,* "instructed ignorance," the complicated tentativeness of those who expertly know that they know not, and somewhat exactly why. What Nature has to tell—and plainly it is much—our expert inquirers are better equipped than ever before to find out, and they are pushing ahead with enthusiasm. But their inquiries just now are very technical ones, conducted in very difficult terms; and in spite of their most friendly readiness to help us, we plain folk will not easily get from their fascinating but tantalizing accounts all the present guidance we require. Something simpler and nearer home is what we need, at least as a point of departure.

Shall we look then to God, who once was said to be "not far from each one of us"? Is He the base line from which our thinking and living must proceed? Today, to put that question at all seems to many a well-meant but unmeaning anachronism. It may be true or be not true, for all we know, that "God's in his heaven." Celestial observations are not easy just now. But here below, in the sickening lurch and swirl of our muddled world, He most plainly is not. Of thus much, disillusioned millions are sure: sprightly skeptics and tired radicals, cultured humanitarians and disinherited waifs of the old order; aggressive Marxists, humanists, instrumentalists, and opportunists who hope to usher in the new. Indeed, even theologians— the most assured, the most vocal, and the most brilliant group, at least, of Protestant theologians—are now proclaiming that God is indeed not "here" as we have been taught to suppose. We who have called ourselves liberal, modern Christians, assured of His nearness, now find ourselves charged all along the line with well-meaning folly.

6

And certain of the words of more than one of these groups have the disconcerting ring of truth.

Let us remind ourselves, for a moment, how this has come about. Say we modern folk like our forebears have been stirred, now and again, by a strangely moving story of God born in the reek of a stable and nailed to a cross between groaning thieves, and thereby triumphant. (I mean not the decorous stories we tell our children at Christmas and Easter. I mean the evangel that broke its way through the Roman Empire and unseated the ancient gods.) Say the inmost core of life, strong and sweet and caustic as flame, has seemed to us at times to be in that story, and that we have hoped against hope that it might be true. Even so we have not wished to be sentimental fools. We have learned what we could, therefore, about men and the world; we have separated out mythical and legendary strands and speculative accretions in the tale; and we have seen its miraculous light and music fade for the most part to a dim, far-off halo behind a handful of emerging facts. Not God, it would seem, but a very human prophet of Nazareth was crucified under Pontius Pilate; and in sober fact no one was born in the Bethlehem stable at all. So for us the first crude power of the story has been drained away; and we will not delude ourselves into thinking that it can be easily restored.

But the scholars and thinkers who thus with one hand have taken away the old talisman, with the other have offered us a surety more suited to modern minds: the assured presence of God immanent as Law and inner Life in Nature and in Man. On this view, "the starry heavens above and the moral law within" not merely proclaim God: they are God, in whom also we live and move and have our being. In our several degrees we plain·folk, then, are vessels of Deity, filled to divers levels with God Himself—though ordinarily we use discreeter language to veil so considerable a claim. Moreover, a world thus alive with God cannot be to us other than a favorable world; whether with the idealists we regard it as through and through good even now, or whether with various pluralists, realists, and pious naturalists we hold it in the main good, and steadily growing better. This last way of thinking, indeed, has had an especial vogue, so simple and reassuringly modern it obviously is.

> "Some call it Evolution,
> And others call it God."

So, in a sentence, many a liberal of the early twentieth century has comfortably believed. So we have been recompensed for the passing of the old strange tale. What need, truly, of incarnation and crucifixion in a world simply and beautifully full of God, as the waters cover the sea?

Very modern, yes; and smooth and comfortable as an ocean liner. Icebergs and storms are not modern. Neither are human stupidities, brutalities and miseries, and fierce loves and heroisms and hates. They loom slowly or suddenly out of the darkness, and suave theories go to pieces against them. Then boats put off, and go this way and that, and the sea takes on a different look. One is aware now of its power, as never in the calm days up on the sundeck; and one's thinking takes fuller account of ice and wind and fog, not because one likes to think about them, but because they can no longer be ignored. If the words of the Marxists and Barthians are impressive just now, it is mainly because they have had their eyes open to the plight we are in. Not their passionate rhetoric alone, but facts and logic make their words carry weight, now that more of us are able to see the disturbing facts to which they

8

point. And further weighing of the facts, as we come increasingly to see what they are, must help determine how far we can follow their judgments and their proffered guidance.

Both are certain that liberal religion is a hopeless wreck. Its faith in the decency and educability of human beings under past and present conditions has been childish; its trust in gradual progress ludicrous; and its talk of an immanent God either delusive tommyrot or blasphemy, according as one sides with Lenin or with Barth. Moreover, the whole complacent philosophy of Hegelian idealism and evolution and what not that has underlain much of liberal theology is dismissed with scorn by dialectical materialists and dialectic theologians alike. But having thus abandoned ship, they are laying essentially different courses. Hard-headed followers of Lenin forswear dependence on divine powers (including, in practice, the supposed "dialectical" progressions of matter by which more doctrinaire Marxists have set so much store), and pin their hopes to revolutionary human intelligence and will. Disciples and associates of Barth, on the contrary, denounce all dependence on human powers, and put all their trust in the transcendent "God Who Is God."

Which way, then, shall we go? With the one or the other of these confident crews? With the battered liberals or the grim conservatives who still do not envisage disaster? Or upon some other course than any of these?

One more remark, and we shall set about seeking an answer. Say that with these merciless critics, we have been driven to relinquish a too easy assurance that God is in us and we are in God, and all is well. What has either of them to offer us that squares better with the facts and with our needs? Marxism says: "Man disillusioned, and a world

9

in which strong men can work." Barthianism says. "God infinitely remote, Whom disillusioned men can worship." Both good, say we: but each lacking that which the other puts foremost, and both lacking something we must still keenly desire, however disillusioned, if we are fully alive to what it means. No doubt if nothing better should offer, we could go with one or another of such companies and do our part, as others are doing. But if without self-stultification we can recover in some live form what was once moving and heartening in the story of the Word made flesh, life would be the better for it. No doubt man the worker, self-reliant, clear-headed, and devoted to the well-being of his class, would be a good shipmate (supposing ourselves to belong to his class) in this sort of world. No doubt God at an "infinite distance," God hidden like stars behind fog, must be an object of adoration whenever (or if ever) faith comes to us that He is there. But stout shipmates and far-off stars are not enough. Surely one is right to ask whether, besides these, there are stable magnetic fields that somehow permeate storm and calm and fog and ocean and all, unseen but steady and reassuring. If such there be, they would not steer for us: our eyes and hands must do that, with all the blundering to which human hands are liable. But they would enable us to recover direction from time to time, and to maintain sanity and rational hope. To know that one must sail where there are no magnetic poles would be a nightmare, in spite of some bold talk we hear. But given the poles, and some sort of compass to say, "There, or thereabout, lies the north," even ordinary sailors can make shift to live, or it may be to die, like human beings.

So much for preamble. Now to our task. We must try

throughout to keep a middle course between the enunciation of abstract principles, and the attempt to deal expertly with details of fact and technique. The prime concern of theology is to help keep men rightly oriented in the midst of actual living; especially as regards the basic human attitudes and dispositions which constitute morale, and the basic structure and flow of the universe with which human dispositions must align themselves or end in failure. Neither abstract principles nor detailed techniques and facts are foreign to the theologian's concern, but he must not yield to the temptation to devote himself, as a specialist may and must, to the intricacies of either the one or the other. Always at the risk of ridiculous errors, to which the expert in abstractions or in details is less exposed, he must try to see how facts and principles illuminate one another, so as together to give indication of the way in which human life should turn.

In these brief chapters we shall be trying, naturally, not to present in review an entire theology, but rather to explore in part one main line of argument which seems of importance; reminding ourselves of a number of very familiar principles, and following out some of their more apparent consequences. The outlines of a sort of theology may appear now and again, but we must hope at best for no more than rough orientation. Where so many of the relevant data are inaccessible, and where specialists do not yet agree even as to what is open to inspection, exactitude plainly is not to be had by inquirers like ourselves.

CHAPTER ONE

THE DAY'S WORK AS VOCATION

To seek in the everyday life of plain people for intimations of God should suggest at once to begin with the day's work and the yearly round. For it was there, primarily, that among much simpler folk religion was grounded. There were overtones of deity in hunting, fighting, and fire-making; in the seasonal routine of ploughing, planting, and reaping; in all labor and rest from labor; in birth, maturing, marriage, and death. When Hesiod wrote of the gods and their impact on human life, he called his book *Works and Days*. The Hebrew psalmists and prophets could picture Yahweh or his Servant as a shepherd, and the Messiah of the new age was reared in a carpenter's home. Festivals and holy days were rooted in the seasons of work, which they were meant to celebrate, purify, and enhance; both by enlisting the gods on behalf of working men, and by putting the workers in mind of the gods, their goodness, and their demands. When these sabbaths and rituals became pious formalities detached from everyday life, prophets and thinkers alike denounced them as play-acting and sham, despised by the very gods they professed to honor. Here as elsewhere, these men were saying in effect, what by nature and of right belongs together cannot by man be put asunder without vital damage to both the severed parts. A secularized, self-centred daily life on the one hand, and formalized pious occasions on the other, become scarred fragments which neither taken separately nor added together can be a living whole.

But their protests, by and large, were unavailing. The separation of work and worship went on, as indeed in some sense it had to go on, as civilizations developed. So that in our day it is precisely with such disjoined members, secularized work and detached worship, that we have mostly to deal. Bewail it as we may, the crude wholeness of primitive life is gone, and unless we relapse into barbarism it cannot, in its crude form, be recovered. There are those, in the Orient and in the West, who for the sake of a finer spiritual life desire that we return to a village polity and a handicraft economy. Most of us cannot share that desire. Whatever one may think of the sprawling monstrosity called modern civilization—and I trust none of us thinks of it more highly than one ought to think—it is hardly possible not to see spiritual gains of the first importance, for work and for worship alike, that have come with the displacement of simpler by more complex stages of human life. Work at its best has gained in objectivity and clarity of conception, precision of method, and integrity of appraisal, with the progressive elimination of irrelevant supernaturalisms. Where once men were quick to see capricious divine or diabolic influences at work in the weather, the course of a disease, or the shaping of a character, and spent energy uselessly in trying to circumvent or to propitiate them, we have learned in some measure to keep our eyes on the job, and to do better work in consequence. Worship too has gained some degree of freedom from the crasser sort of utilitarian employment for human ends, as we have begun to learn not to pray for rain, nor to pledge votive offerings for release from peril; and the advance in human understanding and control of nature, which many have feared as presaging the death of religion, has at least cleared away a vast underbrush of devil-fears

13

and devil-worships that choke the path of high religion in those simpler cultures which we so easily idealize. To go back, deliberately with Gandhi or inadvertently with the Fascists or by way of a large enough war, would for us no more obviously serve the cause of fine spiritual life than it would serve the cause of better public health.

Yet with all that, one may share acutely in the ancient prophets' disquiet over the separation of religion from everyday life, and of worship from everyday work. Two tendencies, both understandable and both regrettable, have led to the most unfortunate aspects of that separation. First, with increasing diversification of what once was communal life, religion tended not unnaturally to become a special rather than a pervasive interest. And like other special pursuits it came to be regarded as primarily the concern of a distinct vocational group, clerical and monastic, whereas for most people it was expected to come in mainly on special occasions, from outside the daily round. Which is to say that for most people, busy with everyday living, religion has become increasingly unreal, or at least unfamiliar and irrelevant. Secondly, as human ingenuity has extended the sphere of man's control over nature, the lives of a growing number have come to be spent more and more entirely within the artificial environment thus produced, and their attention occupied more and more continuously with the multiplying evidences of human prowess. When this preoccupation has taken the form chiefly of incurious or superficially curious exploitation, rather than appreciative understanding of human work and its products in their essential interrelations with one another and with Nature, the world has come to be for the plain man a shrill medley of garish, up-to-date details rather than, as in earlier days, a dimly apprehended and deeply moving whole. The sidewalks of New York and the "Century of Progress" are indeed, as critics so often remind us, at a far remove from Hesiod's rural Hellas, and the villages and countrysides of first century Galilee. To our city-dwelling millions religion is likely to come, if at all, as the verses from Job on "Arcturus, Orion, and the Pleiades" came in at the opening of the Chicago display in 1933: a vaguely agreeable, but obsolescent and none too relevant reverberation of once profoundly meaningful words.

Of this degrading sterilization we who intone the words are aware, with acute discomfort. Children of image-breaking ancestors, we have no desire to be numbered now somewhere with crooners and bedtime-story tellers, among the minor professional entertainers of our time—among the *hypocritai,* the "play-actors" whom genuine spokesmen for God so deeply scorn. We have publicly confessed and deplored this unreality in our worship, and in our theology and ethics, and have sought (not without some success) to avoid it. We have tried to be simple, honest, and humane in these matters; to avoid fulsome pretense no less than emotional inebriety. But something plainly is lacking which our forebears did not lack. To wit: body and bone for these scrupulous spirits of ours. Refinements and avoidances have not been enough. We must begin to fear becoming spiritual starvelings, fed on discriminating words, thoughts, misgivings, regrets, and on artificially insulated, diffident efforts at reform. Not so our Protestant grandsires, to look no further back. Their sinewy piety knew plenty of restraints, but nothing of thin-blooded diffidence. Their very doubtings were robust and urgent self-tortures; and the restraints they laid on themselves and on others were just the reverse side of driving, confident wills. Not deficient in spiritual discernment, albeit to our notion far from irreproachable in either taste or judgment, their religious living had also vigor that we may well covet and emulate.

None would doubt that its ultimate ground was an overwhelming faith in God. But as to the concrete, proximate conditions of such faith and such vitality, judgments differ. Some have pointed to the stringent Puritan self-discipline, and have recommended to us more of such rigors for ourselves. Some have thought the Reformers' zeal essentially sprung from certitude as to a peremptory Word of God, sounding in the Bible or through it; and urge that to recover such assurance we disavow the premises and the major findings of modern Biblical scholarship, or else accept and then nullify them by an ingenious dogmatic *tour de force.* I doubt that either of these counsels gets to the root of the matter. Such vitality as those men had and we need must spring, if it is to be lasting, not primarily from prohibitions nor from dogmatic abstractions, but from a positive, realistic, and fully concrete faith that lays hold at once of what seem to the believer fruitful working principles and generous masses of fact; and that can be sustained by actual, whole-hearted effort to realize these principles in practice. To remind us that Cromwell's Ironsides and Bradford's Pilgrims were sternly disciplined is pertinent, no doubt; but we need still to know why they were ready to endure such discipline, and what concrete ends it subserved. Restraints are meaningless apart from positive drives. To extol faith, moreover, in contrast with feeling and with phantasy and all pseudo-knowledge, is salutary indeed; but pure faith, *sola fides* in the extreme sense of empty alertness, *Hohlraum,* intent waiting, can no more prompt and guide actual human living than the Kantian formal imperative which it so much resembles, and even faith "that the Word of God is God's Word" [1] * is still far too abstract. We need, as our ancestors needed, to be possessed by a positive concrete conviction— a form filled with engrossing, inexhaustible content—if we are to recover that real and effective sense of day-to-day urgency, opportunity, and obligation for want of which the thinner sorts of Christianity have come to compare so badly with what we have been told of working Communism at its youthful best.

I

A. One way to such unifying and living conviction as we need, I believe, was rediscovered and rightly marked, though far from fully reopened, by the much-discussed Protestant teaching about vocation. Against the regnant monastic ideal of the mediæval Church, which held up the lives of celibate clergy and religious as more pleasing to God than the lives of ordinary folk engaged in doing the ordinary work of the world, Luther and Calvin followed and overpassed the lead of certain mystics and mediæval preachers in applying to these common pursuits the impressive term *vocatio,* that meant "divine calling." [2]

(1) It was the term that in various tongues had been used from St. Paul's day to signify God's bidding ("election") of Christians to eternal salvation. From one point of view this was a hidden, eternal decree; from another a gracious summons addressed directly to the inmost heart and mind of every believer. The Church was made up of all those "summoned" from the world in this manner; hence its name, *ecclesia.*[3] In one passage, however (I Cor. 7:8–24 and uniquely in verse 20), St. Paul had used the

* A superior figure refers to the notes on p. 253.

term *klēsis,* "calling," to mean not the inner call but the outward conditions of life, the status—marital, ritual, social—in the midst of which, to this believer or that, the inner call had come. "Let each man abide in that calling" —in that status, as married or unmarried, circumcized or uncircumcized, bond or free—"wherein he was called," since these outward conditions in God's eyes count for nothing. When the Latin translations were made, the term *klēsis* here as elsewhere was of course rendered *vocatio,* and a tenuous Biblical basis provided for the later doctrinal development. But this passage, and particularly the unparalleled use of "calling" in verse 20,[4] remained through most of the middle ages virtually unnoticed.

(2) Another usage, however, came into increasing prominence from the fourth century which in a quite different way associated the inward "call" with a certain outward condition of life: the status, namely, of monks and nuns, "the religious," who separated themselves from a Church grown soft and secular, in favor with men rather than God. Not believers generally but professed ascetics now felt themselves "called," like Abraham, to a separate career upon earth: to go out from their homes, renouncing earthly ties, and to become chosen "soldiers of Christ" and, like Abraham, "friends of God." The inward call was, for them, a personal call to "perfection." But perfection meant nothing less than utter love toward God, and involved the renunciation—as Matt. 18:8–9; 19:12, 21 seemed plainly to advise—of all that might divide or divert such love: in short, of all earthly ambitions and affections. This inward "call" to perfection and, by transfer of meaning, the overt adoption and practice of the monastic life which it implied, was what *vocatio* came to mean ordinarily in mediæval parlance.[5]

Toward the close of the period, during the fourteenth
and fifteenth centuries, the more expansive vision of certain mystics headed by Eckardt and Tauler, with their un-
conventional perspective of things human and divine, led
to a fresh appraisal of life outside the cloister. Dissatisfied,
like the monks of a thousand years before, with the conventional piety of their day, including now that of the mon-
asteries, they too felt themselves "called" to a higher perfection: to become "friends of God" who experience the
actual *visio Dei* and union with Him even in this life. On
the one hand, this called for a more complete withdrawal
from earthly things, a more thorough self-abandonment,
than even monastic asceticism by itself implied: ascetic
practices were at best only preliminary to the mystic vision.
On the other hand, some of the mystics roundly asserted
that this highest level of perfection was possible not only
for monks but even for the humblest laborer—the man
flailing corn or braking nettles;[6] and that therefore an
earthly occupation wherein such a one toiled faithfully and
lovingly in service of his neighbor could be for him, no less
truly than life in the cloister, a medium for the vision of
God. To such occupations Tauler, in a stirring sermon on
Ephesians 4, applied directly the term *Ruf,* "calling"; and
his example was followed by other Dominican preachers
and by plain folk in sufficient number to establish this
novel usage in familiar speech by Luther's day. But the
superiority of contemplative to active life, of the faithful
monk living in accordance with the evangelical "counsels
of perfection" over the faithful layman obeying only the
"precepts of the law," even the mediæval mystics did not
question; and the traditional term *vocatio,* unlike the vernacular *Ruf,* seems to have been reserved still for the monastic or clerical calling.[7]

(3) It was the Reformers who took, not at first without evident hesitation, the further drastic step that wiped out these distinctions. Monastic austerities for the sake of excess merit they rejected as worse than useless; and they affirmed with a new radicalness of meaning that only through faithfulness in the task providentially ordained for him could any man obey God as far as a man may. To this everyday task and station Luther now applied the emphatic and distinctive vernacular term *Beruf,* Calvin the corresponding *vocation,* and both the traditional *vocatio.* Not that what a man can do with his hands and brain is in itself pleasing to God, but that all God requires of any man—faith and obedience—can be shown by each of the elect in that place, whatever it be, to which the divine will has assigned him. Their set doctrinal statements gave more attention to denying the merit of monastic "good works" [8] than to praise of ordinary labor as such. But in certain of Luther's more spontaneous utterances,[9] in one notable passage in Calvin's chief work,[10] and more generally in their diverse but kindred modes of living, Luther, Calvin, and their like-minded contemporaries set the example for a genuinely new estimate of everyday life and toil. It was a fresh and authentic, though still not fully comprehended nor completed, approach toward reassertion of the ancient premise that worship and ordinary work belong together; that the adoration of God should be integral to, and not sundered from everyday life. Its intent, and in a measure its effect, was once more to make common things clean.

In a measure, only. The full logical and practical import of such doctrine for social organization could not be appreciated when feudal thought-patterns had only begun to break down, nor its full import for theology and ethics while polemic was still at fever heat, and persecution be-

fogged issues that called for the utmost clarity of judgment. In consequence, the doctrine was inadequately conceived in both Lutheranism and primitive Calvinism, and
the way was prepared for a warped and one-sided development later, when it was forced to closer grips with a rising
new secular culture. In the first place, the prime concern
of this really bold teaching was ecclesiastical and theological reform, but definitely not economic and social reconstruction. In Luther's mind its implicit social radicalism,
like that of his great cognate doctrine, "the common (*all-
gemein,* universal) priesthood of believers," was counter-
balanced by an economic and political naïveté and a profound religious conservatism that precluded, for him, such
revolutionary inferences on behalf of the common man as
thoroughgoing insurgents could draw. Calvin's more
strenuous ethic and more realistic political attitude led him
into far more aggressive participation in secular affairs
than Luther ever attempted. But as regards practical bearings of the concept of earthly vocation, his express teaching
also was that of one who had only begun to move out on
this new line of thought, and gave no hint of the powerful,
far-reaching social leverage such doctrine could have in
less sternly repressive hands.[11]

This failure to associate theological with social reconstruction was no mere inadvertence. Rather, it reflected
a definite theological conviction which both Reformers
shared, and which in itself constituted a second and more
basic limitation upon their move toward enfranchisement
of the common life: the conviction that man and his
works are as nothing before God. Neither, rightly enough,
was willing to concede man's ability to find salvation
finally in or through this created world, or indeed to do
anything of ultimate worth by and for himself alone.

Both, pushing thence to extreme (though not fanatic) lengths their exaltation of God and depreciation of man, moved away from what might have been a fuller development of their fresh and vital conception of earthly calling, to less full-orbed—and I think also for our day less fruitful, and in the long run less tenable—positions. Luther, in revolt against every vestige of "salvation by works," took the direction of quietism; Calvin, fearing and hating "idolatry" that would put creatures into the place of God, moved rather toward asceticism. Both these tendencies were as natural to early Protestantism as to any other intensely earnest religious movement. In each a resurgent spirit of religious realism got partial expression, and both contributed in full measure to the sweeping ecclesiastical and cultural changes wrought during the sixteenth century. But other deep-seated forces also were at work, against which both main forms of early Protestantism set themselves stubbornly: forces which appeared in neo-pagan humanism, secularism, the new sciences, and the adventurous restlessness which even then was hurrying Europe into the "modern" age. With these neither the Lutheran nor the Reformed Churches nor the Protestant sects and their descendants, even until now, have come to any satisfactory *rapprochement*. Lutheranism prefers to stand aloof from them; on occasion is ready to oppose their intrusions into its own preserves; but thus far has not succeeded in (nor greatly cared about) understanding, coworking with, nor effectively guiding their development. Calvinism and certain dissenting groups, some of which are now of major size and prestige, have entered into a kind of halfway covenant with the modern world, which is satisfactory to neither party, and gives rise to continual misunderstandings and recriminations from both sides. In the process, the good name of Protestantism has suffered, alike on "spiritual" and on "secular" grounds.

(4) How this has come about is a question debated of late with much animation. Contemporary discussion usually sets out from Max Weber's well-known and warmly disputed theory of the part played by "ascetic Protestantism" in the rise of the modern industrial and commercial order. With the question that has exercised most of his critics—whether "the Protestant ethic" has been a cause or merely an effect of the advance of western capitalism—we are not centrally concerned. Whichever was cause and which effect, or whether as seems more likely[12] each reacted on the other, there is no dispute as to the plain fact that during the seventeenth and eighteenth centuries, changes of major import for both the Church and the world accompanied the spread of Calvinism and sectarian Protestantism on both sides of the Atlantic. During those two centuries, while middle-class capitalism and parliamentary government were on the rise in northern and western Europe and parts of eastern North America, a more aggressive and individualistic type of Protestantism[13] largely came into the ascendant, and among other doctrines, the concept of earthly vocation was given a fresh turn. It is common knowledge now that conspicuous among those who worked and fought for the new economic and political order were congregations, conventicles, regiments of rough men whose pastors were admonishing them to "prove" (test, verify) in devoted, effective action the reality of their "calling" as God's elect. Against these "Neocalvinists" and other "ascetic Protestants," and the various forces with which their efforts were aligned, whether in battle, in debate, or in trade, the old order

could not stand. There is no way to prove that their religious convictions, and specifically their belief in earthly vocation, was an important factor in this victory, though few informed observers would doubt it.[14] But there can be no doubt that the victory had fateful consequences for the concept of vocation.

By these men and their descendants, the concept was invested with unprecedented meaning for the common man, and fixed in the language of everyday living. To work in one's vocation or to follow one's calling was no longer an abstraction which theologians and preachers talked about: it was what the plain man did, when he went from meeting-house or chapel to carry on the daily round. Once more, as in ancient times, God was served through common toil.

B. But to advocate now as a way of life what the term vocation thus came to imply is to court either indifference or protest. The word and the doctrine have lost their savor, and that in large part through the very prospering of those who formerly professed to live by them. For reasons to some of which we shall give attention shortly, their successes in the affairs of this world imperiled their consciousness of obligation toward God. As the new economic and political order became dominant over considerable parts of Europe and America, the conviction of earthly calling cooled into a prosy axiom of middle-class life, vaguely and tacitly taken for granted by everybody rather than consciously held by a determined, devoted group. It has lost thereby its earlier claim upon active, spirited minds. We still speak of our daily pursuits as vocations and callings, bearing unconscious witness to the permeation of ordinary speech by a once novel and daring

24

theological usage. But the words have gone stale. The
magic is drained out of them. Three hundred years of
modern commercial and industrial life have left them
drab and secularized, as "common" as the ad-writing and
face-lifting to which we now so glibly apply them. Indeed, if a sensitive person think at all of their old religious
connotations, it is almost certain to be with embarrassment
or with distaste. At every turn, whether we read the calm
pages of Weber or Tawney on the rise of modern capitalism, or the livelier comments of Mencken and Lewis on
their fellow Americans, the urbane, candid reporting of
Lincoln Steffens, or the tense, earnest, fiercely intelligent
diatribes of Scott Nearing, we are made aware how very
far from vindicated by the course of events, how naïve,
inept, and morally ambiguous the old Protestant teaching
on earthly vocation can seem now to one not biased in
its favor. The day has gone by in which it could serve
forthwith as a rallying-cry for heroism, or a steady urge to
pious, self-denying toil.

(1) For the halfway covenant of Neocalvinism and the
sects with naturalistic liberalism, semi-democratic politics,
and modern business has involved compromises very
damaging to middle-class piety and ethics. Laymen ad-
vised by their pastors two and three hundred years ago to
seek assurance of their heavenly calling, or at least freedom from harassing doubt, by diligent labor in an earthly
calling found that advice good. Their lives were stabil-
ized, their worldly ventures prospered; and their self-
confidence and pride increased withal. Increased until
they were ready to face any interference in their affairs,
even by their own parsons and parliaments, with the
same stubborn opposition they had offered in time past
to the overthrown feudal dominations of Church and

State. Their affairs, moreover, they construed increasingly in terms of secular wisdom. "To make the best of both worlds was the part of prudence, and of the two worlds that on which our feet are planted is, at least, nearer and more submissive to our control. Divine providence is doubtless to be acknowledged, but it is highly desirable to supplement Divine providence by self help." [15] The Enlightenment and the Industrial Revolution in Europe, the conquest of the wilderness in America, augmented still further this rugged individual self-reliance and helped to diminish the clear conviction of dependence on God. Romantic efforts to re-establish it through appeal to feeling proved abortive.[16] A new prideful nationalism, expanding into economic imperialism, spread round the world. The result of all by 1900 was a western culture near the opposite pole from what Luther and Calvin had intended or could have tolerated: a regnant secularism, inimical to all aspiring and militant religious faith. Sober middle-class capitalism, that once despised and bitterly resisted innovation with which the Puritans had sturdily cast in their lot when it meant a break with the past, had now come itself to be entrenched as the established order, unmindful of its humbler beginnings and almost devoid of that genuine if narrow piety that had marked its earlier years.

One need not take too literally the gloomy words in the last page or two of Weber's initial essay. If he were writing them now, they would hardly take the same form, but their very excess of dolor has the value of heavy underscoring:

"The Puritan wanted to work in a calling; we are forced to do so. For when asceticism was carried out of monastic cells into everyday life, and began to dominate worldly morality, it did its part in building the tremendous cosmos of the modern

26

economic order. This order is now bound to the technical and economic conditions of machine production which today determine the lives of all the individuals who are born into this mechanism, . . . with irresistible force. Perhaps it will so determine them until the last ton of fossilized coal is burnt. In Baxter's view the care for external goods should only lie on the shoulders of the 'saint like a light cloak, which can be thrown aside at any moment.' But fate decreed that the cloak should become an iron cage. . . . Today the spirit of religious asceticism—whether finally who knows?—has escaped from the cage. But . . . the idea of duty in one's calling prowls about in our lives like the ghost of dead religious beliefs.

"No one knows who will live in this cage in the future, or whether at the end of this tremendous development entirely new prophets will arise, or there will be a great rebirth of old ideas and ideals, or, if neither, mechanized petrifaction, embellished with a sort of convulsive self-importance. For of the last stage of this cultural development, it might well be truly said: 'Specialists without spirit, sensualists without heart; this nullity imagines that it has attained a level of civilization never before achieved.' " [17]

Thus an acute and learned student of sociology and religion in 1905, surveying the recent past and looking toward the more remote and problematic future. This bloodless horror, this "mechanized petrifaction, embellished with a sort of convulsive self-importance," is of course no actual state past or present, but rather such a "brave new world" as Aldous Huxley and Bertrand Russell have imagined in their more prophetic books: the apotheosis of secularism, the abomination of desolation, to which our present may indeed, but let us hope need not, finally tend.

The actual present, however, is far enough along this road to give ample room for skepticism about the good influence of Protestant teaching and living since Cromwell's day. A fair summary, I think, of sober critical judgment

now would be that John Doe's business in the modern
world is business; that calling it a vocation or otherwise
solemnifying it has not lessened its egoism; and that so
far as the Protestant attempt to bring God's will into it has
now any recognizable effect, it is mainly to augment in
personally honest, shrewd, successful men their natural
probity and self-satisfaction, and to keep them free of some
now forgotten misgivings about the dignity of trade. It
has fostered at best the theory and sincere practice of what
is called stewardship, at worst sanctimonious money-grub-
bing, and nearly always a complacency quite unwarranted
by the actualities of modern life. A harsher critic may go
further, as critics in plenty have done from the beginning,[18]
and hold that the doctrine of earthly vocation is through
and through equivocal and unworthy of honest, intelligent folk: at best an attempt to serve both God and mammon, at worst a mask for unscrupulous egotism and
exploitation.

(2) To these charges of ethical and religious compromise, a second objection must be added, less injurious but
hardly less prohibitory if true: that whatever its merit in
the past, this doctrine simply is not suited to the common
life of our time and the probable future.

(*a*) It presupposed, in the first place a living belief in
the reality of God. Luther and Calvin could assume that
without debate. Catholics and Protestants alike subscribed
to the Nicene Creed, and even the anti-trinitarian heretics
believed whole-heartedly in one supreme God. The vital
issue was not whether there is a God, but what God demands of men; and the doctrine of vocation came directly
to that question without raising the more basic one at all.
There were unbelievers, no doubt, but those upon Christian soil found it best to speak softly.[19] Today it is no

longer so. We believe in God in the face of sincere and out-
spoken doubt or denial, not in its absence nor by virtue of
its forcible suppression. Marxists, humanists, and various
radical groups deny, casual pagans ignore, and many
deeply earnest Christians have recurrent doubt, that the
God of Nicæa or any supreme God exists. How shall we
urge upon all these to hearken and do God's bidding?
What can vocation mean to them in the way of divine calling or of religious faith?

(*b*) Next, besides presupposing belief in the reality of
God, the Protestant doctrine of vocation presupposed also
belief in the worth of the individual man, and especially in
Puritan times, first-hand experience of his actual growing
enfranchisement. That was, for men of the North, an
epoch of ostensible and largely genuine emancipation, economic and political as well as religious. The theological
concept of *die Freiheit eines Christenmenschen* had a
worldly correlate in the actual breaking of various traditional bonds, and the liberation of men into a new freedom. Upon this coincidence the doctrine of vocation laid
hold, at once seizing an opportunity and meeting an urgent need. The opportunity was the sudden opening of
widened perspectives of life for the ordinary man; the need
was for a discipline to give moral framework and stamina
suited to the conditions of his new liberty. It was then
theological realism to interpret the plain man's fresh measure of economic and political enfranchisement as involving
at once opportunity and duty to grow in obedience to God.
Theory was relevant to the actual state of affairs. But now
that same theory would face a very different set of facts.
Today ordinary men, we are told—which is to say the
small business and professional man, the farmer, the white
collar employee, the hired worker, and their families—

confront not widening but narrowed perspectives of life. Machine tools that finally ensured the triumph of middle-class capitalism have now mechanized the lives of all but a privileged few who live within its sway. Most of those who work are slaves now to subways and steam whistles; and these leave less· marginal energy and freedom for savoring the present, and dwelling on the future, than even field laborers had in· the· old régime. Moreover, the part of the ordinary worker in much of modern industry and trade has·been trivialized to the point of boredom and pre-clusion of self-respect. Snipping endlessly the pieces of cheap cloth for shoddy garments; punching endlessly the paper and split leather soles for bargain shoes; feeding end-lessly the rods, wire, and sheet metal that become ten-cent hardware; selling endlessly cheap merchandise in a cheap market; finding romance in cheap movies and wood-pulp magazines. Who is fool enough to look for God, even if one were sure there is a God, in this dreary modern ware-house?

(c) Finally, and most ironically of all, the Puritan doc-trine of vocation presupposed work to be done by every-body, through every working day of every year. Sunday for rest; week days for incessant labor in one's calling. But now the machines overflow periodically the channels of trade and glut the markets until the wheels choke almost to a standstill in the accumulating backwater; while men wait helplessly, month after month, like victims of another flood,. until the surplus of goods can· subside and traffic can move once more. How shall men follow a vocation and labor in a calling when, for years at a time, elevators and warehouses are clogged and the wheels are still? Casual and pointless "made work" is no answer; for requi-site qualities of labor in a calling, in the Puritan sense, are regularity and productiveness. But work precisely of this character is what the machines appear month by month to be making ever more uncalled-for. In our own country we have now reached a stage at which, unless drastic changes are effected, unemployment on a disastrous scale unmistakably threatens to become chronic. When 65 per cent of the average number of workers employed in 1923–25 can turn out goods at 92 per cent of the average production rate in those years, as they did for a time in June, 1933,[20] the case is clear. No return to 1925 "normalcy," not even another peace-time boom can cure unemployment now, so long as our existing economic habits continue essentially unchanged. Why, then, in the name of honest and vital religion, preach universal labor in an earthly calling now? What reality can such a doctrine have for our time? Why not rather turn one's back on the whole sorry tangle, confess the ambiguous development of Protestant thought from 1600 a sad mistake, and declare that theology has nothing to do with these wordly affairs except perpetually to condemn them all?

(3) That in effect is what the "crisis theologians" are doing, with impressive vehemence and admirable one-sidedness. In their view the true faith of Luther and Calvin and the Bible stands uncompromisingly apart from the dominant and disastrous secularism of modern life and thought; for being rooted in the eternal transcendent Word of God that is beyond and apart from all history, it stands necessarily apart from any transient phase such as our own. For them the term vocation, *Beruf,* takes on again its lost radiance. But that is because it speaks to them once more of an All-transcending God who bids lost man to repentance and to life beyond death, not because they find new values in the daily round of contemporary liv-

ing.[21] On the contrary, they insist that only by rejecting resolutely all the busy, sentimental-egoistic ways of modern men, and standing still to hear in utter humiliation the accusing Word of God, can we be saved out of the quicksands of our pretentious, ephemeral time.

The warning is opportune, beyond doubt. No religion bred of a particular cultural system, let alone of the spiritual thrills of particular individuals, can call an age to repentance and proclaim that the Kingdom of God is at hand: in short, be a religon. Something like the old Catholic or the old Protestant faith, impatient and virile, is needed for a fresh start. But the start must be a fresh one. No mere reassertion of Calvin's or of Luther's or of St. Paul's thought will serve,[22] much less a reassertion of one side of it alone. That their faith in a divine calling was for these men a faith by which to live devotedly, their own living proved. But that their *doctrine about* divine calling was or is an adequate guide for others to live by, sober theory must doubt and subsequent history seems clearly to have disproved. They and their first offspring, in their respective generations, were in some wise flame-touched insurgents, bent on drastic change in the Church and a new life in the world, full of aspiration, hope, and power. But their later descendants, down to our own day, have shown far more generally a bent to reactionarism in both Church and State, either because they have stood committed to an existing order, or because they have thought to serve God better by standing aloof from every human system than by trying to change any. That commitment to things as they are, in a perennially imperfect world, is tantamount to failure of moral and religious aspiration seems plain; but a spirit of contempt for such a world keeps its idealism and aspiration unsullied at the cost of cutting the nerve that

joins faith and hope to cumulative action, with the unhappy consequences for both worship and work on which
we have remarked. Far better than the smug conformity
that has disgraced so much of modern Christendom is the
courageous protest of 16,000 German Protestant pastors,
and of Cardinal von Faulhaber and his Catholic associates,
against a sacrilegious tyranny. In its courage no less admirable, and in its insight at crucial points more penetrating, is Karl Barth's own intransigence in face of both
Church and State. But all these are exhortations to stand
fast: indispensable in a world threatened with madness,
but insufficient for our continuing need. We listen still for
voices calling in terms of our own day to go forward in
the name of the Living God.

II

But which way is forward? There are voices in plenty
crying "Lo, here!" and "Lo, there!" How can we know
whom to follow? Wherein has traditional Protestant
thought gone amiss, and how shall we recognize a more
excellent way?

A. Let us digress for a moment and try whether we can
align a landmark or two, before attacking this last question directly.

(1) Socrates in the *Phædrus,* engaged in describing
the first principles of rational discourse, is made to say:
"If ever I should come upon a man who is able to discern
the one and the many as they are, I would follow 'in his
steps as though he were a god.' " [23] Here, stated in abstract,

speculative form, is recognition of the perennial enigma as to the nature of unity and plurality, and the relations between "the one" and "the many," that towers like Everest at the end—never reached—of every philosophical inquiry. Of the world or of any part thereof on which his attention is fixed, the speculative thinker is forced to ask, sooner or later: "Is it *one?* or is it *many?* How far and in what sense one? how far and in what sense many? And with what consequences, for thought and for action?" The opposing theoretic poles between which speculation upon this issue may range are, of course, radical pluralism on the one hand, radical monism or singularism on the other. To the former, reality would consist of infinitely numerous, wholly discontinuous items, themselves without internal unity; to the latter, of a single uninterrupted whole, without radical diversity or interval of any sort. For reasons that need not delay us here,[24] neither of these theoretic poles has in fact been successfully occupied by an actual system of thought, though some thinkers have ostensibly held the one extreme position or the other,[25] and some have moved so far toward the one or the other as to leave "common sense" far behind. In practice, the pluralistic terminus is usually some form of atomism or monadism; the monistic, some form of organicism or panlogism. The atomist or monadist views the world as made up of discrete units which do not interpenetrate, but whose relations one to another are all "external" relations. Each is what it is, independently of the rest; and its nature remains essentially unaffected by the presence and behavior of the others, to which it is, in this sense, at most "externally" related. The organicist or panlogist, on the contrary, views reality as a unitary system in which every part is "internally" related to every other part and to the whole, after the manner of organs in a living body, terms in a logical schema, or thoughts in a living mind. There are no independent units, discontinuous from their neighbors or capable of existing apart from them; but each is what it is wholly in virtue of its place in the whole, and every change in its relations with its neighbors involves a change in its own essential nature and behavior. Intermediate views which stand at neither of these termini are none the less, like them, compelled to deal, expressly or tacitly, with this same problem of individual separateness and organic wholeness. All such views, of which Plato's is one, agree in maintaining that reality exemplifies both wholeness and separateness, real conjunctions and real disjunctions, held together in a perennial tension that is partly but not wholly amenable to logic. Such views all seek the one in every *many,* and the many in every *one;* and are judged, in some important measure, on the score of their success in thus bringing to light something of the manner in which reality is ordered. But they differ widely in detail, both in the degree of their general approximation to atomism or to organicism, and in the particular combinations of emphasis upon wholeness or separateness which appear in their treatment of particular concrete problems.

Now theologians also are constrained to deal with concrete theoretic problems about "the one" and "the many," of a peculiarly complex and urgent kind: problems concerning the nature and behavior of human selves as individuals "saved" or "unsaved," concerning their relations with one another and with their cosmic environment, and above all concerning the nature of God and His relations to the cosmos and to man. In so far as they seek to deal with these matters coherently, theologians no less than philosophers are likewise compelled to deal, expressly or

35

tacitly, with this same pervasive problem of wholeness and separateness. No short recourse to intuition nor to revelation can avoid it. For on the one hand, if such appeal be made in furtherance of rational discourse, that expedient in itself either poses the problem in acute form or presupposes that a tenable attitude toward it has already been defined. On the other hand, mere acceptance and reiteration *ad hoc,* apart from rational discourse, of intuitions and alleged revelations cannot fairly be called theology at all; which, however well justified in setting out from supposed revelations, cannot be content simply to rest therein. To be a theologian and not merely a devotee means to take up the burden of rational analysis, exposition, and argument without which *theologia* is a misnomer. And once that burden is assumed, the ubiquitous and always in some way crucial problem of "the one and the many" must again and again be faced.

This is one landmark—the more remote and speculative one—by which our inquiry will be guided. We need a working doctrine which deals more reasonably than that of the Reformers and their successors has done with the perennial tension of individual separateness and organic wholeness, in the world as it is and ought to be.

(2) But such an abstraction is all but meaningless apart from a concrete setting, or rather a series of them. We need proximate landmarks also, and these are to be found only in particular matters of fact and of worth. Superior though it be to any prior theory in its conception of ordinary work (and this I believe to be so), the Protestant doctrine of vocation has proved defective still as a guide to our understanding of and practical dealing with human actualities. Not only does it do needless violence to reason, but also it has shown too great readiness to ride rough-shod

over everyday values and facts. This deficiency and our
need of continual effort to overcome it can be illustrated in
detail only by repeated reference to particular factual situations, some of which we have noticed and others of which
will be noticed hereafter. But in more general terms it
may be said that the fact and the actual conditions of *advance*—growth, development, progress, or what you will—
in the world as we find it require to be convincingly dealt
with by any theory, philosophical or theological, which
seeks the allegiance of folk who for better, for worse, are
constrained at present to live in this world, not some other.
To call progress a fact is, of course, a recent and to many
competent minds a dubious kind of assertion.[26] There is
no need to haggle here over the question whether human
life as such can be improved in all respects and without
limit. I doubt that the question so stated has any clear
meaning, and share fully the skepticism of those who smile
at brave talk about human perfectibility and "progress on-
ward and upward forever." But that in specific ways both
the conditions of human living and human responses
thereto can be changed for the better, on any reasonable
definition of the term *better;* that such changes can be
made available for a larger rather than a smaller portion
of those who are alive at a given time; that such specific
advances have in fact been made; and that they suggest
ways toward further desirable changes: this is not open to
doubt. It is advance and the conditions for advance, in this
sense, that will be used to provide a series of nearer landmarks for judging whether a given theory seems to be on
the right road.

To drop the metaphor: it will be held here that a philosophy or theology must, as rational discourse, be judged
formally and ultimately by its coherence and discrimina-

tion; and that as discourse about the actual world, it must be judged materially and proximately by its sagacity in dealing with particular matters of fact and of worth. We are taking as touchstone with respect to the former the universally recognized, capital problem of identity and difference, unity and plurality, wholeness and separateness; with respect to the latter the complex fact of advance, growth, progress, and its conditions in this unfinished world of fact and worth. Neither sort of judgment, neither criterion, is feasible or meaningful without the other, any more than one landmark can determine a line of march, or an algebraic formula without a logbook the progress of a ship toward port. Both must be constantly employed together.

Theologians doubtless may, as some now do, hold with respect to what we have called progress that improvements in food supply and shelter, protection against disease, and provision of opportunity for learning, for meaningful work and enjoyable leisure, for free and voluntary rather than forced and blind self-devotion, are mere "civic" improvements without theological significance. By all who think thus, the notion of human progress is disparaged as unimportant or illusory in comparison with some transcendent absolute, and certainly as no fit touchstone for a realistic theology. This issue will be constantly before us henceforth, and it will be held that such nullification of everyday human concerns is no less to be deplored, on factual, ethical, and theological grounds, than the smug secularism against which it rightly contends. A valid theology, it is urged, must be one that keeps in view a continual *tension* of absolute and relative, perfect and imperfect, ultimate and approximative; whereas if either of these poles be nullified, or if no relations other than wholly external ones can obtain between them, significant tension must be impossible.

B. Into these matters we shall look more fully in succeeding chapters. But for the moment let us take note here in preparing to judge the Reformers' and their successors' doctrine of vocation, that they themselves have in fact been participants in a noteworthy human advance. One need be no zealot for the modern capitalistic and *soi-disant* democratic order to see genuine advance in its growth at the expense of the feudalism, more picturesque and in some ways more genial and humane, but far less widely responsible, productive, and socially promising, which in the West it has largely displaced. I conceive that theology must be concerned with such change and with the need for more and other such changes, no less than with an eternal order that changeth not. But traditional Protestant theory as it stands can give no intelligible account of such progress either as fact or as ethical objective, and no adequate guidance toward such further advance as plainly is required.

Why and wherein this is so may be suggested by glancing at the manner in which new unities, and with them new separations, were defined in Protestant theory and practice as these bear, especially through the doctrine of vocation, upon everyday human strivings and their outcome. It will be convenient to make this brief critique centre about Neocalvinism (Puritanism and the like), whose prevailing temper—to us most familiar—is that of dogmatic, prosaic, practical rationalism,[27] in contrast with the poetry and cultus mysticism that has been so important a factor in typical Lutheran piety. But the tendencies worked out overtly in the later Calvinist and nonconformist Protestant communions cannot be understood without repeated reference to the older Protestantism from which they all grew, partly by accretion, but partly by continuous development of what was already implicit. We shall take into account also, therefore, the older Protestant thought.

By common consent, predestination is regarded as the central, most distinctive doctrine of Calvinism: the "effectual calling" or "election" of some to unmerited bliss; the rejection of others to a perdition which all have merited, and from which the elect are saved only by the grace of God—in no part by their own worth. Here Calvin stood upon common ground with Luther, and with Augustine, to whom both Reformers looked back as representing the true doctrine of the Church before monks and schoolmen had perverted it. In its primary form the doctrine is a vivid deliverance of religious faith, the impulsive judgment of one convinced that he has been "saved" by God's power, not his own, from vain struggling and despair to assurance and hope, which he deserves no more than his neighbor to whom it does not come. St. Paul seems to have left it at that, and except when they were pressed by polemic necessities,[28] Augustine and Luther for the most part did likewise. But both, on occasion, and Calvin more consistently than either, pushed the religious conviction of unmerited grace into a cosmic context of universal, arbitrary divine determinism; and this theory colored profoundly their thought about God, and man, and all that pertains to both.

(1) In principle, no doubt, this doctrine of universal providence was quite as basic to mediæval as to reformed theology. Both these drew directly from St. Augustine's

thought, for whom that doctrine had come at last to be
centre and circumference. But between the mediæval
and the reformed developments of the doctrine there
were differences of a clear and important kind. The theological mainstay of the late mediæval Church was the
daring and masterly thirteenth century system of St.
Thomas Aquinas. For a time after his death, while
lesser men purveyed his thoughts more or less by rote
and the competing influences of John Duns Scotus and
William of Ockham were still fresh, Thomism had suffered eclipse. But in the fifteenth century, abler men
had turned to it once more,[29] and together with Scotism
(which was in truth rather its complement than its
contrary), it was defended as "the old faith" (*via antiqua*)
against Ockhamist "modernism" (*via moderna*). Luther
sprang from the Ockhamist wing, and against him and
all his works it was naturally "the old faith," and especially Thomism more or less diluted with Scotist positivism, that the Council of Trent and the Jesuit apologists
reaffirmed, and that today still forms the main fabric of
Roman Catholic doctrinal theology.

St. Thomas had made bold to reinterpret the Augustinian doctrinal tradition in terms largely drawn from
the newly rediscovered scientific and philosophic works
of Aristotle. In so doing, he had brought systematic
theology into closer and more consistent association than
had any previous Christian thinker, with the details of
an elaborate system of natural science and philosophy;
and he had given it, moreover, a definitely pluralistic
turn, away from the Neoplatonic monism to which Augustinian tradition and, still more closely, Christian
mystics and Averroists had tended. He still gave first
place among theologians to St. Augustine, and he still

affirmed without ambiguity control of the world in every detail by divine providence.[30] But in his view, providence is mediated through finite beings: through angels, men, and natural forces acting in accordance with contingent natural laws. To these "secondary causes" he calmly ascribed an importance which most theologians even until now have not been quite ready to concede them. He expressly held, it is true, that lower beings are "moved" by higher, not *vice versa,* and in particular, that the spirit of man can be "moved" only by God, not by any created being.[31] But this referred to ultimate, prescriptive causation. Proximately and contingently, an individual is led, for example, into this occupation (*officium*) or that by "natural causes," which give rise in different individuals to "diverse inclinations" toward this way of life or toward that.[32] On scrutiny of the natural world-order, viewed in the light of certain logical principles,[33] he grounded his basic proofs of the existence of God, and his confidence was serene that what reason can elicit by careful examination of nature will accord with what faith must accept on the basis of revelation, in the Scriptures and through the Church.

(2) Against this venturesome linking of theology with natural philosophy, the Reformers reacted with vehemence. It had already been criticized with skeptical acumen by the *"moderni"* who followed William of Ockham, and later with telling literary irony by humanists like Erasmus. But it had withstood the first attacks, and in the fifteenth century, as we have noted, was gaining ground. Neither the acute Ockhamists nor the humanists, even the most idealistic, had any compelling alternative to offer. The *via antiqua* could be riddled with their criticisms, but not by them overborne, because they

had not with all their negations a *via moderna* of power. The Protestant leaders had: a full-blooded new mode of life, together with vehement reaffirmation of pungent Augustinian doctrine—or rather, of like doctrine adhering more closely to the plain meaning of Scripture than Augustine himself had come, restated in terms of the new era, and fired with the living convictions of resolute men. This meant by no means a complete abandonment of scholastic—even of Thomistic—thought; but it did mean abandonment of the cool philosophic attitude of St. Thomas, his confidence in human reason, his interest in the details of the natural order, and a great part of his thought about the relations between God and man, and especially about the Church and its relation to the world. Distinctions that seemed important to him and to the mediæval Church were ignored or denied to exist; and new chasms were opened which had far less emphasis in his thought. Moreover, besides the theories of St. Thomas the Reformers assailed, with even more bitterness, current popular views and churchly practices which claimed warrant in such theology as his. A new contour map of the providential order of things emerged, with a new distribution of alleged unities and separations.

(*a*) First, as regards individual character and conduct, the Reformed doctrine rejected the atomism of everyday mediæval ethics, with its particularized and externalized sins and good works, merits, and indulgences.[34] The unit of conduct for this older theory had been the single act, with its particular *intentio* or purpose, and its particular set of circumstances. Given a knowledge of these, the act could be judged separately, its proper meed of merit or penalty assigned, and the transaction closed; so as to leave the way clear for subsequent acts, each

43

likewise to be judged and dealt with on its several merits. The life of the ordinary believer as thus conceived was, in the easy-going, unsystematic, impulsive feudal manner, a succession of fresh starts and separate successes or failures; for which the sacrament of repentance made appropriate provision. To the Reformers, on the contrary, the unit of ethical life is not the act, good or bad, but the agent. Instead of atomic acts, they stressed the unitary core of individual nature and will from which acts arise,[35] and the year by year explication thereof in the unity of a disciplined, well-ordered life. Hence the importance, for them, of regular labor, year in, year out, in a definite calling; which provides the outward conditions for cultivation and proof of the internal wholeness of a regenerate nature and will.

Both Luther and Calvin agreed in thus shifting the emphasis from act to agent, and in discarding the apparatus of absolution and indulgence which was appropriate to the earlier view. Luther did not turn his back altogether upon those persistent cravings of blundering, unheroic humanity which the Catholic theory and praxis had recognized: cravings for repeated disburdenment, forgiveness, and a fresh start. He conceded freely that sinful lapses are inevitable even for men of faith, and urged retention of the confessional as an aid to pious living. The Calvinist trend was far more severe, with no encouragement to human weakness. One's life stands or falls as a whole in which every act, every moment is crucial; inasmuch as in it the whole man, saved or damned, gets expression. As in early Stoicism, the demand is for rigorous, rational self-control, and to offend in any point is to break the whole law: a hero's moral creed or an archangel's, inspiring—and impossible for

44

ordinary men. Plain folk need to be called to a unity of
life beyond any piecemeal "works righteousness"; but
normally they are not, and without grave damage cannot be, fused into such hard, single flames as Calvin's
doctrine demands.

(*b*) While thus declaring the individual person a unitary being, accountable for every moment to God, this
doctrine tended at the same time to establish new conjunctions and to open new chasms, in theory, between
the ordinary man, his fellows, and his world.

(i) First, as to social relationships, it has been easy to
exaggerate the divisive tendencies of Protestantism, and
to romanticize into a theoretic model of unity what had
been in fact a very loosely ordered mediæval Europe.
Actually, neither Empire nor Church had been a well-
organized whole, except on paper. As regards the Empire, genuine civil unity had depended on vigorous personal rule and a fabric of individual allegiances such as
only an exceptional ruler could maintain. The rising tide
of modern nationalism with its less narrowly personal
loyalties became as truly an advance in actual, as it was a
decline in nominal, unity of political life. As regards the
Church, temporary papal schisms had been merely the
most obvious outward and visible sign of internal conflicts that were incessant: acrimonious rivalries between
Italy and the North, between curia and council, between
monastic and mendicant, secular and regular, orthodox
and sectary, that neither began nor ended at the Reformation. Moreover, deeper-seated than any of these, and
in a way underlying most of them, was the fundamental
disjunction already remarked, between clergy and religious on the one hand, and ordinary laity on the other.
Between these two broad "levels" (*gradūs*) of life, once

more, an essential cleavage lay: between those to whom mere "safety" (*salus*) and those to whom "perfection" appertained. Protestantism in so far as it wiped out this disjunction—a change even now, of course, far from complete—moved toward more genuine unity in its conception of the Church. In respect of polity and doctrine, moreover, it was only the sectaries who at first stood for extreme individualism or separatism.[36] And if in these matters the Protestant movement later came largely to follow their lead and has fostered, or at least tolerated, open "sectarianism," it may be doubted whether even this, in the long run, is more disintegrative to social wholeness than attempts to maintain a specious ecclesiastical unity by force. A reunion of free churches conceivably might embody a higher level of conscious and meaningful unity than the Church hitherto has ever known.

Yet though all this be true in fact, it is also true that in Protestant theory the central concept of predestination, the direct, secret, arbitrary calling by God of the elect, one by one, leads readily to an anti-organic conception of the individual's relation to society.[37] Not how well a man loves his neighbor and bears his part in the common life, but whether he is the beneficiary of an inscrutable divine fiat determines unconditionally his lot, in which no one, not even his closest and dearest, can have the least share. In strict theory, work in one's earthly vocation is not primarily for the sake of contributing to the common life; though given a complex division of labor, such contribution is a fortunate result and further justifies the practice. Work in one's calling is primarily a way of expressing obedience to God, and secondarily of discovering to oneself and to others evidence of God's favor—that is of one's enrollment among the elect—according as one's diligence issues in

46

prosperous and tranquil life. There still persisted in Protestant doctrine a lingering shadow of universalism or some kindred humane tendency, in the notion of a "general calling" of all mankind, from the highways and hedges; but it was only a shadow. The vivid and vital thing was the "effectual calling" of this or that certain individual, beside which the "general calling" was practically of no account. Far more harshly and finally than the old disjunction between "spiritual" and "secular" life, this new one between the elect and the lost divided mankind by an impassable gulf; the more awful because arbitrary and unseen.

In Neocalvinism and in certain of the sects these consequences were most clearly drawn, and translated into practice. Primitive social solidarity as of clan or tribe was gone; humane philosophies were in disrepute; and no concrete sense of mankind as bound together *for good* in world-wide, worth-fraught kinship—not even so imperfect a sense as our own—had been achieved. Only in its fatal derivation from Adam was the whole race kin, and in being snatched singly out of that fellowship of death lay each man's one hope of life.

(ii) In like manner the new concept of vocation dealt with the relation of the believer to the whole scene of his earthly living. Here also time-honored distinctions were repudiated and new ones affirmed, but in no very clear nor consistent way, and the results for both theory and practice were confusing. Here, if anywhere, grounds for the charge of moral equivocation must be sought. But I think a fair scrutiny will at least make one aware of the uncommon difficulties that beset any attempt, however honest, to find a way through this twilight zone where flesh and spirit meet. The Protestant thinkers attempted, at any rate, for better or for worse, a fresh approach to the baffling alternative: world-denial or world-affirmation. The principle, "Ye cannot serve God and mammon," had of course been basic to Christianity from the beginning. That principle, while the apocalyptic hope was yet strong, had naturally prompted the Christian community as a whole to sit loose to the present age, not necessarily with the ascetic's repulsion, but with the preoccupation of travellers nearing a goal. When that tense expectancy waned, and the Church as a whole became identified more closely with the secular order, it is understandable that a division should have taken place within the Church itself, between monastics who rejected the world with what now became true ascetic contempt, and ordinary Christians who more or less frankly accepted the world and made their occasional obeisance to God in the form of confession and penance. But the true *contemptus mundi* is not easy for ordinary flesh and blood to maintain, even in a monastery; and in spite of successive reforms, undertaken in deep earnestness, secularism appears to have had the upper hand with most Christians, monastic and non-monastic alike.[38]

Now the Protestant reformers sought to end that anomalous situation by abolishing the monastic division between Christians who accept and Christians who reject this world. All Christians are to stand henceforth on one level. But it is not easy to define what that level should be. Not the frank self-indulgence of pagan Humanists and Libertines, obviously. Not the professed, and oftentimes genuine, renunciation of monks and mediæval clergy. And not the archaic, millennarian adiaphorism of the radical sectaries which turned erratically now in the one direction, now in the other, as special revelations came in. A subtler attitude than any of these was formulated in somewhat different ways by Lutheran and Reformed groups: an attitude in which world-affirmation and world-denial are combined in a new way. Man is a bond-servant of God, set to labor here or there in His earthly vineyard, for God's sole glory. Neither in Lutheran nor in Calvinist theory is the work itself of intrinsic importance. Simply it is a task associated with that earthly station to which a man is assigned by God, and in God's sight one man's task is no more important than another's. The Lutheran with his more consistent reliance on "faith alone" could take a more easy-going attitude toward the earthly vocation, neither insisting too sternly on perpetual toil, nor disparaging the natural pleasures of healthy living. But the grimmer Calvinist thought urged men to labor without ceasing, and decried relaxation as conducive to enjoyment in which it recognized an ever-present temptation.

It was a paradox of this latter view, noted with some dismay by Protestant leaders, that while thus decrying luxury, it tended strongly to increase the productivity of pious laborers and the wealth of pious employers, and provided no adequate safeguards against the new perils which it thus helped to produce. The fact is, it had no coherent and realistic insight into the connection between ethical ideals and economic facts. Instead of seeing these as closely interrelated, it sought to deal with them in arbitrary isolation, and could therefore make no satisfactory appraisal of the far-reaching economic and social changes in which its own adherents were participating. Of human progress as having intrinsic worth it could entertain no thought, because of its determined theocentric absolutism; yet its peculiar blending of worldly zeal and other-worldly self-denial was helping to bring about the very phenomena of which it could give none but a strained, unnatural, and self-defeating account.

At the same time, this way of conceiving a man's relation to his work involved another disintegrative paradox, only less painful than the terrific sundering between saved and damned. Now that the old comfortable distinction between ordinary Christians and those called to a "spiritual life" of perfection was gone, the obligation to "be perfect" rested upon every believer, in every sort of earthly calling. But many a calling—magistrate, soldier, hangman—plainly required of those who followed it a mode of life in conflict with the precepts of the Gospel. As Christian, one must love one's enemy; as public servant, one must destroy him. Luther recognized this conflict between private and public duty, but found no way to alleviate it. Calvin, for whom the antithesis of law and gospel was far less apparent, drew no such express distinction as Luther's between private and public obligation.[39] But explicit or not, the conflict was there. Men were asked to be perfect without such aid as monastic seclusion once gave. Men were bidden to follow the callings, of all sorts, divinely ordained for them, and to practice in the midst of their often brutal requirements the command to be perfect. For the tough-minded, such a dilemma need not be unmanageable: brutality in a good cause has never lacked virtuous and willing practitioners. But for Christians of finer sensibility, the new demand brought inescapable conflict and pain. "Moral man and immoral society were at war in the individual."[40] In some sense, of course, this paradox is rooted in the basic conflict between what is and what ought to be; and the Reformers' teaching merely brought it with new harshness

into view. But the paradox was made more gruelling by
their representation of the existing social order as, in its
main outlines, ordained by God—the very God whose
law of love that order and its duties made one violate.

(c) A similar awkward conjunction of unitive and
separative tendencies appears, finally, in the Reformers'
account of relations between created beings and God. On
the one hand, as we have seen, in contrast with philosophic
Schoolmen like St. Thomas and with mediæval church-
men generally, they asserted with new vehemence the
direct and determining impact of God's will upon each
individual, each event, and brushed aside as unimportant
or as mischievous both natural causes and priestly minis-
trations.[41] Thus every man depends immediately and
wholly upon God, and Him alone, for his every act and
impulse. Yet on the other hand, in contrast with mediæval
mystics and the enthusiasts of their own time, the Calvin-
ists in especial emphasized quite as vehemently the total
otherness of God over against all created things; and the
externality of that miraculous Word by which, in Jesus
Christ and the Scriptures, He reveals Himself to the elect,
to whom alone He grants arbitrarily the gift of faith.
The paradoxical total effect of this doctrine was therefore
to present God as at once more and less accessible to the
plain man than hitherto. It assured him that philosophers
and clerics had no better access to God than he; but this
really meant, as it turned out, that no one had access from
man's side to God at all, nor even the power to make a
first feeble step toward Him. Only the elect, arbitrarily
chosen from God's side, can have His gratuitous and oft-
times strangely hidden aid, which leaves no room for genuine co-working and which in principle takes the form
of overruling all that "the natural man" may feel im-
pelled to undertake.

51

What chiefly distinguishes this teaching from that of Aquinas is its ruthless slashing out of middle terms, and its bringing thereby to sharp focus the hitherto partly obscured meaning of uncompromising belief in divine foreordination. Aquinas also had professed that belief, as we have seen; but by regarding the divine will as mediated (though everywhere none the less immediately present) through "second causes," and by holding that in detail these latter act not necessarily but contingently, he softened for human reason the paradox that helpless man can disobey Almighty God, on whom his every act wholly depends. Calvin forces the paradox relentlessly into view —and stands by it in despite of love and logic.

This reason-defying assertion of both rigorous externality and arbitrary immediacy pervades, of course, the Calvinist doctrine of earthly calling. Whereas Aquinas could hold that a man is "inclined" to this or that earthly station through the working of natural causes, and a modern theorist likewise would stress the importance of individual aptitudes and social needs, the Reformers saw in each man's lot an arbitrary assignment by direct divine fiat, that took no account of natural and human reasons. Divine reasons doubtless there are, but God keeps His own counsel, and permits no slightest approach from man's side, whose part is not to understand but to obey.

If this doctrine with its forced unities and disjunctions bids defiance to man's theoretic reason, it is hardly less unmanageable in its implications for human action. It can provide a stimulus of extraordinary power to determined insurgents and warriors, convinced that they are fighting with the irresistible support of the will of God; but it can also be taken by prosperous later generations as sanctioning if not sanctifying a *status quo* full of inequities, held to be determined by powers beyond human control. This is by no means peculiar to Protestantism. For example, Marxism, having begun likewise as an insurgent faith, has passed also through a time of domestication during which its theoretical determinism was used to justify the practice of moral *laissez faire*.[42] Just as Calvinist clergymen have defended slavery, so Marxist Social Democrats have supported a World War, because what is to be must be, and all is ultimately for the best. But plainly a doctrine so engulfing in its theoretic, and so equivocal in its practical, import can provide neither explanation nor guidance for specific advances such as we have here been concerned about. And if, like the Protestant dogma, it conceives the determining Power as arbitrary and inscrutable, its logical affinity is rather with a general anti-rationalism and conservatism than with such persistent prosecution of specific inquiries and experiments as that by which, in large part, human progress comes about.

Such doctrine, perhaps we may say in summary, is for strong, hard, unreflective men of action rather than of thought and feeling—disciplined fighters, pioneers, traders, wreckers of an old order and shock troops of a new, in a world that is to be subdued. But when far-sighted, humane, appreciative planning and building are to be done, in a world that needs so far as possible to be understood and loved and not merely exploited or condemned, another concept of vocation is required.

III

Let us see whether we can frame one, in terms of our common life today. It must be realistic, in the sense that actualities are to be faced and so far as possible taken fairly into account, not ignored nor explained away. Yet it must go beyond bread-and-butter realism, not palming off mundane efficiency as the substance of piety. It must deal honestly with things as they are, and yet demand not only more than most men achieve but more than men can achieve, or else merit the gibes of worldly hypocrisy-hunters and the censure of all honest servants of God. Such a concept of vocation, I suggest, may be approached by way of three converging lines, each of which can be drawn here only in terms of somewhat general principles, to be later developed in more concrete detail.

A. One obvious way of approach is objective and in a sense rigoristic. A vocation must be regarded first of all as *a systematic and persistent doing of needful work.* For humankind, this world is not a paradise and never will be. On our race, above other creatures of earth, is laid a burden of labor, the bearing of which however can become for man, tool-maker, talker, and thinker, an opportunity for life having new dimensions beyond those of inarticulate animalism. Labor then, manual and mental, appears to be a primary and universal condition of man's survival as man, and of his chance for good human living. To this common task and promise all men, in principle, are called.[43] It is a "general vocation," not a "special vocation" in the Calvinist sense. We all are called to become fully human selves, and as men and women to work in a world unfinished, urgent, and full of unexplored resources and demands.

But this requirement needs to be examined a bit more closely. Not every sort of activity will serve for such human maturing. Needless drudgery and competitive sport, for example, are not enough; though often we say of others or of ourselves that we are working, when blind drudging or strenuous playing would be the fitter term. The work that makes full-grown men and women is intelligent and persistent effort to meet the needs of living things, with due regard to their relative urgency and worth, by coping with the exactions of an environing world at least partly ordered and intelligible. Both drudgery and play doubtless may come into it as subordinate factors; but persisting vital needs and the right ways of meeting them in concrete situations must be the primary concern. For a mature worker, pleasurableness, profit, prestige, self-realization, even merit before God will all appear secondary. An exigent and partly intelligible reality has its hand upon him, and he cannot and will not do other than hew to the line, as far as he is able to see where the lines run. Such a one learns of necessity to move out on solid earth, beyond personal subjectivity and caprice, for neither vital needs nor other facts and laws of being are subject to his whim. What needs to be done and how it can best be done are always matters of fact and of law, to be discovered, not improvised; and to these a real worker must learn to adapt his wishes and his deeds. Here is the analogue, in our view, of Calvin's stern concept of Providential rule, with a somewhat similar mingling of intelligible order and arbitrary givenness. But the order is here taken to be progressively discoverable and understandable by man, not hidden in the secret counsels of God nor ultimately contingent on arbitrary fiat; and there is no assertion of rigid individual predestination—a matter to which we must give further notice in a moment. For such a view as this, discipline falls naturally into the place which, as the word signifies, it should hold; as one factor,

55

namely, in a difficult and often enough painful process of *learning*. But however difficult and painful, human learning can be diverse and progressive and therefore endlessly interesting, not monotonous nor mechanically predictable; for both needs and methods are susceptible of seemingly endless diversification, expanding from simple roots—a craving for food, a prying with a lever, a cry—into the rise and fall of human cultures and civilizations.

If throughout the course of such complication the basic pattern of significant work could have been kept clear, for every one concerned, I suspect a doctrine of vocation would today require less apology. But it has not been so. In the process of cultural diversification, the basic pattern tends to become obscured or displaced. Real needs and sound methods from time to time are lost sight of, and pleasure, profit, prestige, or hoped-for divine favor come to be primary rather than secondary concerns. But unless one despair altogether of human reason—without which it is hard to see how we could go on living—one must suppose it possible to get back at least now and again a clear sight of the basic pattern, and to search out some of the consequences, theoretic and practical, which it seems to involve; and therewith to recover a sense of the urgency and import of work.

B. Meanwhile, consider a second way of approach, correlative to this first one. A vocation may be regarded further as *an absorbing, inclusive, and purposeful putting forth and development of an individual's own constituent powers.* This is, so to say, the reverse side, the view from within, of that outward thrust of energy in labor whose objective aspect we have been examining. Looking from without, we have said: "There is work to be done, in which every responsible adult should have a hand." Looking now from within, we say: "There are diversities of gifts, and the call to work must be in some sense not only a general but a special calling." Not in the traditional sense, however, that some are called and some not, but in the simple and obvious sense that each is called to live not his neighbor's nor his nation's nor his church's life, but his own. The general call to live and work cannot be understood by a man at all save in terms of his own capacities, native and acquired; nor can his response to it take any other shape than one compatible with his own overt and latent powers. Both his apperception and his response are unavoidably and uniquely his own.

This, I suppose, is one obvious factual basis upon which was reared the doctrine of individual predestination; and so far as that doctrine is concerned to insist on the reality of ineradicable differences between persons, and on their importance as determining, at least by way of limitation, each man's response to the common task, plainly it is well founded. So far, however, as it asserts further a total absence of genuine contingency in nature and of genuine autonomy in human thought and action, it goes beyond what the facts at hand seem to imply, and I think beyond what sober ethics and theology require. It seems better, therefore, to regard the concrete entries of diverse individuals upon their several callings, and their diverse conduct therein, not with Calvin as the outcome of direct, external, and arbitrary divine fiat; nor yet, with more recent evangelical leaders, as individual responses to specific, direct divine promptings mystically or miraculously conveyed; but rather, with St. Thomas, as the outcome of each man's responding, within the limitations of his own nature and character, to the operation of manifold natural and social causes.[44] The ultimate status and meaning of these latter are no doubt to be inquired into further: one may well doubt that they are ultimate or exhaustive of reality. But in any event, if this notion be correct, each person should be expected to find and follow his special calling by a sort of human gravitation, albeit exploratory and in some measure purposeful rather than mechanical; and in a well-ordered society, ways should be open for such exploration and adjustment. When it is not so, human resources go to waste, needed work that might have been done goes undone, and misfitted individuals fail of that fulness of life which is the correlate to effective and satisfying labor in a suitable calling.

As a focus and framework for developing selfhood, I think there is clearly no substitute equivalent to absorbing and cumulatively significant work. It is at this point more obviously than at any other that the ordinary man may find saving truth in the great religious paradox of losing one's life to find it. Not many of us, by and large, are likely to join the small company of genuine martyrs who, in purity of heart, lay down their lives for an invisible hope; and it does not make for clarity when we talk as though all of us could or should be living all the while on that high plane. For most of us the carpenter shop must come before the cross, and we shall do well if we learn to be faithful over a few things. But given a really engrossing task suited to his needs and powers, the individual who is not content to live and die an amateur has a chance to find himself through a natural, healthy sort of self-devotion, by learning to sink momentary impulses in long hard pulls, and incongruous wishes in a desire for good beyond what a trifler would ever see and beyond what even master-craftsmen will ever achieve.

He can learn also, if he be teachable, the patience of one who knows disappointment, and the understanding of one made keenly alive to human weakness; the astringent honesty of a workman who hates and fears sham—fears it the more if he also is not innocent of it; and the inward steadiness and hope of one who has put forth his strength against the pressure of actuality and has known his blade now and again to take hold and cut with the grain.

But this is saying, of course, what a vocation may and should be for one who labors in it faithfully, rather than what the day's work now usually is for an ordinary worker in fact. We must return to this problem in the next chapter.

C. Finally, a third approach to the concept we are seeking may be suggested in some such terms as these: a vocation should be *a willing contributive share in the world's work and the common life.* If the words of preceding paragraphs have seemed to strain at the moorings of fact, this third statement plainly is rising on the wings of imagination. For most workers in the modern world could not now honestly view their work in such terms as these. Yet given the nature of man as social animal, this statement only makes explicit what is implied, I think, in the first two; and in principle what it requires is that we seek to realize on a larger scale and in wider contexts what has repeatedly been realized on a small scale within simpler cultures. Let us review briefly a familiar modern panorama, to see in what sense this is true and what light it may throw on our present task.

In a primitive or a pioneer household or in a village not yet converted to the Industrial Revolution, occupations do have an organic and contributive character. The division

59

of labor is sufficiently simple and apparent so that each worker can see how and why his part must fit into the whole. It is important for our theory not to romanticize at this point. In neither a frontier household nor a rustic village is life idyllic, and there is plenty of untamed egoism to mar such harmony as a too innocent observer might expect to find. But the fact is that, like it or not, the members of such a household or village must work together or perish. It is that kind of world, and under the pressure of common necessity, aided in such cases by physical proximity and biological kinship, there has in fact developed within such households and villages at least a requisite minimum of both practical co-working and conscious, willing participation in a common lot. The wilderness or the countryside is at once opportunity, challenge, and compulsion to communal living within each small group.

On the other hand, as between one frontier cabin or one village and another, no such conscious unity need ordinarily obtain; and except on occasions of common rejoicing or common peril, it usually has not obtained. One curious and equivocal special case has been provided by regional fairs, trading post assemblies, and other gatherings for buying and selling. But these have been specious exceptions that prove the rule. For in them, what our too innocent observer might take to be light-hearted, neighborly merry-making is in fact a jovial mask for the serious antagonisms of competitive trade; somewhat as in our day hard buyers and sellers, before and after driving a bargain, engage in ceremonious handshaking and exchange of witticisms and cigars. A too barefaced egoism cannot easily get its way in either a rude or a mannered society; and egoism finds it expedient often to appear in the guise of neighborliness and co-operation. But real neighborly and co-operative living has been found hitherto mostly within small groups rather than large ones. Both the need of it and the imaginative basis for it become, in the former, more quickly and clearly apparent.

But the problem is posed for us now, directly and insistently, in terms of large groups also. After the frontier came machine tools, and a time of swift physical expansion. The cabins and the villages and growing towns over great expanses of territory were linked rapidly together for purposes of trade, without regard to the more primitive lines of social unification and division. Too rapidly by far, and too ruthlessly, for anything like the old felt unity of household or of village to broaden also, and overtake the new competitive rush for places in the sun. Indeed, even the old unities themselves tended to be broken up, as the work of household loom and of village mill and forge was scattered among a hundred factories in a score of distant cities.

For a while the competitive rush found an open road for its steam-driven, steel-shod progress, and there was felt no inclusive pressure of common necessity to force the development of actual co-working and conscious solidarity on the new larger scale. There were for a while, moreover, no adequate media for swift interchange of news, and the nurture of unitive imagination (both basic to what is called "public opinion"), among people widely separated in space. For the time being, neither natural process nor human intelligence was at all obviously furthering a new, inclusive unification. *Laissez faire* was preached, and lethal competition practiced. The former as theory disparaged conscious effort to co-ordinate production and trade with human needs, over wide social areas, and urged

61

instead the maintenance of an open world market and reliance on natural processes of supply and demand to preserve a balance. In practice, competitive business flouted both co-operative planning and natural law. Competing groups engaged in private seizure and exploitation of natural resources, and in getting exclusive political grants, franchises, and tariffs, to the death of free trade; while instead of co-operative planning for the common good, the practice was for stronger corporations to grow at the expense of weaker, in destructive rivalry with their competitors, and in comparative disregard of unorganized consumers and workers. Thus theory and practice alike conspired in support of rugged economic individualism. And though the latter as practiced was very far from what *laissez faire* as theory called for, and though a succession of painful "crises" gave notice that all was not as it should be, spectacular progress of a kind was being made, and the harsh practice continued.

Primarily, this progress consisted in the development of more efficient production, through improved machinery and methods, and through more strongly centralized organization within the powerful production units which distinguish modern industry. As in a feudal village, within each of these corporate units (composed often of many smaller units merged under central management) there was division of labor, directed toward a common end; and there was in each a roughly hierarchic system of control. But for most workers in the modern plant, repetitious, machine-like tasks replaced the more varied activities of the older handicrafts; and workers became, in effect, replaceable parts of a mechanism over which they had no control, in which they had little or no autonomy, and with whose owners and other members they had far less concrete and lasting personal relations than villagers had had with one another and with their overlords. Within the corporate unit, forced co-working could usually be maintained, when necessary by discarding, or threatening to discard, human parts which did not fit. But voluntary participation, based on each worker's imaginative grasp of his place in a measurably satisfying whole, such as the life of a household or village had been, was now far harder to achieve than in time past. Human loyalties survived, even in so unfavorable a climate. But either they attached themselves to workers' organizations (trade unions, political parties) which intersected the big business units, and loosed somewhat their hold on the worker; or else they took the more primitive form of that blind loyalty which, in any culture, binds simple folk not only to what deserves their allegiance, but to whatever is familiar and specious enough in its claim. In the former case, the worker's life was painfully disunified; in the latter, his growth as a person impeded; and in neither event was the concrete wholeness of village life reproduced in more modern terms.

On the other hand, as between one modern industrial or commercial unit and another, there was no more socially valuable co-operation than once there had been between rival towns. Since among competing business groups joint action for the sake of the common welfare was ordinarily regarded as not thinkable at all, co-operation among them for the sake of greater economic efficiency was discouraged, and at length forbidden by law; and when practiced in fact, by recourse to financial linkage, it accentuated rather than relieved the social destructiveness of irresponsible competition by increasing the magnitude and prowess of the combatants, the numbers of people dependent on them, and the magnitude of the booms and depressions in which their contests issued.

The reasons for these recurrent crises, and whether and how they can be avoided, are of course vexed questions, difficult in themselves and fogged besides by the heats of partisan struggle. But even among laymen, certain elementary factors in the problem have come, thanks first to Karl Marx and then to his critics, to be widely recognized.[45] Improved production meant most obviously having more goods to sell, in return for a given expenditure of productive effort: so far a clear gain. But it meant also, in an unplanned capitalistic economy, that more and still more goods (especially of the more durable kinds), in a constantly mounting total, *had* to be sold in season and out of season, if all businesses were to be run at a profit. The alternative was net loss and eventual bankruptcy for producers who could not fulfil this new rigid requirement, and for sellers of services (labor, transportation, public utilities, and the like) which depended upon the continuance of industrial demand for what they in turn had to sell. This life-and-death requirement to make sales in perpetually increasing sum was new: a correlate of the modern factory and financial system. It was rigid partly because of fixed ratios in the behavior of machines; partly because of accepted habits in the behavior of men. But also it has been, by reason of a growing sum of rigidities which operate in the existing order,[46] impossible of continuous fulfilment. Hence, intervals of very painful readjustment have to be endured, whenever a slackening of demand in some major group of industries threatens them with loss. To avoid immediate loss, they resort to reduction of operation and output, hoping to stay within the existing demand. But their own demand for materials used in making their products is thus lessened, and other factories suffer. Men are thrown out of work, and their buying power reduced, with damage to still other industries. Securities fall; credit and confidence shrink; and the spiral of deflation runs its course.

Whether the just word for this unhappy periodic condition be "over-production" or, as seems more likely, "under-consumption," [47] the only apparent cure would be a generally expanding market, and provision for prompt redirection of men and machines from an area of failing demand into an area in which new demands are forthcoming. In time past, an expanding market was provided in general by continuous increase of population. For a given product, new markets could be sought, roughly, in either or both of two ways: through commercial or territorial expansion abroad (with government aid), and through intensified competitive salesmanship at home. But now neither of these methods, if conceived and practiced in the customary way, can longer be counted on to produce results commensurate with their cost.

The plight of those who seek new foreign trade is well known. In most parts of the world the ways to new markets are now blocked by *No Trespassing* signs and by tariff walls, guarded by grim modern guns. To push ahead now in the old reckless way means to risk large-scale war. But war can be tolerated less and less safely as civilization grows more complex. Step by step with technological development of industry goes increasing intolerance of anarchy. In principle, the case with respect to anarchy is unchanged: Given a world in which at a given time and place, too great a failure in co-operation makes life (or good life) impossible, anarchy is always a perilous (though within limits a proper and beneficial) self-indulgence. What is new today is the enormously heightened threshold below which, it would seem, purposeful co-operation cannot safely fall. A measure of non-co-operation that would be tolerable in a pioneering or an agricultural society, with its sparse habitation, local self-sufficiency, and slow tempo, plays havoc in an industrial society in which great city populations depend from day to day on vast, intricate systems of production, transport, and distribution to keep them alive. It seems plain that, whether we realize it in time or not, on the far larger scale of industrial cosmopolitanism, no less than within the microcosm of frontier household or self-sustained village, an inclusive common necessity is operative: a pressure comparable to that which has forced the smaller economic units to develop requisite minima of internal solidarity. The steel-incarnate logic of our machines, working ever more productively (and, on occasion, more destructively) within their finite, earth-bound setting, seems now to be urging us in despite of all our divisive habits toward such consciously realized unity as only within our time has become at all vividly conceivable.

It is not strange that from our first blundering approach toward world polity, for which we have been most inadequately prepared, our leaders and peoples are in recoil. The newer media for developing lively "public opinion" (which might better be called public sentiment) on a large scale—telegraphic news services, syndicated journals, talking pictures, radio networks—have been devised and used mainly to further the interests of commercial and national groups; and with honorable exceptions, mostly among journalists, they have too often served partisan demands before truth and humanity.[48] The case for worldwide co-operation is yet to be effectively presented.

Moreover, it does not yet appear what form a world organization may best take, nor whether within our life-
times a successful approach thereto can be made. But no
one can seriously doubt that the pressure toward such
organization is heavy upon us. We are in a world which
requires that, if we are to live well, enjoying the resources
of modern knowledge and skill, we shall learn how to
live together, in the largest groups as well as in smaller
ones.

Economic nationalism, I judge, is not a live alternative
to such self-discipline. It is both proper and needful that
in all countries we try to cultivate more intelligently our
respective home markets; but we shall not thereby escape
the silent, relentless demand that we go on to more inclusive community of life and work, even at home, than
has yet been attempted. For new markets at home must
mean numbers of people with new buying power who
lack such power now. In most countries, the curve of
population growth is flattening out, and stability seems
probable in less than a century.[49] But even if, under natural or artificial stimuli, the curve should rise sharply
once more, that would not in itself provide new markets.
What modern sellers need is not merely more people; it
is more people who can buy. But the great mass of people
everywhere have only their work to offer in exchange for
goods, and when the value put upon their work grows
smaller rather than larger, they must buy fewer goods,
not more. In an economy of competition conducted primarily for immediate profit, the exchange value of a man's
labor must decrease if the demand for it grows less. But
the development of highly efficient machinery tends periodically, in presence of the rigidities mentioned above,[50] to
decrease the demand for, and hence the competitive mar-

ket value of such labor as most men have to sell; and to decrease, therefore, the proportionate amount of goods they can buy. Under such conditions, instead of growing larger the home market for consumers' goods, and so indirectly for capital goods, must tend to grow smaller. Strenuous and costly selling campaigns, in these circumstances, become wasteful and self-defeating. The whole process of production and trade must slow down, until a partial redistribution of buying power has been effected by non-competitive measures, such as charity and special legislation. In other words, conventional competition in the home market has to be rescued again and again from its own *impasses,* with cruel discomfort for all concerned, by resort after all to non-competitive means. Add to this picture of self-frustration two further details: that charity and legislative relief, indispensable as life-savers, are yet a poor substitute for the regular employment which profit-oriented competitive industry and trade have thus far proved unable to provide; and that even in "prosperous" intervals, it is said by competent engineers[51] that we get far less than full value from our producing and distributing machinery because of waste and artificial restraints, which have thus far proved inseparable from competition primarily for profit, and a type of management directed primarily to that end.

These difficulties should not be misconstrued into grounds for economic pessimism. There is no apparent reason whatever to suppose that, as regards production and use of goods and services, we are caught in a closed circle of hopeless frustration. The bogy of general and permanent over-population has passed, and the bogy of general and permanent over-production appears to be no more substantial. Over-production is always specific, not general; and there will be always, so far as one can now judge, an economic and ethical "frontier" [52] in the needs of men for better food, housing, equipment, education, and new safeguards and stimuli for better living. But this "frontier," which is biological and spiritual rather than spatial, is far less easily kept accessible and effective as a growing-point than the geographical wilderness which once served both to hearten and to discipline earlier pioneers. Conventional habits and vested claims continually get in our way. Bent on immediate profit, competitive advantage, or simply the maintenance of what has become familiar, we fail to see where at a given time the line of actual need runs, and waste our effort in trying (by high-pressure sales methods, and the like) to push forward somewhere else, where at the moment there is no "frontier." Or, seeing real needs—as in starvation years one cannot help seeing them, and as in any year men of broad-gauge imagination will always see them—we yet find it impossible to get our goods and services across to those who need them, because habits and vested claims of a secondary kind block the way.[53] We shall find a perpetual growing-point in human needs, which collectively are inexhaustible, only when we find ways to orient the energies of machines and of men with reference primarily to these needs as such, rather than to any objective less basic and inclusive.

This, I venture to think, is economic as well as ethical realism. It is not the case that industrial and commercial competition as hitherto practiced has approved itself a "practical," if not a moral, success. Rather, it has shown itself incapable of conducting successfully its own affairs in its own chosen way, without benevolent first aid on a colossal scale. The paralysis of our American banking system in March, 1933, might well be kept in public memory as a time of humiliating judgment upon prideful rugged individualism. Human needs persist and will persist; and an economy directed broadly and flexibly toward their satisfaction might well avoid the convulsions that periodically imperil our present order. What is more, such an economy might succeed in using machine tools and skilled organization so as to banish economic anxiety far and wide, and to free men and women for growth in areas of living from which now most are shut out.[54] Its success would then be at once "practical" and moral. But however that may be, thus much is certain: so long as we continue to see our economic problems piecemeal, and to let our energies be diverted from grappling with them to fighting one another, we shall achieve neither practical nor moral triumph. Bitter defense of vested claims and obsolescent special interests must give way to more clearsighted and inclusive loyalty; else we shall continue to miss not merely spiritual enlargement, but even that "prosperity" for which we try in vain to sell our birthright.

Whatever we might wish or hope, the world we are in does not in the long run tolerate irresponsible self-seeking, by groups any more than by individuals. The required minimum of co-operation in a machine-equipped culture is not obviously different in kind from what it is in a simpler one, and in extent it is far greater. If we desire, then, to live with full advantage of our newer resources of knowledge and equipment, we must develop once more, in our new and wider context, a "contributive society" in which every one who will may work whole-heartedly, with assurance that his work, great or small, is needed and valued as a contribution to the common life.

To do needful work, then; to lose oneself and find oneself therein; to participate thus in a common task and a shared life: this, and the summons to it, we shall mean by vocation. Such doctrine professes to begin not with wishes nor with dogmas about God nor about man, but with what appear to be facts and likely inferences therefrom. It commits one neither to blind support of the *status quo* nor to indiscriminate revolt against it in the name of inscrutable authority. Rather it sketches out a group of related principles, professedly suggested by the actual behavior of men and the world, which may serve to guide in part a serious effort to live in the world as it is and toward a world as it ought to be. It seeks to make place, in principle, both for organic interrelatedness and for individual differences and autonomous selfhood, while insisting that neither the one nor the other is at all adequately realized now. While steadily refusing to look for a kingdom of heaven on earth, past, present, or to come, in which men would be gods and life one grand sweet song, it steadily hopes for a time when more men can be more fully men, through conscious participation in a meaningful common life, freed from some of the crippling drudgeries and irrational fears that have hampered our race in the past and still are heavy upon us. Its hope is not mainly in human nobility nor in human intelligence; seeing that both, for all their promise, are as yet at least far too sporadic and fragile to carry the fate of mankind, and moreover that both are themselves grounded in a world-order vastly more ancient and inclusive than they. Rather, its hope is first of all in what that world-

71

order may portend: that order which with silent condemnation and promise calls mankind back, again and again, from the bogs of unbridled competitive war to the road of contributive work. Not dogmatically but quite soberly, in part though not wholly for reasons which can be examined in the third and fourth chapters, it regards that call as coming ultimately not from men, nor from dialectically moving matter, but from God.

CHAPTER TWO

WORTH AND THE ACTUAL WORLD

There is no more evident and no more important fact of human experience than the widespread discrepancy between what ought to be and what is. The simpler contrast between what one wants or likes and what one can get is more obvious, to animals and immature persons, and at times to all of us. But for civilized adults, the disparity between what can be thought fine and what is forthcoming in fact is not less evident, and is much more crucial. One may learn to accept calmly, even to welcome, frustrations of particular desires, though they be one's own, as conducive to growth in wisdom and stature; but one cannot without moral abdication become indifferent to disparities between possible better and actual worse. Come to terms with a world deeply infected with such discrepancies one must, or go mad; but acquiesce in them one may not, and keep morally sane. Here is a theme made for satirists and pessimists; a standing provocation to moral crusaders; and a paradox which religion continually must seek to resolve.

In our talk of vocation we have already become involved in this puzzle of actual and ideal, and must face now some of its difficulties from the special standpoint of that concept. We must try still to keep clear our task as theologians, whose primary practical concern is human morale and orientation. We must not try here to develop a general theory of value, nor to devise detailed ways and means for achieving such values as seem to us generally worth seeking. We must try steadily to talk, that is, neither as axiologists nor as would-be social engineers. Indeed, we can give here only incidental and fragmentary notice even to the question what values in particular are to be accounted of especial worth. Our present concern is to follow here and there, in the tangle of principles and facts known to us, some of the implications of whole-hearted belief that work conceived and practiced as vocation is basic to good life and religion; and to elaborate, clarify, and test that belief in the light of those current tendencies which seem most relevant and at some points most inimical to it. The discussion thus begun will be continued in the fifth chapter, in which among other matters we shall inquire how this conviction may bear on the urgent problems of social criticism and change, and help to define a stable attitude toward the persisting tension between what is and what ought to be.

We have argued that the day's work and the yearly round, now as in more primitive times, is a *milieu* within which religion for the rank and file of mankind must be strongly rooted. We have held that only so can fragmentation of life and sterilization of both work and worship be overcome. To that end we are urging rehabilitation and development, as working doctrine for every day, of the religious concept of earthly calling, now in general disrepute. In this chapter we shall consider that doctrine as a partial expression of what has been called religious realism; and shall give our attention in turn to what may be called vocational ideals, and vocational realities.

I

The theological tendency of which this doctrine professes to be one phase is that currently known as religious

realism. Its characteristic approach to the apparent tension
between actual and ideal may be indicated most briefly
by comparing it with three alternative tendencies, and
by taking note of certain of its constituent factors. Confronted, then, by the actual which seems not ideal, optimism tends to accept the actual and defend it as somehow fully good; pessimism tends to reject it as incurably
bad; academic skepticism tends to acquiesce in it
as simply beyond human power to evaluate in either
way. In distinction from all these, religious realism un-
dertakes to criticize and endeavors to change the actual,
in the conviction that it ought to be and, in principle, can
become better than at any specifiable moment it is.

On the other hand, religious realism has common
ground with each of the three alternative views named,
as a glance at four of its constituent factors may show.
(*a*) Basic among them is the outward-looking attitude we
call by such names as belief, affirmation, conviction, "animal faith," which I think in fact though not always in
theory is characteristic of realism in all its forms.[1] The
religious realist believes that confronting him is an actual concourse of things, persons, and events which has
both a history and a future; he finds that in seeking to
understand, evaluate, and come to terms with all these,
he is constrained to recognize defining forms or characteristics, some of which assume for him the special guise
of ideals; and he believes that both facts and forms, whatever be the status or mode of being assigned to either,
transcend in their range to an unknown extent the range
of actual human observation and thought. (*b*) In reflective elaboration upon these beliefs, he works out a theology
which affirms in one way or another the ambivalence
of the actual, the ambiguous status of the formal and

ideal, and the inability of either actual or ideal as it stands to provide the basis for an intelligible account of the relations observed to obtain between the one and the other. The actual is ambivalent in the sense that always and everywhere within the range of human experience, it exemplifies both goodness and defect. The crucial line marking off better from worse cuts not between one group of things or of persons, and another; as though some were sacred and others profane, some a true Church, a fellowship of saints, and others unsaved children of this world. The crucial line cuts rather through the midst of every occupation, every human group, and every man's own living, best and worst alike. Nothing actual is nor conceivably can be ideal. On the other hand, a form or ideal has ambiguous status insomuch as it is pertinent to and partly exemplified by, but not identical with nor completely present in any actual thing or event. And neither actuality nor ideality as such appears yet to have provided by itself a sufficient reason for the inter-relations in which we find these two modes of being to occur. Both seem to offer clues and intimations to follow out as well as one may, rather than satisfactory self-explanations. It is in trying to follow out these clues that the speculative theologian may be led to affirm as cognate with the demands of reason such belief in the reality of God as he is likely to hold in the first place upon other than logical grounds: a God who in some sense is kind to the unthankful and evil, and yet sternly exacting toward even the best among actual persons and things. (*c*) But there is in religious realism, thirdly, a strain of moral energy which often is impatient of these nice distinctions, and which, seeing merely gross in-equalities of worth between the doings of one man, one group, one occupation and another, seeks to throw its strength against those which appear to be the worse. (*d*) And there is, finally, a strain of skeptical reserve and critical doubt, acutely alive to both the defects of the actual world, and the futility and presumption that dog both reflective theory and aggressive reform.

To the religious realist in certain moods, indeed, his more cautious neighbor the skeptic seems to be in an enviably strong position. We all know that the vagaries of human behavior have never been easy to set right, nor even to judge rightly. For one thing, it is always easier for theorist or reformer to recognize aberrations elsewhere than in the area of his own vested interests, and it is always pleasanter to grasp at the mote in some one else's eye than to do something about the beam in one's own. For another thing, even sincere and courageous attacks upon plain abuse close at hand, including such as may be of profit to oneself, are liable to one-sidedness in conception and to unforeseen warping in outcome. Hence there is presumptuousness in every human attempt, even in such mild talk as this, which aims at positive redirection of thought and behavior in the complex tangle that constitutes an existing culture. And hence also there is persuasiveness in the academic inclination to refrain from any decisive speech or action, and to prefer the more sheltered rôle of the onlooker. One who does not feel and understand this impulse to distrust human judgment, especially one's own, as liable to presumptuous error has not, I think, seen very far into the actual, painful disabilities of creaturehood. But what the academic skeptic, of course, often does not let himself see is that since he too is human he cannot stand, godlike nor ostrich-like, outside the stream of human conduct, and that his effort to do so is itself a commitment, like any other liable to be wrong. The mood and attitude of skepticism is, then, a needed antidote against speculative and practical excesses; but no more than any other mood, nay in the long run much less than any other, can it become a complete way of life.

Again, the theologian must take full account of the moral reformer's problems, insights, and active impulses, and must seek to appreciate and illuminate, rather than to ignore or to eviscerate these and their methods and objectives. The moral reformer, conversely, and the man of hearty "animal faith," granted they can learn from hard experience, must become aware of the need for reflective understanding and sober critical judgment, lest their affirmations and efforts be needlessly and culpably near-sighted. In religious realism, an effort is made to deal fairly with all these diverse demands; and a considerable measure of neatness and finality is sacrified, for the sake of maintaining touch with substantial masses of fact and with urgent practical concerns, though neither present facts nor short-term obligations can be permitted alone to dictate the theologian's view.

II

It is of this theological tendency that the doctrine of vocation professes to be a partial expression. We shall be engaged now, for the most part indirectly, in adjudicating that claim and certain of its implications. How far, first, can that doctrine be thought congruous with religious realism, or what deserves to go by that name? Is the doctrine realistic, in the sense of being relevant to the existing state of human affairs? And is it in any honest sense religious, or does it, in effect, recommend us to honor God by serving mammon, and give the name of piety to sanctimonious egoism? Further, what value has the doctrine for contemporary living? Does it, on the one hand, offer specific guidance in our present quandary as to what needs to be done, and how it should be done? Does it, on the other hand, offer help toward re-establishment of morale and general reorientation? What difference, in short, would it make to any one if he should try to live by such a view?

A. Let us begin with a brief look at what may be called here vocational idealism: the ethical and quasi-religious demands of good workmanship.

(1) Certain of its positive demands have been noticed in the preceding chapter. (*a*) The first is objectivity. Inasmuch as every serious worker finds himself at grips with actual, exacting, and at least partly intelligible situations, he finds that there is permanent call for outward-looking intelligence, and for some measure of honesty and integrity on his part, if he is seriously to meet their exactions. There is call, likewise, for energy and persistency; and for a continual self-commitment to the job, which draws him continually out of his private imaginings and wishings into a public order, an actual concourse of things, persons, and events, which is not subject to his whims, but which is to some degree responsive when he applies himself to it seriously. (*b*) A second demand on the workman, which he may or may not successfully meet, is for that combined plasticity and resourcefulness that is needed for learning and growth, without which work can never be more than conscientious drudgery. This involves a certain pliableness and

amenability; what von Hügel called "endless docility to fact." [2] It involves also conscious self-discipline, in response —but not passive response—to discovered environing conditions. And with these it involves a measure of vitality, endurance, and active resource that will ensure recovery from disappointment and from injury, and at least occasional triumph over obstacles and recouping of defeats. (*c*) A third demand, at first sight less intrinsic to work as such but, as we have tried to show, in the long run not less inescapable, is for co-operativeness and contributiveness. The primary need here, in a human group trying to keep alive, is of course for actual co-working that shall not fall below the minimum required in a given situation; but for full human living, the demand is also that the need for such actual co-working be acknowledged consciously and accepted voluntarily, so that it takes the form of conscious responsibility and participation.

(2) Correlative to these positive demands are certain essential antipathies which are a no less important part of what we are calling vocational idealism. (*a*) One of these is rejection of sham. Pretentiousness and obsequiousness, sham "service," fake "art," and scamped "work" are negations of all that decent workmanship stands for, and repugnant to every decent workman. (*b*) A second is distrust of egotism, whether of the individual, of a group, or of man as man. Individual egotism commonly takes the forms of subjectivism, caprice, and inconsiderate selfishness, all of which plainly conflict with working requirements. The point is not, of course, that individuals cannot profit in certain ways by selfishness: obviously they do. The point is merely that such behavior is in conflict with essential implications of respon-

sible workmanship, without which in the long run men cannot survive as men, and which, on the other hand, offers values in the way of growth and enhancement of personal life such as even a selfishly inclined individual can ill afford to miss. Group egotism, so familiar just now in theory and in fact, likewise violates a principle of sound workmanship by its clique, class, national, and racial antagonisms and exclusions, and by its proclivity to arbitrary as against instructed and disciplined government within the group. The peculiar egotism of man as man which issues in sentimental or in theoretical glorification of mankind, avoids some but not all of the perils of individual and group selfishness, and increases the handicap to sound workmanship by encouraging a tendency to vague abstractionism. No less than egotism of the individual and the group it tends to distract the thoughts and efforts of a worker from doing needful work to seeking self-aggrandizement, whether in fact or in fancy, and in either case to the detriment of what as worker he finds needing to be done. In so far, moreover, as such all-too-human estimates of the value and dignity of man tend to go beyond sober realism and to be overestimates, they open the door to falsity and sham. Egotism and sham, indeed, almost always go together; and together they constitute what seems the very core and proper essence of impiety, and a gross denial of what one should mean by vocation. Straightforward recognition of solid human values, alike in the individual, the concrete group, and the human race, is implied in all doing of work and in the theory of religious realism, and will be defended here against current disparagements; but inflated egotism is inimical both to sound work and to valid religious theory.

More archaic than conscious egotism and pretense, and perhaps literally underlying both, are two other modes or conditions or tendencies of human behavior, which may even deserve to rate as original sin, if one be interested in such matters. They are tendencies which clearly man has in common with simpler organisms, and I venture that from them are engendered much of the human misbehavior which we deplore and find difficult to eradicate. Both are ever-present and ever-tempting alternatives to the difficult and painful way of rational, responsible behavior; and against the dominance of either, vocational idealism is by its nature on guard. (*c*) The first is a bent toward anarchic, irresponsible self-indulgence: a Janus-faced principle of chaos which shows itself now as lethargy, now as undisciplined violence. From its influence no son of earth seems to be free. It drags, a dead weight, against every move toward fuller life and a more decent world. No doubt in our queer space-time medley, inertia too has its uses, and at the human level a good deal can be said for those who only stand and wait. But it needs to be said with discrimination. To stand and wait may be actively to refrain from ill-timed action, or it may be passively to evade unpleasant effort. The former is of the essence of rational behavior; the latter undermines, in its amiable way, the whole structure of human living. Doubtless indolent men are less offensive neighbors than rapacious or violent ones, in whom the same irresponsible drift toward chaos appears in harsher guise. Doubtless, too, causes for lethargy of body or of mind can be found in climate, fatigue, malnutrition, hormone deficiencies, bad heredity, wrong education, social disorganization, and should be sought out and remedied when possible. But none of these palliations, though they must temper

82

our judgment of individuals, classes, and cultures, can alter the broad human fact. However caused and however manifested, complacent lethargy is quicksand, whose still waters are ever-present death to the spirit of man. Those who complacently hold as ideal for the few a gentleman's life, unsullied with labor, and those who look with tranquillity upon recurring stagnant floods of unemployment for the many, have forgotten how civilizations and decencies have settled out of sight beneath just such tides of disintegration, deceptively quiet at first, but at last dark with violence. However often we forget it, life at the human level rests on the co-operative doing of needful work; and among us we have to keep such work going, and such spirit in the ascendant, or revert to animalism. In face of that stark fact, there seems no rational place among men for purely decorative leisure classes nor unemployed masses, large or small. For leisure, yes: good human life at every level has need of it. But lives given up to leisure, no, since men are not Epicurean gods nor ravens nor lilies of the field. They need work, not to keep them alive merely, but to keep them human. And aggressive demands for work instead of alms are just now a welcome sign of vitality among idle men who have had their fill of idleness but who still prefer work to violence.[8] Work is a genuine, violence a spurious, alternative to inactivity, however readily in given situations it may be explained and excused. This point we shall need to examine further in the concluding chapter. (*d*) Meanwhile, we note here finally another closely related archaic tendency to whose dominance a vocational ethic is of necessity opposed: the tendency to stiffening or stereotyping of behavior which, indispensable as a subordinate factor in learning and growth, means

83

senescence or deformity if it becomes dominant. In its proper functional setting it is a check upon irresponsible caprice; but whenever among men its automatic operations, in either individual or group, supplant adaptive rational control with rigid habitual conformity, the outcome again is likely to be lassitude or violence, or both. Against such stiffening and mechanizing, the vocational demand, as we have seen, is for plasticity and rational adaptiveness.

These, in the abstract, are some of the claims of vocational doctrine to be considered as seriously idealistic and not time-serving. In its demands for objectivity and rational self-commitment, for teachableness and growth, for co-operativeness and contributiveness in a persistent effort to meet real needs in accordance with the exactions of a real world, it plainly goes far beyond what most men and women now can claim as achievement. Moreover, in its intrinsic opposition to sham and to egotism, to the irrational lethargies of indolence and violence, and to the dominance of rigid mechanism in human behavior, it may be held without undue absurdity to stand so far upon common ground with the most exacting of ethical and religious thought.

B. It is time now to raise the question of vocational realism: to look in the light of these demands at contemporary working life in some of its familiar aspects, and to see whether our doctrine deserves to be called realistic. Let us begin by asking what dispositions or modes of behavior actually show themselves where men are at work. It will be understood, of course, that what are here called occupational dispositions do not fall into fixed, sharply distinguishable types. They may and do appear in endless variation and combination, and this list may easily be extended and varied in such fashion as to bring into relief other modes of behavior than those here chosen for emphasis. Moreover, we are not now concerned with the task of explaining, but rather with that of describing and roughly evaluating human conduct. The point is merely to remind ourselves of some ways in which human workers go at their work, and it is enough if the dispositions referred to seem roughly recognizable in fact, and the interpretations put upon them appear to be reasonably fair.

Let us take note, then, of six more or less variant ways in which men do work:

(1) There is first a disposition which one may call, with Lloyd Morgan, "natural piety," [4] though some would call it, perhaps, stolidity. This, I presume, defines the normal attitude of the simplest, least self-conscious laborer toward his job. There are mouths to feed, and work to be done: timber felled, land cleared and tilled, harvest gathered, food cooked; or else coal to be dug, fires tended, concrete poured, freight handled. A steady round, for the most part, with little room for questions of why and wherefore. Immediate needs are self-evident, and ways in which they can be met make their appeal directly and unequivocally. So when things are going well, one may work and rest with a pervasive and mostly inarticulate thankfulness, or when they go ill, with mingled frustration, resignation, and obstinate hope for better times; but in neither case with any inflated sense of personal dignity, nor on the other hand with any nervous doubt that the work is worth while and worthy of respect. The question just does not arise.

(2) Hardly less simple-minded but appreciably less

simple-hearted than such natural piety is a sort of half-naïve solemnity by which it is often displaced and caricatured. In a society like ours, whose pursuits have multiplied and become minutely specialized through hit-or-miss competition, many occupations develop which cater only to minor or vestigial or fictitious human needs, or to needs which for æsthetic or other reasons are not held in high honor, or even to no clearly specifiable needs at all. Methods, likewise, come into use in this occupation and that which violate traditional tabus, or otherwise tend to put those who practice them on the defensive. One consequence is growing vocational self-consciousness and inflated but uneasy self-esteem, troubled by doubts as to how one's calling may appear to others. The comfort to be had in such cases from suitable incantations is well known, and no one who has himself tried their inflationary, sedative, and hypnotic properties need wonder at the current vogue of grandiose phrases and gestures on every hand. Prominent realtors convey choice locations to leading restaurateurs. Physicians and other clinicians divide their nomenclatorial prestige with beauticians and cosmeticians on the one hand, morticians on the other. Erstwhile stockbrokers become investment bankers, and their customers' men consulting economists and financial counsellors. The gay science of advertising, grown fat on appeals to fear, sex, and snobbery, devotes its splendid resources of applied psychology, imaginative literature, and the plastic arts to public-spirited efforts on behalf of national prosperity. All of which Babbittry is naturally deprecated by aloof intellectuals who subsist on salaries or royalties rather than competitive profits, for which they have their scrambling done vicariously, and defer to one another as authors, educators, critics, and authorities on

this or that; by ardent white-collared reformers in shining
armor, and black-hatted public servants on marble ped-
estals; by professional proletarians who agitate, demon-
strate, demand, and pass resolutions overwhelmingly,
with glib talk of a united front, world revolution, and
classless society; by eloquent and popular ministers of this
church and that, to whom each more expensive pulpit
is an opportunity for larger service to the Kingdom of
God; and by earnest theological lecturers, who like to
fancy themselves single-mindedly serving truth and right
as associate professors of something in a university. *Hypocritai*—play actors, all of us, in our times of half-naïve
solemnity; like the Pharisee who prayed his incredible
prayer in the temple.

But not all workers are thus virginal, or demi-virginal;
at least not all the time. Some are disillusioned spoilers
or victims; and some are responsible workmen who find
life and joy in their work.

(3) The tough-minded individual for whom his occupation has neither intrinsic worth nor fanciful glamour
is apt to manifest toward it an attitude of predatory cynicism. He intends to get from it what he can and give to
it only what he must, with no self-deluding nonsense
about "service" or other polite humbug. Publicly of
course, in job-hunting or in labor disputes, in advertisements or in after-dinner speeches, he may use the fulsome language of more innocent folk as camouflage; and
sometimes he may even partly believe it himself. But
fundamentally he is immune to such weakness, and may
be frank enough to say outright, "The public be damned!"
At best his occupation is for him an exciting sport, in
which he carries on private combat against competitors,

big and little, with profits and power to be won; at worst
a racket, in which he fleeces the employers, fellow-work-
men, employees, or customers, and sells short the stock-
holders, who are fools enough to trust him. He takes
pride in not being innocent, though often he is more
naïve than he and his admirers suspect.

(4) Equally disillusioned but less able, callous, and efficient are the very large number of workers and would-be
workers who today are humiliated and hopeless: battered
victims of a world that seemingly has no decent work for
them to do. Many of them have had ambitions, many
have had ideals. But stretch-outs and layoffs have scrapped
them. Some are old men at forty or forty-five, shouldered
aside by the growing surplus of youth. Some are already
victims of that surplus at sixteen, before they have ever
held a job. Some have jobs in which they can find no
satisfaction: jobs of which they are ashamed, or by which
they are physically damaged, nervously exhausted, and
spiritually numbed. Pessimism, cynical or submissive, is
their lot, unless in youthful vagabondry and early death,
or human friendship, or in some miracle of self-sacrifice,
a part of them may find some reason for living. Or unless
they yield again to illusion, and dream of prosperity
around the corner. Or unless revolutionary passion, feeding on their frustration and despair, should fire them to
violence with blind, reckless hope. Or unless decent and
sufficient work be provided for them, by a social order
goaded and frightened into fuller awareness of what these
things mean than any conservative society hitherto has
shown before it was too late.

There remains a disposition for our purpose the most
important of all, which may appear at either of two

roughly distinguishable levels: the disposition of conscious
and voluntary responsibility of one who works with vigor
and not without satisfaction.

(5) The more ordinary level of such working is that
of the trained workman, skilled or unskilled. Whether his
hand be clumsy or clever, the genuine workman's heart
responds positively to his work; which becomes his un-
pretentious contribution toward making the world somehow more fit to live in. He takes pride in knowing his
job, whether road-mending or garage work or plumbing
or preaching. He knows, to some extent, what it is for
and how it should be done, and he tries honestly to develop skill at doing it. Moreover, like every honest and
vigorous man, he is keen to get rid of the hindrances that
stand needlessly in his way, so far as he can see what
they are. He is impatient of charlatanry in his own field,
and resents being forced to do shoddy work, or to work
under needlessly bad conditions, or for less than a decent
wage. His attitude may be, and commonly is, complicated by greed, envy, belligerence, and the rest of the
seven deadly sins; and his sense of values outside the field
of his limited competence may be poor and twisted. But
one who has any claim to the title of workman has
learned at least something of integrity, self-control, and
self-transcendence, whether he has words for them or
not.

(6) When such workmanlike competence and conscious responsibility reaches the level of technical master-
ship and intense love for one's work, the workman
becomes an artist, in the fine basic sense of that word.
Not a finicking precisionist, nor a temperamental show-
man, nor a manufacturer of pretty or romantic or classical or realistic art objects, but a doer of exceptional in-

sight, skill, and devotion. Such a one may work in any
of a thousand media: metal, cement, and stone; soil and
growing things; fluids, fabrics, living bodies; words, tones,
abstract symbols; desires, movements, concrete feelings.
He may have any occupational label, or none. His
artistry is not in his title nor his rank, but in his working and, deeper than that, in the dispositions from which
his working springs. He is one who loves what is he is
doing, and still more what he is trying to do; not with the
indiscriminate gush of the sentimentalist, nor the submissive acceptance of the fatalist, but with the exacting
and impatient, long-suffering but never-resting love of
one who is slave to a good beyond all that he is or has
or can be or do, and whose work is a struggle to open
ways by which envisaged goods and, beyond them, goods
yet unimagined, may become incarnate, within reach of
human hands and eyes.

C. If now this is a fair sampling of what can be said
about men at work, how shall we evaluate it? Can a
religious doctrine of vocation be fittingly applied to such
factual stuff as this? A first trite judgment is of course
that such human behavior is not simply good nor bad, but
as we have said inherently ambivalent. Running through
it in all directions are telltale marks of infantilism, premature hardening, and spiritual deformity, side by side with
marks of spiritual vitality and integrity.

(1) Plainly it bears the marks (*a*) first, of perennial
immaturity, which is itself, again, both good and bad:
since it keeps a way open for growth, yet through its
indiscipline, irresponsibility, and lack of insight, hinders
us and makes us hinder one another from fuller living.
The industrious ant, the busy bee, are not immature.

Neither are they models for men to follow, whose life would cease to be human once it hardened into uniformity. Yet we pay heavily for our protracted childhood. We pay in wasted energy, with business men racing to see which can set up the tallest slum-footed skyscraper in New York, and communists planning a hideous monument in Moscow still taller, in token of the superiority of a proletarian leader. We pay in stagnation and parasitism, with Palm Beach and the Riviera sucking wealth and strength alike from play-boys who spend and toilers who make possible their spending. We pay in unintended destruction and death, with solemnly irresponsible statesmen, arms-makers, and publicists time and again jockeying irresolute peoples toward war. The coils of that sluggish serpent, original sin, the lethargy of mind and will which slips over so naturally into violence, lie about us in our infancy.

(*b*) But premature senescence also is apparent in human behavior. Most of us bear in one way or another the marks of spasmodic effort to put away childish things and become defiantly adult, once for all. The discomforts and indignities of immaturity prove too painful, and we have sought to add forthwith a final cubit to our stature and be done with the disabilities of being children. But things as they are, the result of such effort, when it is not wholly a failure, is more or less unevenly arrested growth, and therewith shortening of our perspectives both of value and of recognizable fact. Such stoppage may take the form of contempt for the world and man, and may show itself in ascetic renunciation, sneering disparagement, or cold-blooded exploitation: the way of the anchorite, of the cynical satirist, or of the insensitive spoiler. Thus one may avoid the pain of repeated disillusionment. By having one's heart hardened, whether by accident or design, toward the world and men, one becomes less vulnerable to betrayal. But contempt has this effect only because it makes alien and null that which is despised, and so it cuts off possible benefits no less than possible hurts. One can learn nothing from that which one holds in contempt, and one's room for growth toward the very maturity one covets is thus far curtailed. So one is become prematurely old, through grasping at maturity before it comes duly to hand.

A similar cramping of outlook may come about in what appears to be a precisely contrary way: to wit, through unwarrantably high prizing of things and of human persons. The sensualist, the miser, the devotee of buying and selling, because their hearts are set upon things and respond to nothing beyond these, put limits to their own growth and hamper also the efforts of their children, neighbors, and fellow citizens to grow further. They are those smug realists who care more for sparrows in the hand than for an eagle on the wing. They can truckle to wealth and power, make tools of their weaker associates, and fight by means fair and unfair to keep possession of what they have, whatever values may be at stake, because unlike more imaginative folk, they do not know how great the world is and how stupid a possessor of some small part of it can be. Their love for things is good, so far as it goes; sparrows also are to be prized for what they are. But so far as it is entangled with ignorance and contempt for what cannot be had in hand, its power to generate growth toward genuine maturity is checked. So likewise with an undue attachment even to human beings. Very much has been said among liberals, humanitarians, and good Christians, and now quite espe-

cially among Humanists, about the supreme worth of
personality. With much in the spirit of such affirmation
one must concur. Surely a man is of more value than a
sheep; and human institutions should be made for men,
not men for institutions. Surely also a man must think in
human ways. But to make an entire theology or philosophy out of one such principle, giving man the supreme place in one's scale of values, is to risk the
sentimental unrealism against which Marxist and Barthian polemics are now so effective, and against which
Spinoza and the Stoics had already argued with telling
weight. Again the trouble comes not with love for men;
that is something we need far more of, not less. The
trouble comes when we fail to look beyond man, and
pride ourselves that in such refusal, we have come of age.
The fact is now, as it has always been, that unless there
be something greater and better than both, there is no
obvious ground for optimism about either the goodness
and power of men or the ultimate worth of things. To
stop with these is to stop short of that maturity which is
able to recognize and accept for oneself and one's kind a
subordinate place; which shows itself in "a willingness to
be ignored."

Throughout these last few paragraphs we have been
close upon what was called earlier the essence of impiety
in human living: to wit, egotism and sham. These are
the characteristics of overt human behavior that are most
impossible to reconcile with any religious concept of vocation. How can one call that an offering to God which is
so plainly a deliberate grasping at profit for none other than
oneself? And how can pretentious fake-science, pseudo-
art, and mock-altruism be described without blasphemy
as labor in a calling? The answer must be: These are not

and can never be anything other than ignorant or brazen denials of all that we mean by vocation.

(2) But it is time now to turn the glass the other way about. If egotism and sham are the antithesis of piety, it follows that the development of genuine piety in daily living must involve persistent attack on just such offensive modes of behavior as these. To urge that one live one's daily life as a vocation is not to recommend that one honor God by serving mammon, nor that one sanctify with a phrase whatever actually goes on. Not all things are clean; the tension between what is and what ought to be cannot be relaxed; the things that are Cæsar's must still be distinguished from the things that are God's. But that does not mean that this world belongs to Cæsar and some other world to God. It means that the servants of God in this world have obligation to resist self-aggrandizement and pretense wherever it crops up, in industry, politics, individual living, and social affairs; recognizing freely that perfection is not to be looked for here, but refusing to acquiesce in the finality of anything less.

Against egotism and sham one who holds his work as a calling will oppose a steady effort to keep the basic pattern of human work clear: needs to be met, methods to be sought out or devised and followed with sincerity, integrity, and teachability, and without pretentious display. I am presuming that thousands of men and women are working in this fashion, some of whom would call themselves religious and some of whom would not. My concern at the moment is not to argue whether those who do not are unwittingly religious, or religious in spite of themselves, for that sort of discussion is endless. My concern is rather to urge that such work is fit to become one basic factor in a full religious life; and that both the work,

and the worship by which it should be supplemented,
would gain by such integration. It is fit to become a basic
factor in religion because, over and above any descriptive
virtues it may possess and any valuable results it may
achieve, such work demands continually self-devotion or
self-transcendence on the part of the worker: a daily
exercise of unstudied faith, and hope, and normally of
love. At the simplest level, of inarticulate, unselfconscious
labor, religion must be such as inarticulate folk can give
themselves to: a matter of heart and of muscles, mainly,
rather than of words and ideas. At the level of conscious,
responsible workmanship, both morality and religion also
will be conscious: a recognition of needs, of values, of
means to their realization and of hindrances that stand in
the way; and then conscious devotion in word and deed
to doing what needs to be done. At the level of artistry,
self-transcending devotion is carried as far, I surmise, as
in any known mode of human living, mystical contemplation not excepted. Even the mystic can yield up to the
experienced Other no more than all his human powers,
and these the rare artist in any craft learns to devote for
hours, days, years at a stretch to the compelling tasks that
will not let him go. Indeed, in so far as mysticism at less
than its very best tends to subjectivism, artistry (which
has always an outward reference) may claim a certain advantage. Herein are faith and hope and love at white
heat, fit for the worship of God because they are at once
so devoted to and so critical of what is man's. Yet even
here one must be on guard against any assumption that
the rôle of theology is simply to mirror and approve an
existing state of affairs. Theology worth the name has
never been content to report on existing human behavior
and conform to its demands. Rather, it has persistently

confronted human behavior with demands by which humanity is bidden to acknowledge itself bound and judged. Taking the concept of vocation seriously as theological doctrine commits one not to placid acceptance but to drastic criticism and attempted amendment of things as they are, even at their present best.

(3) Yet plainly a serious demand for change must be relevant to the existing state of affairs; and there are current just now three less favorable estimates of man, particularly of the ordinary man, and his doings, which would cut the ground from under this whole train of thought so far as it lays claim to any realism and practical relevance.

(*a*) The first is a cynical pessimism which would depreciate human life and interests, and the values in which they terminate, by reducing them in theory to simple functions of subhuman processes. This is the familiar line taken long since by the true Cynics, those biting "dog-philosophers" who, after the manner of Diogenes with his bitterly ironic lantern, stripped down complacent man to the quadruped level. For what is man, and what are human needs? In sum: digestion, excretion, reproduction. To see this is to be done with pretenses about human dignity and human values. Thus too the more savage monks of the Christian middle age, who pictured the human body as so much offal and dung, and the human soul as though it were a foul odor. Thus also the literary pessimists, old and new: Dean Swift, whose monarch of Brobdingnag judged mankind "the most pernicious race of little odious vermin that Nature ever suffered to crawl upon the surface of the earth," and who tried in clinical poem after poem to disgust his readers with human love; Carlyle, whose reductive word on the anatomy of orches-

tral music is in its way final; and now Ernest Hemingway, for whose emasculated soldier the sun also rises;
Joseph Wood Krutch, under whose honest eyes, when he
wrote *The Modern Temper,* heroism and tragedy had
faded out of human life with the going of religion, and romantic love itself paled into a chemical reaction; Aldous
Huxley, before whom jerk, puppet-like and brilliant,
living organs and conditioned reflexes in the shapes of
men and women: a brain, a mouth, muscles, loins, taut
nerves.[5]

But this recurrent effort to discredit man and all his
values by declaring them subhuman is after all a *tour
de force,* more valuable in its way than its authors could
in full consistency admit, but needing to undergo correction from time to time in the face of quite everyday
facts. In the first place, these critics who care enough
about mankind to berate human folly stand above their
own criticisms, and hold fiercely to values of their own.
Diogenes looks down with grim pride on the self-
indulgent Alexander the Great; Swift and Carlyle are
tortured idealists; and through the work of many post-
war cynics, hatred of sham and prizing of bitter truth
runs like undying fire. To criticize is human. A quadruped really has no use for satire. And to expect others
to read and understand one's criticism is to suppose that
others also are human. The earnest critic's attempt to
repudiate all values, or to deny appreciation of them to
others whom he seriously addresses, must inevitably fail.
In the second place, a healthy idealism can well stand and
profit from being reminded that men are animals, in
whose behavior subhuman mechanisms are an ever-present part. Of course we have bones and muscles or we
could neither stand nor go, as Socrates having chosen to

remain in prison cheerfully recognized.[6] Of course hunger and sex drives directly or indirectly initiate very much of what we do, and gross physiological explosions are factors in our richest emotional experiences. And of course every one of us, some more than others, has sunk repeatedly to subhuman modes of behavior. An idealism too fastidious to bear the rough touch of fact may need to deny or forget that these things are so; but a more robust idealism can recognize them neither with shame nor with gloating but with candor, and seek to learn how in fact they grow to be included in widening and deepening reaches of life. To affirm that we are animals is not to deny that we are men; and our business here is to learn how to be better men, not blithe spirits. Doubtless our animality often proves a sluggish, treacherous mass, and not an aid to spiritual health. But even so, a realist's prayer will be not "Who shall deliver me out of the body of this death?" but "How shall this body, groaning and travailing until now, be quickened toward new life?"

(*b*) There are Nietzschean and Barthian critics upon us now, however, who are not mollified by reminders that after all we can be men. For to them humanism at its very best is most self-centered and illusory. To be human is matter for weeping, not pride; and to follow after humanly chosen values is vanity, and a striving after wind.[7] Now as warning against the sentimental egoism of our kind, this is excellent, as we have more than once remarked. But in so far as it seeks to discredit values on the score of their human appeal, it is untenable. For on the one hand, the goods recognized by the Nietzschean ethic or the dialectical theology itself must be relevant to human interest, else men could not respond to them without first ceasing to be men and no such earthly rebirth as

any sane philosophy or religion looks for may be expected
to negate man's essential nature. *Der Uebermensch,* "men
like gods," and so on, are good enough stuff for romantic
dreamers and novelists, but not for more sober thinkers
and workers, to use as criteria. Further, relevance to human interest and aptitude must not be taken as equivalent
to subjectivity. The values discovered by men at work
come to light in actual situations, in association with order
which is objectively there, whether particular men are
aware of it or not. The planets did not wait for man to
come, before they began swinging in ellipses around the
sun, or doing whatever it actually is that we perceive and
describe in those terms; and it is with that objectively real
order in their behavior that such value as intelligibility
or truth or beauty can be associated. It is just for this
reason that tastes have to be acquired, naïve preferences
supplanted, value judgments revised; and that goods
hitherto unnoticed come to be appreciated only through
learning, oftentimes painful and prolonged. There seems,
therefore, no rational ground to talk as though it were
somehow derogatory to a professed good if it should be
found relevant to human desire.

(*c*) Last among those who in our time disparage ordinary men and their doings are the despisers of democracy:
the more ardent nationalists, fascists, and doctrinaire communists by whom not mankind but individual men and
particular groups are held in contempt.[8] The nation,
the corporative state, the Aryan race, the proletariat is all,
the individual and the dissenting minority nil. To lump
all these views together and dismiss them in a paragraph
is of course absurd, and probably more unjust to the communist ideal than to the others. For in communist doctrine the proletarian dictatorship is presented as a tempo-

rary stage, not a permanent pattern, even though it be ruthless while it lasts. Whether that stage once established can be transcended without further violent revolution, or whether a communist oligarchy will show itself as reluctant to relinquish power as feudal and financial oligarchies have been, remains of course to be seen;[9] and in the meantime dogmatism is not in place. Three hasty comments may be offered here. First, as harsh correctives of romantic and of too rugged individualism, these extreme collectivist dogmas have doubtless their value. Here, he who runs may read, is the natural reaction from such anarchy as we have practiced hitherto; and the chances seem very large that we shall have more rather than less of such regimentation before we are through. But secondly, to suppose that the human animals we know can be permanently subordinated, as individuals and as occupational, ecclesiastical, and other constituent groups, to a collective despotism is to misread the records of human behavior and misbehavior. Basic drives and satisfactions reside ultimately in individual persons. There is quite as much vicious abstraction in such pseudo-mystical notions as "group mind" and "race unity," [10] and quite as much unrealism in using them as guides to social policy, as there has been in the abstractive, atomistic individualism that has vitiated our western civilization. And finally, so long as the envisaged social whole does not comprise entire mankind, the welding of separate nations, races, or sovereign states into herd-minded regiments uninhibited by internal criticism and divergence, must be of all conceivable ways just now the surest way to general massacre. It may be the way we shall go. More than once men have shown themselves capable of reverting to barbarism, and groping about in the dark for centuries. But in spite of much confident talk, no proof is forthcoming that it must be so. And whether now or millenniums hence or never on this earth, if men continue to be human animals and not machines, it seems necessary to suppose that only a culture that takes full account of concrete individual differences and the unique worth of human selves, as well as the need for collective organization, can avoid the recurrence of major collapse. Moreover, whether or not such a culture can ever be realized, it seems the part of sobriety to work in terms of its demands rather than to work away from it toward either extreme. But that raises the problem of methods and next steps, to which we shall give some notice in the concluding chapter.

D. Meanwhile, it is necessary to bring into this cursory account of things as they now are some special mention, with reference primarily to the United States, of two conditions which seem peculiarly unfavorable to such working life as we are here trying to represent as basic for a realistic theology.

(1) The first is the advancing mechanization of industry as it affects workers who are employed at machine labor, and would-be workers who are forced out of regular employment altogether. It is necessary to clear the air at once of a familiar confusion between machines as such and the way in which they are used. To damn modern machinery as an iron devil squeezing the souls out of helpless human beings has just enough plausibility to fog the real problem. The "Man with a Hoe," that pitiable brute of Millet's and Edwin Markham's vision—of what modern machinery was he a victim? The beggars, thieves, and lepers who swarmed in the horrible slums of mediæval cities; the chattering crowds around public gallows and

guillotine; the stinking inmates of eighteenth century bedlams and prisons; the wild miners of Wesley's England and Wales: what modern industrial methods had brutalized them? Dehumanization did not begin with the coming of the machines; and its chief source, now as in the past, is man's inhumanity to man.

The most important change which the development of machines has wrought seems to be of a very different kind. The most common sort of dehumanization has consisted in making men and women and children live with economic necessity so continually and painfully in the foreground, instead of in the background where it belongs, that there is little chance among them for human life to grow in its other characteristic dimensions. Machines have now made such distortion of human life at once more dangerous and more inexcusable, and the argument for its elimination unanswerable. Such elimination would involve better distribution of output, and better organization for work and leisure.

(*a*) As to distribution, when the economic struggle could be regarded as a contest for portions of a total output whose adequacy to provide for every one was open to question, at least a specious case could be made for refusal to spread the available wealth and leisure so thin that no one would have economic security and freedom, and opportunity for fuller life. If some then had to live subhuman lives, that was no doubt to be regretted, but it could be held unavoidable. Now that is changed. We are being assured by men who should know that the problem now is to get rid of the hobbles with which profit-seeking and a conventional debt structure keep the machinery of production tied, to run the machines with no other restraint than that required to maintain reasonable balance between production and probable need, and to make such distribution that no one need lack the material conditions for decent living.[11] If this be true, it becomes at once doubly clear that not machines, but the habitual modes of thought and behavior of men in positions of privilege are primarily responsible for keeping other men submerged,[12] and that such repression cannot much longer be colorably talked of as a necessary evil. The question seems clearly to have become not whether more humane distribution is technically feasible, but only how and how soon it is to be effected, and the way to a better life cleared of this increasingly inexcusable barrier.

(*b*) The need of change in our organization for work and for use of leisure is even more fundamental. Improved distribution will profit us nothing without improved men and women to appreciate it and make use of it. Here again technology offers indispensable but only indirect help. It can reduce the amount of toil required of a given worker, but it cannot make him a whit more capable of good life. He needs security, self-respect, and such training as may free his capacities for appreciation, and quicken and broaden his imaginative powers. So long as he works with an eye on the clock or on the boss, and finds in his leisure only an occasion for unimaginative indolence, even a four-hour day will drag and vacations with pay will be boredom, as they now are for many wealthier folk. So long, moreover, as he works always by sufferance rather than by acknowledged right, at the mercy always of arbitrary power, an important basis for self-respect will be lacking. But if definite provision were made that his leisure be for him, besides relaxation and play, a chance to learn what he could, with competent guidance,[13] about himself and his job and his neighbors, near at hand and remote in space and time; about other sorts of work than his own, and about their interrelations; about the world of nature, and the satisfactions to be had through woods and water, and some knowledge of the ways of life; about human achievements, failures, hopes, and perils: then he might grow. And if thereby his awareness of membership in a working society and a growing universe, and of passable competence and willingly accepted responsibility for his part in both, should be enhanced, that would be nothing other than what we have called vocation. Already a start toward this sort of thing has been made in Russia,[14] and though only a meagre start, it seems enough to make plain the relevance of such thought as this in a machine age. And if it should be maintained that nothing of this sort can be done in the rest of the world, so much the worse for whatever mode of organization stands in its way. For this sort of thing needs to be done. To take seriously the notion of earthly calling means to help clear away obstacles that now make it needlessly hard for men and women and children to hear the call.

The same principle applies to forced idleness, which, poisoned with anxiety or despair, has none of the values of either work or leisure. How can we justify talk about earthly calling when a fifth of our working population, more or less, can find no work? Not otherwise than by giving that concept in fact a central place in contemporary preaching, teaching, and religious living; and by insistence, in season and out of season, that no economy which makes it impossible for human families to have the sort of security that regular work can provide is any longer tolerable. To say that at present there is not enough work to go around is literally nonsense. What the statement ordinarily means, of course, is that the present industrial and commercial order, loaded with debt and hemmed in by trade barriers, cannot according to the present rules sell enough goods for enough money to meet its fixed charges and salaries, and also pay living wages to all those who want to work. There is all the work to be done that any one has time, training, and inclination to do. The trouble is that under the rules now in force much of it cannot be paid for in legal tender. And that, once again, is not merely for lack of real wealth; not when we have been plowing under cotton and wheat, destroying hogs, and running our factories at half speed to get rid of accumulated stocks of goods. It is not for theologians to say where the trouble lies, nor what in detail should be done about it. These are questions for specialists in social engineering. But it is in place for theologians and preachers to urge upon others who, like themselves, are non-specialists, the need to recognize that human beings, for all their native and acquired patience, will not stand indefinitely privation in the midst of plenty; that the old order needs drastic changing and must change; and that we shall do most wisely if we seek ways to make easier, not to hinder the transition.[15]

(2) Here finally we come face to face with another present condition, which like unemployment has grown to new dimensions in recent years, which is in deadly conflict with all that we have been urging as basic to the good life and the opening of roads toward it, and which stands squarely in the way of our getting even a clear look at things as they are. I mean various current modes of inducing mass behavior by cunning suggestion. There is first our more flamboyant advertising and the industrial and commercial practices which it seeks to embellish. It is bad enough that trashy and harmful goods are made

105

and distributed; worse that unsuspicious buyers are flat-
tered or frightened, by tricky irrelevancies, into buying
them at absurd prices; and worst of all that such organized victimization, paid for by the victims, has come to be
one of the major stumbling-blocks in the way of advance
toward a more honest economic and social structure.[16]
We seem to have reached a point at which even goods of
merit have to be overpraised and decked out in meretri-
cious finery. Add to the advertising openly bought and
paid for that still more treacherous and dangerous stuff,
mendacious propaganda,[17] circulated by way of legislative
lobbies, public utility and food-and-drug institutes, steel
and armament rings, patriotic associations, subsidized
school-books, controlled newspapers, popular magazines,
and whispering campaigns. Add finally the censorships
that keep news out of the news columns, facts about
production and distribution from consumers who pay the
bills, and doings of public servants from the public they
serve.[18] In its extent, costliness and ostentation this
smother of lies and half-truths apparently has attained
new enormity in our time. But in principle it is neither
new nor strange. *Caveat emptor* is not a new phrase,
Machiavellism a new theory, nor spreading rumor and sup-
pressing fact a new practice. On the contrary, methodical
deception has been always and everywhere an important and recognized procedure in destructive competition, whether military, political, ecclesiastical, or commercial. The smoke-laden, gas-drenched mental air we now
have to breathe is the atmosphere characteristic of combat,
and will not be finally cleared until the prevalent ethic
and practice of strife has been definitely supplanted by a
dominant ethic of respected and self-respecting work.
Work and war appear to be, at this point as elsewhere,

natural contraries; and there can be little serious doubt as
to which represents the higher level of human life.

If our purpose in the first two chapters has been realized, we have now before us a number of matters, mostly
concrete, which require next to be given a more general
speculative setting. First, we have tried to describe in
some detail what pretends to be a concept of vocation fit
to be given place in theology and religion in our time.
We have sought to exhibit its community at various points
with the early Protestant doctrine of vocation from which
the term is derived, with that sort of philosophical theology represented by the Thomistic system, and with the
contemporary tendency called religious realism. We have
sought also to suggest its relevance to the practical exigen-
cies of present-day life, particularly as regards the area in
which for most men and women work is actually to be
done: that is, in the area of production and distribution of
economic goods. We have seen that such doctrine is by
no means hospitable to any and every mode of human
behavior; but that, on the contrary, to certain ways of
thinking and behaving, and to certain conspicuous features of contemporary civilization, it is in essence and by
nature opposed, so that one who seriously tries to live by
it must oppose them also, in his own life and where else
they appear. It involves in essence, as we shall see more
fully in the fifth chapter, both love for and criticism of
what is actually at hand, in the light of ideals partly but
never completely realized here; and itself is in essence
the effort to realize such ideals more fully.

But thus far, concerned in the main with a mass of detail close at hand, we have not more than hinted at the
wider ramifications of this vocational concept which give

it specifically religious and theological import. Much
of what has been written thus far might be accepted,
might even be regarded as obvious to the point of plati-
tude, by many who would reject for themselves any
thought of being religious, and by others who, themselves
religious, would deny that the sort of thing we have been
talking about has any essential place in religion properly
so called. To this issue we shall address ourselves now
more directly. The next two chapters will be used in
seeking to show more fully how this doctrine fits into a
wider theological pattern, and the last chapter in sketch-
ing more concretely its place in a religious way of life.

CHAPTER THREE

LIVING MINDS AT WORK AND PLAY

The next part of our task will be to suggest the place of human work in a more general scheme of thought and life. Only thus can our proposed doctrine of vocation show itself as anything more than a somewhat commonplace rehearsal of familiar facts and threadbare admonitions. We must prepare to breathe for a while the thinner air of speculative altitudes, as we venture out further into regions accessible only to inference that is often tenuous and problematic. But we shall begin, at any rate, at the most accessible point: the behavior of human minds in the accomplishment of work. To avoid here, so far as possible, entanglement in metaphysics of unmanageable complexity, let us agree for the purpose of this discussion that by minds we shall mean, concretely, systems of such distinctive processes and other factors as differentiate manlike behavior, whether in degree or in kind, from windmill-like or cabbage-like or earthworm-like behavior. How rough and unsatisfactory such a statement is I am well aware, but as a starting point it has the advantage of permitting us to begin, at least, with the assurance that we are talking about facts, whatever on further analysis the nature of these facts may turn out to be. It has the further advantage of making plain at once the anthropic basis and viewpoint from which this whole argument is conducted, and to which at any point of doubt it should be referred back. How a mind thus understood appears to immediate inspection each of us may observe for himself, since each of us has one or is one. But familiar as minds are by acquaintance, any one of us would probably find himself puzzled to give an adequate account of them by description, or even to specify with confidence where they are and where they are not to be found in the known regions of the universe. For this latter purpose, fairly definite criteria are needed, and from the first critical attempts at speculative thought in the West, suggestions have been accumulating which are meant to help identify minds where they are to be found.

(*a*) The pre-Socratic thinkers generally spoke of soul (*psychē*) rather than of mind, and with some important partial exceptions agreed on two criteria by which its presence might be known: movement and sentiency, which latter they generally called perception (*aisthēsis*). By the former criterion, soul was identified as active; by the latter, as receptive, retentive, and responsive to impressions. But since movement is virtually omnipresent in visible Nature, these thinkers tended at first to recognize soul or animation everywhere.[1] The Eleatic criticism compelled greater caution, and Anaxagoras distinguished between living things and inanimate masses, declared Mind (*Noūs*) the prime mover in the universe as a whole, and held that some things (namely, those that are alive) partake of it, whereas others do not.[2]

(*b*) In general, Plato like his predecessors regarded movement and sentiency as the marks of the soul, but he sharpened the account at both these points. Like the Eleatic masters and Socrates, he distinguished clearly between sense perception (*aisthēsis*) and intellection or thought (*noēsis*), and himself recognized other cognitive processes besides. Like Anaxagoras, but more accurately, he distinguished between animate and inanimate things, and defined the difference by ascribing to those in which soul is present spontaneous or self-initiated movement, to inanimate things only passive or transmitted movement. Further, among spontaneously moving things he distinguished between those whose movements are well-ordered and those whose movements are disorderly, and associated intelligence or rationality (*noūs*) with the former alone.[3] For Plato, then, the presence of mind or rational soul is manifested on the one hand by intellection, with or without sense perception; on the other hand by orderly spontaneous movement. No well-ordered movement apart from mind; no mind apart from soul; no soul except where movement is self-initiated. Rational soul or mind thus described is able, in virtue of its power of initiating orderly change, to function as an organizer, both of souls and living bodies, and of situations in which inanimate things also are factors. With this account Aristotle agreed in general, as regards the criteria for recognizing the presence of soul and mind; though like the earlier Ionian thinkers he more closely identified soul as vital principle (*entelecheia*) with the body which it informs, while on the other hand, unlike Plato, he held that minds or intelligences may exist apart from souls.[4]

(*c*) By certain later thinkers, notably Plotinus and Kant, especial stress is laid on the unifying or synthesizing action of mind as observable in or inferable from perception, memory, and like experiences. Many diverse details are united in a single field of attention, and such unity is indispensable to there being conscious experience at all.[5] This criterion has become familiar in the works of various modern psychologists, particularly of those who like James or Janet[6] have much to say of integration and disintegration; and in modern philosophical theories of mind, no other characteristic is more frequently treated as of central importance.[7]

(*d*) Finally in still more recent work, attention has come to be focused on capacity for learning, or more narrowly for learning which involves the use of symbols, as identifying what we should mean by mind. Thus Hollingworth declares that a mind is a sum of learning processes which involve reacting to parts of previously experienced situations as adequate cues, symbols or surrogates for the total situations of which they once were parts. Such "redintegration" is what we should mean by mental process; and "mind" is a name for such processes organized into growing systems.[8]

In reflection upon this accumulating list, which might well be extended with profit to the argument, one becomes aware that two interests are represented: one descriptive or analytic, concerned to say more definitely what we mean by mind, what it is or how it acts; the other diagnostic, concerned to recognize more discriminatingly the presence or the work of mind, especially where mind if present is not accessible to direct inspection. In the foregoing accounts, descriptive items predominate, most of which have diagnostic value as well. Several of them are summarized in Dodge's formula that minds may be regarded as dynamic, cumulative, and recapitulative.[9] They show themselves always in process; their earlier reactions help to condition their later ones; and they are able to abridge, short-circuit, or telescope their behavior in a variety of ways.

For diagnostic purposes it seems advisable to put into the record another criterion, familiar, obvious, and inclusive, such as archæologists employ in trying to recognize artifacts. One may say that the presence or the work of mind may fairly be suspected as a factor in situations wherein two conditions obtain: first, that the observed combination of details is intelligible, or congruous with intelligent human behavior, to such an extent or in such a way that this apparent congruity cannot well be regarded as entirely a fiction, contributed by the observer; and secondly, that the observed combination would appear highly improbable[10] if considered as the outcome solely of known processes other than those regarded as mental. If we come upon a situation which seems clearly to display intelligible or otherwise humanly appreciable or appropriable order which we have not simply read into it, and which cannot plausibly be accounted for as the outcome of known non-mental processes, it is a fair hypothesis that mental behavior in important respects like our own has helped bring it about. Thus, animals, huntsmen, and kitchen utensils among the stars plainly are fictions contributed by us as observers; triangles described by drifting pebbles are not merely fictions, but neither do they appear improbable if considered simply as outcomes of non-mental processes; whereas fragments of pottery or of basketry, or marks on paper or inscriptions on stone which can direct a reader to the discovery or recognition of facts remote in space or time, cannot plausibly be accounted for without supposing the collaboration of mind with whatever other factors entered into their production.

Assuming now that these are pertinent hints as to what minds are and how to recognize them, let us examine in some detail a situation that may serve to illustrate a number of ways in which they behave. Suppose the need for school buildings to be built and lived in. Suppose the architect receiving from the officers of the school a memorandum setting forth what is needed: so many dormitory rooms, so many classrooms and offices, refectory, social rooms, chapel, to be built in a given place at a specified time, at such and such total cost. Then suppose, after visits and conversations on the ground, the architect with his drawing board, ink-bottle, and instruments, making marks on paper—which is to say redistributing ink by removing drops from the bottle and spreading them out flat along imaginary lines, to make visible patterns, with words and other symbols marked alongside. These patterns and these words and other signs (which also are visible patterns) are not literal copies of things to be seen anywhere about; for just such buildings as these are to be, as yet nowhere exist. Neither are these sheets of paper and ink marks to be any part of the buildings which are to come. Yet by means of these and a multitude of other cues, visual, verbal, kinæsthetic, and so on, the architect is able to assure himself and others before one brick has been laid on another that, barring major accidents, the needs which have been specified will be approximately, albeit never perfectly, provided for. The marks on his paper stand for tons of cement and steel and glass, and for cubic feet of enclosed space. They stand for the tensile strength of steel in girders that must hold up the roof, and for axes of the earth along which upright walls and towers must be approximately aligned. They stand for current market costs of labor and materials, for gangs of men and man-hours of work, for intricate processes of calculation, special skills, and utilities and beauties yet to be realized. But they stand for all these things only in so far as they serve to suggest them, as we say, to an intelligent observer competent for the reading of such signs as these.

One can see by their help only what he is competent to see.

Here now is a committee of the faculty of that school trying to decipher them. Their concern is not directly with tensile strength nor labor cost, but with cubic space and equipment that shall be suitable for future work, and contours that will be pleasing to the eye. They try, in short, to read the plans concretely in terms of specific present and probable future needs, and future satisfactions. There are conferences with and without the architects at which sounds are emitted, gestures made, and additional marks drawn. There are visits to the proposed building site, movements of heads and eyes along the lines of non-existent corridors and gables; tightening of neck muscles, tongues, diaphragms, deltoids, and gastrocnemii; counting movements of fingers and toes; shifting flights of visual, auditory, and motor imagery, in efforts to anticipate the non-existent doorways and staircases and terraced courts. And at length here again is the architect, marking in another floor of offices and seminar rooms, and re-drawing the pulpit in terms of more concrete utility and less abstract beauty, until almost every one is more or less well satisfied to go ahead.

Then after more symbolic communication with builders, contractors and sub-contractors, dealers and employment offices, the actual assembling on the ground of materials, machines, and men. Here now are relatively unorganized heaps of bricks and I-beams and bags of cement instead of paper and ink, to be rearranged by laborers' muscles and steam-driven cranes instead of the draughtsman's pen. Symbols are giving place to things symbolized, possibilities to actualities. But the rearrangement of these more massive materials by these more

115

complex instruments must follow approximately the lines of the earlier symbolic rearrangement of paper and ink; and herein fresh difficulties arise. Steel and cement are less plastic than paper and ink and speech and imagery. Laborers' muscles and contractors' minds cannot be used as simply as one pushes a pen. Laborers and contractors, no less than faculty committees, have to be persuaded and guided, and sometimes persuasion is difficult. But so is making a suitable plan in the first place. From the builder's point of view, the materials, the implements, and the persons (including himself) involved in a task of this sort from beginning to end, have at least this in common: each has its capacities and its limitations for the purpose in hand; each if rightly dealt with is plastic or co-operant within limits, but each also is in some measure refractory to change, and would be worthless for productive work otherwise. Clear understanding, appropriate method, and skilful technique are required to deal successfully with conditions like these. But this is what constitutes work. Working is problem-solving, with a view to future satisfaction. In so far as present satisfactions also come into it, work may at various junctures approximate strenuous play, and no doubt that is all to the good so long as the main goal is not lost to view.

At all events, the walls and roofs go up, and instead of symbolic drawings and possible buildings imagined or conceived, there are actual sheltered spaces in which actual lives can be lived, and further work and play can go on for years to come. In the new buildings moreover are blackboards and paper on which yet other symbols can be marked, to represent anything from the heavens above to the waters under the earth: symbols which may have only play value in present enjoyment, or which may lead beyond the present moment, through processes of actual change, to deferred satisfactions for those who make them or for others who never see them nor know of them, and thus serve as factors in the doing of work.

I

It is time now to examine more closely an individual mind as it participates in such a task of organization or productive rearrangement, both as regards its own career, and as regards the successive sets of environmental situations which it helps to rearrange, in work and play. It goes without saying that the several items here set down serially and as though separate, form in concrete fact a fluid network of interdependent processes. The individual is not separable from his social context, nor from the situations in which his work is carried on. Neither is the cognitive-affective aspect of an individual's mental behavior separable from the various "drives" that keep it going. Always with this understanding our several analyses and discussions are offered.

A. First, then, consider the sort of synthesis or organization involved in the individual's own growth as seen, so to speak, from within: the subjective side of his doings, observable only by himself.

(1) If one try to imagine a single cross-section, say of the architect's conscious life as he sits at his drawing-board, it must take the shape not of a static field, like an instantaneous photograph, but of the brief, vital, conscious event sometimes called a "specious present," a single "attention span" or pulse of living awareness.[11] Within such

a concrete moment a diversity of content is brought together into what Dunlap calls "the peculiar and essential
identity which constitutes the organization of the experience as such." [12] The experience has, as it were, a central
point or "frame of reference," a subjective centre or ego,
to which every item in it is directly referable. Seen from
within, it is "my" experience in all its diverse detail. It is
well known how from preoccupation with this observable
inward unity and its implications as Kant worked them
out arose the amazing philosophic tidal wave of modern
idealism; somewhat as the kindred system of Neoplaton-
ism was associated with a similar analysis by Plotinus
nearly sixteen hundred years before. Now it may be that
these impressive systems present the logical terminus of
any attempt to give due weight to the subjective unity of
conscious experience; but I am not convinced that that
is so, and our course here will be much more modest,
following Kant's analysis somewhat closely at the start,
and proceeding thereafter on realistic rather than idealistic
lines.

What transpires in the architect's field of awareness as
he observes his drawing? Doubtless the apprehension
that here is a visible pattern composed of lines which meet
at definite angles to form a structural whole. And what
mental processes are involved in the forthcoming of such
apprehension? At least three unifying or synthetic acts,
says Kant, which ultimately are themselves unified in a
single act of apperception. [13] There is first a synthetic act
of sensory perceiving, whereby the successive parts of each
line and the several lines of the drawing are apprehended
as forming one aggregate, not as separate bits. Secondly,
an act of memory, whereby other aggregates previously
perceived are now reproduced in imagination as part and

parcel of the present experience. Thirdly, an act of conceptual recognition, whereby the common factor in the previous and the present percepts is grasped and it is seen that the present percept is an instance of a sort already experienced. Finally, these three synthetic acts, sensory perception, imaginative reproduction, and conceptual recognition, must all transpire in a common centre, else no conscious experience can be forthcoming: as, if one subject should receive these present impressions, another should recall a previous experience, and still another conceive a general characteristic of several experiences, no one would apprehend this given drawing at all. And therefore, although none of these synthetic acts nor the subject itself can be observed as such, all of them must be inferred from the fact that the experience of the drawing as such does take place.

Crude though it is in detail, so as to make William James snort in derision of all this cumbersome machinery,[14] Kant's argument seems to me essentially valid. The process of perception—or of apperception, as he called it—is at once vastly more complex and less methodical than he recognized. It is also, as James rightly insisted, much more continuously and intimately unitary than Kant's plodding analysis would suggest. But beneath all awkwardness of analysis and pedantries of language one may recognize that Kant was saying on the basis of careful inference what James, more positivistic, thought could be discovered by simple inspection: that a field of awareness must be *unified* with a peculiar fluid and centralized unity, else conscious experience is inconceivable. Into that unity come, we should say, affective and impulsive as well as cognitive elements: feelings of pleasantness and unpleasantness, impulses to advance or withdraw, emotional cur-

rents of liking or distaste, all in the quivering web of a
specious present, presented to a unitary subject. Nothing
less complex and unified than this is a recognizable cross-
section of human consciousness at the adult level.

(2) Besides such momentary synthesis, a kind of linear
unification of successive segments of experience somehow
takes place also. Not, I think, with due deference to
James,[15] by a simple overlapping of specious presents, but
by some action of a persisting subject; and not I think,
again with deference to the suggestive and often brilliant
work of the newer behaviorists,[16] by the complex actions
of a physical organism alone, unless we are prepared to
assign to its component parts other properties than those
which the physical sciences recognize. Both questions are
too intricate to argue here,[17] and I prefer to go on without
dogmatic assertion, still holding for the present somewhat
closely to the descriptive point of view. In some way, then,
temporally diverse segments of experience are held together, partly through such processes as those we name
memory, anticipation, reasoning, and purposive action,
into enduring, cumulative wholes. But these wholes, likewise, which we call conscious lives, are developed selec-
tively, no less than synthetically. They grow by exclusion
as well as inclusion, forgetting as well as remembering,
abridging and short-circuiting by symbolism as well as
full-length experiencing by actual *Erlebnis*. Space-bridg-
ing, "time-binding," selective, unifying processes comprise
the fabric of an individual life on its subjective side; so
that into each moment of conscious behavior, partial
memories and unnoticed vestiges of the past and anticipa-
tions of the future effectively enter.

(3) This unity of conscious life is like the fluid, shimmering unity of a whirlpool or an electromagnetic field,

in which a relatively stable pattern is maintained through continually changing materials or media. In perception or in thought the data and the symbols that enter into the field of consciousness never rest for more than a few seconds at most, and usually much less; yet the process goes steadily forward. Scraps of words, snatches of music, fleeting images, slight movements of hand or head or ribs or jaws, faint twinges of pleasure or of anxiety—a thousand and one details that come and go may serve to carry, as we say, a train of thought.[18] It is as though one were crossing a river by leaping from log to log, no one of which will bear one's weight for more than a moment; or as though one's attention were like a small dog dashing now this way, now that, looking into all sorts of odd corners, but getting on toward home.

This utilization of evanescent materials to effect solid practical results has a specially interesting illustration in the difference between profitable and unprofitable daydreaming; a special case of the interrelation between automatic and voluntary psychological functions to which Janet gives so much attention.[19] There are persons whose minds can be held to a job of work only by continual forcing, and once released they go meandering off into daydreams of romantic adventure or fairyland luxury quite irrelevant to the day's work that has to be done. For such persons, work is a bore and dreaming a perilous flight from reality—perilous because it is so much easier and pleasanter than the work which, unenriched by relevant fantasy, grows increasingly stale and liable to neglect. A vicious circle thus develops, with real situations growing ever more unpleasant to the person who brings no imagination to his aid in dealing with them, and who therefore tends to find his satisfaction more and more in withdrawal

from real situations into the effortless flights of fancy. On
the contrary, there are others whose daydreams, even
when free-running and not voluntarily directed, circle back
again and again toward the job that has to be done; not
with a sense of continuous strain, but with the freedom
and pleasantness of genuinely footloose fancy, roaming
hither and yonder without restraint, yet turning up again
and again some detail that fits in with the day's work.
Herein is an important difference between the healthy and
the ailing mind. Both work and both play—for a time.
But for the one, play enriches work and both are satisfying; for the other, play impoverishes work by contributing
nothing to it while taking more and more time from it,
until at length that one is unfit to work, and can find
satisfaction only in dreams. The life of the one is unified,
not rigidly nor by what is called "will power," but somehow fluently and dynamically; the life of the other falls
apart.

As a kind of summary of what we have said of the subjective unity of healthy personal life, we may refer to the
account which Hollingworth, following James, gives of
intelligence.[20] In it two factors, these men say, are essential: learning and sagacity. By learning it is meant that
one has come to react to present details, even to meagre
hints, with a complexity of response acquired through
numerous past experiences. By sagacity it is meant that
one's attention is laid open so widely to the present situation that each of many significant cues in it, however
obscure, may have a chance to act as a present efficient
stimulus, and that the several significant cues may act
with duly proportioned effectiveness. Thus one's total
response, in the light of past experiences and present
stimuli, will be inclusive and well-balanced rather than

meagre and one-sided. Herein is manifest the working
of well-ordered and effectively ordering mind.

B. Consider now this individual, whose career we have
been viewing "from within," as another observer may see
him at work, with such additional information here and
there as he himself may be called upon to give.

(1) Productive work involves, we have said, organizing
or rearranging situations which in some respect are to be
made more satisfactory. There must be, then, motives for
such work: to wit, needs to be satisfied. And there are
ends toward which the work is directed: to wit, anticipated events which are somehow envisaged as satisfying.
We have had much to say about needs as fundamental to
sound work, but we have made no attempt to list, classify,
or evaluate them, nor can we do so here. Their name is
legion, and in the complex mazes of human living, now
one, now another may legitimately claim satisfaction.
The discussion in the first two chapters presupposed, however, two things: that there are definitely harmful cravings
and artificially induced cravings which are not properly
to be called needs, and which in general should not be
satisfied—cravings for habit-forming drugs, for exciting
exhibitions of cruelty in which one may desire to take
part or to look on, for bizarre and over-costly finery, for
despotic power and prestige, or the like; and that among
more or less legitimate needs, some, as various psychologists have held, are more fundamental than others, and
in general should have right of way. The need of ordinary
folk to have suitable food, clothing, and shelter, economic
security and self-respect, a chance to do satisfying work,
enough leisure for healthful social life, and a chance to
grow in understanding and appreciation as far as their

own limitations will permit we have assumed to deserve right of way before less urgent needs of more fortunate folk. Something further will be said on this point in the fifth chapter, but into the development of ethical principles and casuistic precepts we shall not attempt to go. And here, all that need be said is that a worker is motived by needs which seem to him legitimate, to strive toward ends which promise to bring satisfaction.

(2) To attain his ends he must organize materials in accordance with an intricate network of structural patterns or forms.[21] (*a*) Some of these forms are exemplified in the materials themselves. Cement has one complex character, steel another, marble, wood, silk, wool still others. Materials are suited for one sort of work and not for another, according as they exemplify this character or that. (*b*) Some of the relevant structural forms are exemplified in the environment rather than in the materials as such. Bedrock will hold up a skyscraper, hardpan an ordinary cottage, loose earth neither. Palms and pines want different climates. City slums are poor places to grow fine citizens. Competent workmen know these things and act accordingly. (*c*) Some of the relevant patterns or forms, finally, are fully exemplified neither in the materials nor in the adjacent environment. They may be symbolized by words or diagrams or images; they may be thought about as possibilities and as ideals; but they are not yet actualized in any approximately adequate way. Yet even these envisaged possibilities are more inflexible in their unaggressive fashion than actual rock itself. Nothing is more stubborn than the multiplication table; and we risk our necks every day on the way some engineer has used his slide rule in computing factors of safety for elevator shafts, high tension power lines, and outside rails

where fast trains round a curve. Structural patterns, whether now exemplified or yet to be exemplified in actual things, involve exactions which good work has to meet.

(3) Appropriate methods, therefore, are demanded: suitable processes for organizing materials to accord with structural requirements. (*a*) There is call first for knowledge on the part of the workman. He must know as clearly as possible what he is trying to produce—though doubtless in planning and in pioneer work he is likely to find out, in detail, only as the work proceeds. But even for planning and for pioneer experimentation which is not to be mere trial-and-error, some fairly clear notion of the end sought must serve as a guide. He must know his materials, the setting in which he is to work, and the standards by which such work as his must submit to be judged. The more inclusive, clear, and relevant his knowledge, other things being equal, the better his work and its product. (*b*) To knowledge he must add skill; or rather his knowledge must grow in part from the appropriate skills. Book learning confronted with a problem in carpentry or in human relations has been sufficiently satirized. Knowledge, we are told, is not enough. But it has not always been clearly seen that what passes for knowledge is often mere verbal skill, and not properly knowledge at all. To have the knowledge required to do metal work, one's fingers and eyes must be educated, not merely one's larynx and ears. When Plato selected pilots and physicians as exemplars of the wisdom a statesman should have,[22] he knew what he was about. Pilots and doctors carry much of their knowledge in the form of nice eye-hand co-ordinations for which no amount of lingual dexterity is an equivalent. The expert knows the "feel" of

good material, good tools, and good craftsmanship. His skill is not mere dexterity; it contributes indispensably to his knowledge, and to his competence as a whole. Here too the need for both learning and sagacity is plain. To say this is far, of course, from belittling verbal skill where that is appropriate. An old friend of mine wrote a book called *Workmanship in Words*,²³ and with good right. There are jobs that need to be done with words, and cannot be done otherwise; and for these the man who knows words, their powers and their limitations, and how to handle them, is (other things equal) the man for the job. To have knowledge and skill in words is good; to confuse skill in words with knowledge of politics or of human hearts is bad. (*c*) There is over and above knowledge and skill an inclusive working attitude to which I shall give more attention in another chapter. There is time here only to label it and pass on. Let us say, for one aspect of it, critical realism; and for another, something of the faith, hope, and love that mark idealism at its best. There is more than a little absurdity in leaving these terms standing here all alone, but there is no help for it. They belong here, and later we shall try to see why.²⁴

(4) The rôle of mind in this work of organizing materials in accordance with structural patterns to satisfy needs has been touched upon at many points of detail. Let us venture now a summary dictum in language familiar to theology. In such work mind, let us say, is both immanent and transcendent as regards the actual present situation. It is immanent in so far as it enters into direct causal and stimulus-response relations with what is actually here now. It is transcendent of the immediate situation in so far as, by way of symbolic behavior, it takes account also of what is not actually here now. Some of the

factors not actually present have been, are now, or will be actually existent: some in the past, some in the future, some spatially remote or perceptually inaccessible at the present moment. The age of dinosaurs, the year 2000, the other side of the moon, the feelings of my neighbor: all these have been, are, or presumably will be actually existent, but in responding to them now by way of symbolism, I am responding thus to many things that lie beyond my present perceptual field. Moreover, in symbolic behavior I habitually respond likewise to non-actualities: to possible events (in the sense of abstract possibility or conceivability) which may never transpire; to ideals which may never be actualized. Explain or interpret it as one will, in this definite sense mind transcends its present perceptual field; and we could not plan and carry out purposed work otherwise. Thus has our inspection of minds at work drawn us into metaphysics. But we must go further before it will be evident that this is also theology.

II

Let us turn now from minds as individual to minds as social, and examine two basic modes of social behavior: communication and co-operation.

A. Communication takes most commonly (1) the form of efforts to convey detailed information by conventional signals, and this process is full of instruction for any one concerned to observe human minds with discrimination. The need for it arises from the fact that minds are individual as regards their immediate experience and need to be social as regards practical co-working, and ultimately as regards felt companionship also, if human life is not to lose most of its savor. In our building illustration, the use of signals as a medium of mental commerce appears so often that the story could not be so much as begun, still less carried forward, without presupposing its lambent presence at every step of the way. Without it there could be no school, no committees, no architects, and no building. The needs felt by students and faculty would remain private to each as an individual, and no common understanding nor common enterprise would be feasible. How then does one communicate with another?

(*a*) We have seen individual minds engaged in rearranging perceptible materials: putting ink on paper, chalk on blackboards, air currents into spasmodic movement, and so on. When one of these perceptible changes is such as to direct the attention of another to something which I observe and want him to observe, that gesture or sign may serve as a medium of communication, whether it be merely a shout and a pointed finger, or an intricate set of articulated sounds or of marks on paper. The first step in communication of specific or detailed character, then, is effecting a change in some common environmental medium which shall be perceptible to another, and calculated to arrest and direct his attention. (*b*) The signal is not itself, however, except in rare instances, that which I want to communicate. It will fail of its purpose if it should catch and hold the attention of the other so steadily that he sees or hears only the signal itself, and not that to which the signal is intended to point. An automobile horn so loud and startling as to rivet the pedestrian's attention upon itself may paralyze him in the path of danger instead of directing him away from that path. On the other hand, a signal of the crudest kind which gets the other to see what I want him to see has served well its function as a medium of communication. The subtlety required in signals of this sort will increase with the subtlety or inobviousness or complexity or remoteness of that to which I try to direct some one else's notice. If a mass of color, a gross movement, or an ordinary spatial relationship is to be pointed out, simple gestures of hand or head may suffice. If a nuance of tone or of posture, a logical disjunction, a refinement of manners or morals, an ideal possibility be the object of attention, much more elaborate symbols are called for. But in every instance in which detailed information is to be conveyed, the meaning, not the signal as such, is of primary concern. (*c*) Moreover, it is essential to recognize that in the cases thus far considered, there appears to be no literal transfer of content from one mind to another. I cannot implant bodily a piece of knowledge or of feeling in my neighbor's mind. What I may do is to try to arouse and re-direct his attention in hope that once he sees what I see, he may respond to it somewhat as I do, and that our two minds may thus be brought into effective correlation with one another, as well as with the environment which we share. But such hope will be vain unless he to whom I speak or write or otherwise give signals is able to decipher or decode, as it were, the sights and sounds which I put before him, and also to identify that which they seek to point out. I must be able to count upon sufficient sensitivity and sufficient learning and sagacity in the recipient, else there is no hope that my signals will be effective as cues to appropriate response on his part and that communication will thus be effected. He must understand my language, and be able also to recognize that which I desire him to notice, else we are cut off at this particular point each from the other. I do not talk in polysyllables to a child, nor expect a tone-deaf friend to find beauty in the Choral Symphony. From the simplest gesture of hand or eyes or voice up to the most elaborate work of art, these requirements hold. Detailed communication requires two, and defect of learning, sagacity, skill, or responsiveness in either will impair its effectiveness. For each must have his own experience: no other's can be transplanted into his mind.

(2) Besides such deliberate communicating of detailed information, there is another level of social interplay more limited in range but often more profound in emotional and moral import. This is communication of one's personal presence and intimate character. For very much of ordinary human intercourse, this sort of communication is obviously irrelevant. When I order a ton of coal, my tastes in poetry and the dealer's favorite pastime are matters that need not come into the discussion. We should never get our work done if we should wait for intimate acquaintance with every associate. Doubtless a working minimum of confidence in one another's ordinary integrity is needed for any sort of social living, and to that extent our respective characters and philosophies are matters of common concern. In our day, however, a man's unique private self is hidden, for most of those who have dealings with him, behind a more or less standardized public self; and we deal for the most part with reputations, credit ratings, trade names, and official titles rather than with known persons. But with respect to some few individuals, at least, there is insistent need for continual approach toward more intimate and complete mutual understanding. It is not enough that we shall direct one another's attention to this and that aspect of our public environment. There is need also that our at-

tention be drawn now and again to one another as persons, who engage in public activities but who also live private, inwardly pungent, ultimately unsharable lives, and need intensely to be acknowledged, understood, and cherished as fellow-beings.[25]

(*a*) To communicate one's presence as a self, needless to say, is not a separate transaction, carried on apart from the communication of objective items. But it goes beyond such impartation of details in two ways. It involves that my neighbor convey to me an impression of some unity, consistency, and coherence in so much of his behavior as I can observe, so that it shall appear to me as a more or less integral system of behavior, and not merely a farrago of atomic events.[26] It involves also conveying that there confronts me here and now an actual *other individual* in essential respects like myself, but different; inwardly quite as real, and definitely *not* one with me, but centred about another ego and having a character and career of his own. A real other ego—a *thou*—must be apprehended and accepted by me not merely as a convenient point of reference for such present behavior as I observe, and a presumptive guaranty of its continuance. Rather, a real other person will become for me again and again a locus of behavior that is *un*expected, out of accord with my picture of him and constraining me again and again to revise, it may be with much discomfort, my own thought and behavior. Herein is his real otherness most sharply manifested, and his potency for giving pain and sudden joy. In this real otherness also is grounded his unique worth as an individual self, whose character and career are nowhere else to be found, and whose very being is fraught, for an appreciative observer, with poignant value.[27]

(*b*) When now we ask in what way this fact of personal presence, over and above the details of observed behavior, is conveyed, our notice is drawn to another aspect, presumably a more archaic and surely a basic aspect, of human communication. First of all it seems to be a fact, account for it as we may, that the healthy human animal is incurably "realistic" in his working epistemology; in the sense that he spontaneously and incorrigibly supposes himself surrounded by things, persons, and events which are other than he. From this basic tendency it is extremely difficult, if not quite impossible, to free oneself by taking thought. One may suppose it rooted in the prompt and primitive response—call it "animal faith" [28]—of a sentient organism as such, moved by an environment on which (at first unwittingly) its life depends; a type of response which survives in man as animal and is contributory to his survival. One may suppose its initial crudity lessened with the development of powers and habits of discrimination which are of later growth in organisms than the basic reactive tendency.[29] One may recognize and welcome its further testing and restricting in man by critical reflection, brought to its most conspicuous development in the trained positivist or skeptic. Crude native realism clearly affirms too much, and its assertions are too cocksure. It needs sharpening and discipline. To avoid being taken in too easily by specious appearances, on the one hand, one must learn to examine all sorts of presented data with nicer attention to detail, ferreting out the significant clues which are not at first apparent. Thus one learns to read between the lines of editorials and news stories, and to probe after unavowed motives in human behavior. To avoid, on the other hand, bondage to unchastened, immature "wishes" in oneself, and the illusionism that comes of naïve "projection" of unexamined wish-fulfilments, one must learn to recognize wishes for what they are, try to discriminate between those which do and those which do not bear up well under both logical and practical testing, and accustom oneself to that progressive modification of wishes in which growth toward spiritual maturity so largely consists.[30] A reflective, critical "realism," in short, must supplant the immature, too-naïve kind. But to say all this is not to discredit nor to dispense with the archaic tendency to affirm, in deeds if not in words, a real *other* over against oneself. It is significant that even in highly trained skeptics (witness David Hume),[31] the tendency flares up quickly in response to the touch of other persons in the give and take of practical living. It is significant that its diminution or loss is often an important symptom of mental disorder, associated with diminution or loss of ability to get work done and to make the adjustments needful in everyday life.[32] Genuine solipsism would seem more likely to indicate psychasthenia than subtlety; and one may doubt that a race of solipsists could have survived and reproduced itself until now. "Belief-ful realism"[33] seemingly is bred in our bones, and however we may need to prune and train it, there is no ground for supposing it can or should be rooted out of healthy human living.

But granted all this in general, how does a human person convey to another his individual presence in particular? (i) In the first instance, I presume, by causal impacts. The mode of social intercourse examined in the preceding section[34] was mainly of the sort in which signals are so used as to direct the recipient's attention away from the signal and the signaler toward some more or less remote object. More primitive, one may suppose, is the mode of intercourse in which direct causal impacts rather than symbolic signals predominate. The touch of the mother's breast, the pull of a helping hand, or the blow of a fist is not a mere symbolic gesture: it is a causal impact in which the presumable presence of an agent, helpful or harmful, friendly or unfriendly, rational or irrational, is at first more vividly conveyed than by any gesture which should seek to direct attention away from rather than toward the immediately present event. An embrace, a thwarting or chastisement, help with a burdensome load, a gift or deprivation: all these in their varying guises are causative contacts in which the life of the recipient is changed for better or for worse, and in which his attention can scarcely fail to be directed more closely upon the presumed agent than would be the case in other circumstances.

(ii) Yet these contacts also, intimate and direct as they are, not only stir massive and direct responses in which emotion is likely to be prominent, but also function as symbols; else the recipient's attention would be fixed solely upon the event—the touch or blow or pleasurable stirring—and not become aware of the agent as a real present entity at all. This blow is a cause of pain and rage, but also a sign of an enemy; this handclasp a cause of tactile perception, felt pressure, and heightened tonicity, but also a sign of a friend. On the other hand, words and other expressly symbolic acts come to have, among persons accustomed to their use, consequences for life not inferior in impressiveness to those of many cruder causal impacts. The physical efficacy of a spoken word, even a scream of pain, impinging on a listener is slight; its capacity to stir response may be very great and very

134

far-reaching. Evidently the distinction between causal and
symbolic advances by one person toward another is a
relative and variable one; and in a concrete instance of
human communication, both aspects I doubt not will
ordinarily appear.[35] Both, moreover, must contribute to
one's perception that a human self confronts him, and
to his perception of what that other self is and does.
Words without deeds here are empty; deeds without
words, without *logos*—heedless, inept, casual deeds—too
often are blind, and leave the recipient blind. But deeds
in which a clear meaning is embodied, in which a word
becomes flesh, are revelations. And living words, too—
calm speech offered as a gift to one in need of clarity;
bold speech against vested wrong, or in defence of imperiled right—such words, being words *of life,* are revelations also. Through them, living minds come into
view as real individuals.

(iii) There is still another factor, besides all considered
acts or words, without which communication of personal
presence and character would fall far short of presenting
us one to another as individuals: to wit, those subtler cues
which, in large part unknowingly, one person gives to
another who sees much of him in varying circumstances.
Unlike the deliberate signals by which one conveys detailed information, these are such evanescent gestures,
facial expressions and bodily postures, tones of the voice
and chance turns of speech, lights in the eyes and color
in the cheeks, silences and omissions, as only one more
sensitive to them than a casual acquaintance will be apt
to understand or perhaps even to notice at all. Here
again, in pre-eminent degree, the need for sagacity, in the
sense of openness to subtle signs and inclusiveness and
nice balance in their interpretation, is apparent. One

comes, then, to live in a world with persons who are not merely talking pictures and lay figures, only as one is exposed to causal impacts in which, by long acquaintance and sagacious reading of subtle clues, he discerns other selves as agents and as subjects other than himself. Such knowledge is never, I take it, immediate and never complete. I cannot feel my neighbor's feeling as he feels it. But I can come to know him more and more adequately as I learn to lay my attention open widely to his doings and to interpret with sensitive discrimination and limitless patience, refusing premature foreclosure, the signs of his presence which his doings offer. In strict logic, I cannot be certain that a person is there at all; but in concrete life I find it impossible to doubt the real presence of one of whose presumed activities I am thus inclusively aware. To such knowledge contempt and antagonism close doors; love, hope and faith keep them open.[36]

B. With communication maintained, the way to co-operation is made clearer. This may take forms in which either social control or social companionship is the dominant note, though neither one need exclude the other.

(1) In case the chief stress is on social control, the total situation may approach that in which things are being organized; and indeed we speak of organizing persons, usually with some intimation that they are being treated more or less as materials to be arranged for production of some ulterior end. (*a*) This tendency to dehumanization, already noticed in other connections, is most evident when the method of control is most exclusively coercive. In military organization, political despotism, and industrial control of non-union workers through impersonal corpo-

rations, we have, I suppose, three good instances of such coercive organization. Plainly it is subject to gradations, from cruel tyranny to beneficent paternalism; but the primary principle is autocratic, and the tendency is to depersonalize in one way or another the relationship of governor to governed. (*b*) At a less rigid level, control is exercised partly by coercion, but usually by persuasion. The ordinary household in which small children of various ages require to be kept on the main track by their elders until they can safely take over the controls themselves, or the traditional schoolroom, or the average political democracy will provide instances. (*c*) At its best this sort of control verges toward organization in which mutual understanding illuminates persuasion, and to a large degree displaces coercion. As one's children grow, this is what one hopes for as an intermediate stage on the way to still more complete freedom for them. Coercion is still in the background, to be called on if needed; but one is acutely aware now that one is dealing with persons, not things, and that forced obedience from persons is not the best response.

(2) With growth in mutual understanding, whether among few persons or among many, there comes a shift of emphases within such a group from control to companionship. When each understands, and to a sufficient degree approves, what the others are interested in achieving, and the way they are working toward it, the attention of all may be focused more and more on the work to be done or the situation to be enjoyed, and the compresence of fellow participants therein; less and less on the need to keep this one and that one in line. Thus a group may work and play together, for remote ends or immediate enjoyment or both at once, with a minimum

137

of irrelevant constraint. Moreover, in such a relationship the subtler clues by which one manifests his intimate self are likely to be more freely offered, since one is less stringently on guard among those whom he understands and trusts, and who like and trust him.

This situation seems to me the best that is humanly attainable, and the rarity with which it is now at all fully attained bears witness to the unsatisfactoriness of much of our living hitherto. There is ground for hope in that some measure of such companionship finds its way even now into so many unsatisfactory total situations. But we need not look yet, nor for a great while to come, for coercion to become obsolete and companionship to become the way of the world.

Let us summarize again. Minds, we have now said, are at once individual and social. As individual they somehow organize both private careers subjectively observable, and public situations in which things are so rearranged as more adequately to satisfy experienced needs. In such public activity, minds have occasion to communicate one with another, and to co-operate in common enterprises. Each remains itself in its ultimate privacy; each may respond to others and stimulate others to response; yet none can ever be or become another.

To this situation we may apply now, for the sake of a later stage in the argument, the terminology used earlier in speaking of an individual mind at work. In its own private range, let us say, which includes all the contents and processes of its subjectively observable experience, and all the causal or stimulus impacts to which it directly becomes a party, each mind is actually immanent. In so far as no mind can occupy the viewpoint of another, so as to experience from that other centre the private range of another mind, each as subject is radically transcendent with reference to the other as subject. But in so far as one mind may apprehend symbolically both actualities and possibilities outside its private range, including, we may suppose, other minds and their private experiences; and in so far as in communication a public environment and viable media are occupied and employed in common, though from permanently non-interchangeable points of view, one may speak (with some linguistic qualms) of a relative or communicative transcendence by each mind of its ultimate privacy, and a correlative or communicative immanence—what Plato called *koinōnia,* "communion" or "participation" [37]—in the areas of reciprocal influence and understanding. Here we touch on a speculative frontier, that will need to be revisited in due course.

III

We come finally to the question about which all our time might well be spent, though doubtless we should be even then little nearer to all we desire to know: the place of minds in the world-order. Let us here run swiftly over a wide and intricate pattern, seeking to sketch roughly a working diagram of which some sections can be treated more fully in the next chapter.

A. Consider first mind in evolution, at once a product in some sense, and a participant in the complex processes we call collectively by that name.

(1) The products of evolution as we know it and extend it by conjecture are sufficiently numerous and varied to make a bare list of them, by major families and genera,

look ridiculous; yet no more is possible here. There are first, it would seem, the systems with which physics and chemistry, astronomy and geology deal: the inorganic systems small and large.

(*a*) Whether our probably curved space-time network is itself an evolved product, or whether that question even has meaning, I do not know. Alexander takes space-time as primordial; Whitehead does not;[38] and we shall not decide. Likewise whether the minor units of matter as we now conceive it, electrons and protons, are in any sense evolved is not known, though competent physicists hold at least that they are probably not indestructible.[39] Even with respect to comparatively large blocks of matter, such as atoms and molecules, whether evolution is a suitable description of the way in which they appear is not known; though here, of course, clear evidence is now ample to establish their destructibility, and on the other hand the periodic table of the elements signalizes an orderly sequential arrangement as impressive as anything the sciences have brought to light.[40] Thus far, disintegration rather than evolution seems most clearly suggested by the evidence at hand.

(*b*) It is when from the very small scale we pass to the very large, and begin to talk of galactic and planetary systems that the concept of evolution takes on more liveliness; though even here it is necessary to be cautious about construing it in terms of progress. But the appearance of order on a grand scale, associated not with static but with swiftly moving masses and rapidly changing material constitution is overwhelmingly clear. The order displayed in these mass movements, however, lends itself well to mechanical description, and so far as the principle of entropy may be supposed to apply, the picture has still rather the look of progressive disorganization than of what we commonly mean by evolution.

(*c*) It is not otherwise when we focus on the earth in its far-off days of flaming youth. That picture too shows dissipation of energy and inexorable slowing and cooling. But in the light of what has come later, it is possible to look back with a biophysicist like Henderson,[41] and note with interest the accumulation in the earth and its atmosphere—a somewhat special adjunct in itself—of large quantities of carbon, oxygen, hydrogen, and water in readily accessible and readily transposable forms; the stabilization of temperature within a moderate range; the development of tidal flats; and a great number of other conditions, some causally related, some apparently not so related one to another.

(2) But only when living organisms appear, no one knows how, do the familiar phenomena of coincident differentiation and integration take the form of what we ordinarily call evolution. Each of these living things, to borrow a French biologist's vivid word, is a "whirlpool," *tourbillon*, in which diversity and rapid, perpetual alteration of matter is associated with notable stability of pattern or form. This structural pattern, moreover, and the behavior associated with it grow increasingly complex in certain strains of descent; and in numerous instances, with increasing complexity of structure and behavior goes also increasing integration or unification. It is in the course of such development as this that minds, as we have been describing them, emerge, and themselves undergo development. But minds develop, as we have seen, not in isolation but in social contexts; and these, no less than individual organisms, have their places among the products of evolution.

(3) Of social development among men we have come to know something, but of social life among our wild cousins, for obvious reasons, our information is scanty and conflicting. Kropotkin sees mutual aid a conspicuous feature of animal life in many species; Briffault cites emphatic testimony to the ruthlessness of living things everywhere.[42] Plainly more light is wanted. But one fact of importance stands out with apparent clarity. Just as man as individual displays more complex variability in behavior than his less articulate kinsfolk, even those so close as chimpanzees, so man's social organizations have complexity and plasticity such as those of no other animal exhibit. Social groups of the family type, the herd type, even the societal type involving regular division of labor, appear among other forms of life. But the most complex of these, the ant-hills and bee-hives, seem as rigid in their organization as primitive human societies were once thought to be. It is characteristic of human society as we know it, however, to combine with a large measure of fixity a considerable measure also of variability; and both tendencies have played and now play their parts in shaping the intelligence, conscience, and tastes of men now living, as these conversely help to make and mar the social patterns.

(4) To speak thus is to cross the line from biology into history as it deals with human persons, movements, and events. And again the suitability of the term evolution or rather, to follow here Hobhouse's distinction,[43] the term progress is open to lively challenge. For whereas in talking of such facts as the biological sciences deal with, it was feasible to construe evolution, with Spencer, simply as increasing differentiation and unification, and although certain lovers of order such as Bosanquet have seemed

willing to stand by that formula as a sufficient criterion also of human value,[44] most of us now are more doubtful that the good can be so simply caught within a phrase, and that twentieth century life at all obviously fulfills that test anyway. Hence, in part, the widespread current dismay and bewilderment among educated folk. We had been taught to believe in progress, and now they have taken away our lord. But not all of human history is taken away. Minds able to think, to learn, to build, and destroy and build again have emerged somehow, and it is they that now pour scorn upon themselves and their achievements. Men have been savages before and perhaps will be again, not merely in metaphor but in sober fact. That does not undo the world that brought human minds to birth and gives promise of sustaining and training them far into the future.

B. In putting to ourselves the picture of human life as it now is, we have become accustomed to nearby, small-scale views. We have been content to stress the adaptiveness of terrestrial organisms and the mechanism of natural selection, all rightly enough, but without giving due attention to the inorganic setting within which organic development transpires. Instead of being staggered and frightened or repelled by the picture of barren reaches of space, moving matter, and hurtling light with which contemporary pessimists try to dumbfound us, why can we not face in all fairness its full sweep and chill and fierce heat, and then ask afresh what minds are doing here at all? Emergent evolution: yes, but that restates the problem rather than provides an answer. Chance? "Natural law"? Blind, "unconscious purpose" at large in the world? Perhaps. These are questions we

143

shall face in the next chapter. The answer which seems
to me least incredible of the answers so far proposed is
the familiar one which Plato wrote into the *Sophist*, the
Philebus, and the last book of the *Laws*:[45] that Mind in
significant measure such as we have sought to describe is
among the first principles of the universe; not merely a
product of evolution but one of its primary grounds.

CHAPTER FOUR

CONCERNING GOD AND HIS CREATURES

When St. Thomas Aquinas wrote the great treatise which Father Rickaby abridged and translated under the title *Of God and His Creatures*,[1] his first section dealt with God but his argument began with creatures. He was unable to find intellectual satisfaction either in uninquiring faith, or in mystical intuitions or aprioristic proofs which leap at once to immediate certainty that God exists otherwise than as idea or in human experience. Rather, as philosophical theologian he placed his chief reliance on what Leibniz later called "the principle of sufficient reason,"[2] and from the existence and order of the world as perceptible and intelligible, he argued to the existence and activity of a Being sufficient to account for the facts observed. He had no quarrel with faith, nor with mysticism, nor with a priori reasoning, each in its proper place. Without rigorous dialectic, no reasoning of any sort worth the name can go forward: a priori dialectic in which it is shown that, irrespectively of any particular experience, from given premises, certain consequences necessarily follow. Without faith, all that reason can discover will be less than enough for man's salvation. And toward the mystic vision as a goal of blessedness, reason and faith alike may aspire for their completion. But to confuse idea with actuality, voluntary assent with coercive knowledge, or end with beginning, St. Thomas steadily holds is not allowable. To reason about God as existing in actuality, and not merely in idea or in experience, one must argue from actually observed consequent to sufficient ground.

Today the mode of philosophical theology which these pages profess to follow, and which in mental temper has more than a little in common with Aquinas, proceeds upon that course. There are, however, two major differences between his philosophical situation and ours. On the one hand, positivistic doubts have arisen as to the cogency of causal argument or, more generally, of the principle of sufficient reason,[3] as referring to anything other than observable connections among observed phenomena. The only "sufficient ground" of a perceived event, many would now hold, is another event of the same sort, itself perceived or perceivable. On the other hand, supposing it legitimate in principle to look for a more ultimate existential ground, basic to what appears but not itself wholly apparent,[4] the difficulty of defining specifically a "sufficient ground" for what we can in fact observe of nature and human behavior has been vastly increased by our growing awareness of the complexity of both these areas. To us it is by no means so obvious as it appeared to Aristotle or to Aquinas—or to Galilei, Locke, and Newton—just *what* the phenomena are that need to be accounted for. "Natural theology" has fallen once more upon hard days; and until (or unless) our thinking about the world of nature moves out again upon a plateau of temporary stability and agreement, the task of the natural theologian is not likely to grow lighter, nor its legitimacy to go unchallenged.

Nevertheless, this effort appears to me in principle sound, and in practice indispensable, unless we are to forgo theology altogether. As to the propriety in principle of taking phenomena as revelation of realities that are not

wholly apparent, we have already had occasion to speak.[5]
Whatever our judgment as to other sorts of phenomena,
those at least which we interpret as revealing the presence
of another person are thereby referred to a "sufficient
ground" (to wit, a rational agent) which is not and cannot be to us wholly apparent. The practical inevitability
and theoretical propriety, in such cases, of assigning observed phenomena to a ground beyond what can be observed, is not, I think, seriously disputed by any one;
even by those who (I think rightly) deny its logical
cogency. In principle, to assign likewise a much greater
system of phenomena to a proportionately greater "sufficient ground" is again to pass a judgment which lacks
logical coerciveness, but which may, for all that, have a
legitimate place in the organization of normal and reasonable living. If nothing more were meant, indeed, in this
latter case, than that such and such extensive and complex
phenomena reveal the presence of an extensive and complex reality of some sort, the statement would ordinarily
not provoke much protest. But when such a judgment
means to affirm, as natural theology does mean to affirm,
that of the observable world-order or of a major part of it,
the "sufficient ground" is *God,* then both its theoretical
propriety and its practical inevitability, as well as its logical cogency, are likely to be disputed.

It is obvious that in this issue the whole problem of
knowledge, in all its complexity, is involved. With respect
to that problem, the tendency here followed is that currently known as critical realism, which has direct affilia-
tion with Thomist thought, no less than with Kantian and
other modern critical theories.[6] As regards the possibility
of arriving at logically cogent knowledge of God by
argument from sufficient reason, I find it necessary to go

with Kant rather than with St. Thomas. Logically cogent knowledge of God, even knowledge that He exists, I think we do not have. Faith rather than logical proof seems what we may hope for here. But faith unexamined by critical reason, once more, is not *theologia;* and such testing of faith involves us quickly in *theologia naturalis*—as Kant and St. Thomas both clearly perceived.[7]

In this chapter, following out further the lines suggested at the end of the preceding one, we shall speak of what apparently is an unfinished universe, of man as product and participant therein, and of God in relation with these. We shall use as a general descriptive scheme the familiar conceptual framework of emergent evolution, with theism as a more ultimate interpretive belief. In so doing we shall claim company, as regards intent and general direction, with such contemporary theologians as Dr. Tennant and Bishop Barnes, with such philosophers as Lloyd Morgan, Hobhouse, Bavink, von Hügel, and Whitehead, and at a greater historic interval, with such patriarchs of thought as Aquinas and Plato.[8] Neither novelty, inclusiveness, nor any sort of authority, needless to say, is here professed: only an effort to be reasonably critical, suggestive, and pertinent.

I

The phrase "an unfinished universe" will conjure up, for one acquainted either with Platonic metaphysics or with the more exact sciences, two ideas: phenomenal flux; and order, pattern, or law.

In the present actual world of events, things, and

persons, both flux and form are exemplified in such fashion that this world has at every moment the look of perpetual incompleteness and partly ordered becoming. In it we are accustomed to distinguish, though not abruptly to separate, the flux of physical events and their metrical frames; the flux of living organisms and their anatomical and behavioral integrations; and the flux of minds at their work and play. Let us glance quickly over these in turn.

A. In the study of physical events, it is now usual to discriminate structural or patterned fields, on the one hand, and particular happenings which occupy or embody them, on the other. The concept of a physical field dates, I believe, from Faraday's discovery of electromagnetic induction, which threw doubt on the classical Newtonian concept of "action at a distance"[9] through empty, inactive space, and suggested instead that space in the vicinity of a magnet becomes full of activity—a "field of force" concentrated along certain definite lines which can be mapped with great accuracy. A similar concept has proved fruitful also in more recent restudy of the phenomena of gravitation, and gravitational fields are now thought of in much the same way as electromagnetic fields; which latter, indeed, may be more highly specialized fields of essentially the same kind.

(1) Physical fields of both sorts are concrete, actual webs of events arranged into definite patterns. When the patterns thus exemplified are themselves isolated for study and abstract description, there results description of a geometrical structure of greater or less complexity. But the study of geometrical structure can be pursued on its own account, far beyond the limits of any phenomena

actually observed; and pure geometries result, which exhibit the abstract, formal relationships which must follow, among figures and magnitudes, from the adoption of one or another of various sets of basic assumptions, or postulates. Each geometry seeks to be internally coherent; each is distinct from every other in its particular set of postulates, and therefore in its resulting equations; and each may properly hold its conclusions to be valid upon its own postulates, whether or not any observable system of events displays in fact the relationships which in theory it has described.

Of such pure geometries, it is common now to distinguish three main "classical" types, and a great number of variations and developments by which these are generalized through removal of one or another of their limiting postulates.[10] First among the three "classical" geometries is Euclid's, concerned with figures and magnitudes in a space of zero curvature, in which plane surfaces are spread out flat, and solids have three dimensions. In it, a "straight line"—the shortest path between two points—is the straight line of everyday common sense, more exactly defined. Any segment of it will lie exactly along any other segment, and if one or the other be turned end for end, one will again lie exactly within the other. It is postulated (among other things) that such a line can be prolonged to infinite length without returning upon itself; and that in any plane, given a straight line and a point outside it, one straight line and only one can be drawn through the given point so that it will not intersect the given line, though both be prolonged to infinity. The spatial field thus defined is open in all directions; but the variety of figures which can be described in it is rather sharply restricted by certain of its postulates

—notably by its narrow definition of straightness, and its assumption about parallels.

The other two "classical" geometries drop these restrictions and work out the relations which obtain under more general conditions. Lobachevski abandons the "parallel postulate" and defines a spatial field in which through a given point outside a given "straight line" in a surface, an infinite number of "straight lines" can be drawn which will not intersect the given line, though all be prolonged to infinity. Under these more generous conditions, a fresh set of definite relationships can be defined and a self-consistent non-Euclidean geometry formulated. In it, plainly, a "straight line" is not what Euclid means by a straight line, but rather a certain curve—a "geodesic line"—and the spatial field as a whole is "curved"; but it is still an open field, in which a line can be prolonged to infinite length. Riemann takes a further step, and explores the relations which hold within a spatial field in which no line can be prolonged to infinite length. Such a field is not merely "curved," but its curvature is such that the field is finite: every line drawn through it, if sufficiently prolonged, returns upon itself; and in its curved surface, no two "straight lines" can be so drawn that they neither coincide nor intersect. Like "great circles" on the globe, every geodesic line in Riemann's space either coincides with or intersects every other which lies in the same surface. These non-Euclidean geometries make it possible to define the relations which would remain constant, or invariant, if figures constructed under one set of conditions were "transformed" (by projection, or otherwise) into corresponding figures in which some but not all of the previously defined conditions obtain. Such geometries, therefore, are more highly generalized—or less highly restricted—than geometries in which the number of postulates is greater.

Beyond these three "classical" geometries, still further generalization is being achieved by dispensing with still other assumptions held by all of the three theories thus far noticed. Thus, all of them assume that a measure of length (a yardstick of some sort) can be moved from one part of the spatial field to another without variation in length; so that a rod which measures twelve inches in one part of the field will measure off twelve inches in another also, whether along a straight-edge or along any of a wide variety of curves which, however they vary in shape, are invariant in length. Now Weyl and Eddington have abandoned that assumption also, and are exploring a still more general system of relations which would hold if a measuring rod carried from *A* to *B* through one part of a spatial field should have at *B* a different length from that which it would have if carried from *A* to *B* through another part of the spatial field.[11] These investigators, in short, are asking what relations may still hold good not merely in a homogeneous but also in a heterogeneous spatial field, in which even the length, as well as the shape, of a measuring rod may vary from place to place.

What in detail these successive generalizations of geometric description involve, in theory and in application, only the experts know. I have not so much as a beginner's understanding of it. But even to an untrained layman, one central fact is clear: These theoretic systems bear witness to the fact that among highly abstract forms, whether originally suggested by observed phenomena or defined in the first place by purely theoretic postulates, there obtain invariant relations which can be exhibited in coherent systems of thought. Thus far, at any rate, rigorous order seems to confront the mind of man. But whether observed physical phenomena display any such order is a further question.

The answer is to be sought in two closely associated, but thus far imperfectly co-ordinated inquiries: those, namely, which describe physical fields, and those which describe the units of "matter" that occupy or embody these fields.

(2) The triumphs of field physics in describing the patterns of gravitational and electromagnetic events are too well known to call for more than mention here. What Galilei and Newton began, in the study of gravitation, Einstein seems to have completed so far as macroscopic events are concerned.[12] The behavior of freely falling bodies (excepting very minute ones) can be described, it seems, with a high degree of precision, if they be regarded as movements of one body relatively to another, in a four-dimensional field such as Riemann first defined[13] —a closed, curved space-time continuum, in which the apparently fixed speed of light provides a gigantic measuring rod suitable even for stellar distances. In such a continuum, the lines on which light rays and material particles move would be not Euclidean straight lines, but geodesic curves; and such concepts as absolute position in space and universal simultaneity in time are not applicable. Every movement has to be described relatively to a particular frame of reference: a point on the crust of the earth, or on the sun, or on a certain star. But among the descriptions of a given movement calculated for several diverse frames of reference, definite correlations appear. Invariant equations persist through all the calculated "transformations," and give assurance that gravitational fields thus conceived display intricate order, not chaos.

In like manner, electromagnetic fields have been described with great precision by Clerk Maxwell, whose equations formulated sixty years ago are still regarded as capable of describing, in theory, any event which can transpire within the limits of such a field (excepting again, perhaps, the puzzling events within the atom).[14] These equations are taken to describe the behavior of electric charges and currents, magnetic phenomena, and rays of light as variants of one basic kind of physical behavior, to wit, electromagnetic action. Such action appears to set up disturbances of certain parts of a spatial or gravitational field which differentiate these parts from other parts in which electromagnetic phenomena are absent. On this showing, the homogeneity or uniformity of space-time considered as a physical field is destroyed, as though by the intrusion of alien factors. But this very non-uniformity can, it would seem, be included in a more general geometric pattern of the sort first proposed by Weyl, in which a certain kind of local curvature (warp or twist) in space-time is calculated to display just the relations expressed in Maxwell's laws for electromagnetic fields.[15] Assimilation of the latter, so far as structure is concerned, into a single system with Einstein's gravitational field is thereby presented as theoretically possible for a geometry of sufficient generality.

(3) As regards the dynamic, material, or forcible, as distinct from the structural aspect of electromagnetism, no such assimilation has been approached. The disturbances manifest in magnetic fields are associated always, it would seem, with units of "matter"—electrons, positive charges, atomic nuclei, and so on—which do not reduce to terms in any of these equations. As we have more than once observed, the behavior of these sub-atomic units within the

atom has thus far appeared to defy all precise ultimate measurement and description. In dealing with them, resort must be had to statistical procedures, in which by measuring as accurately as possible large numbers of instances and averaging the results, approximately accurate findings, of relatively high probability as regards their pertinence to an actual event, can be obtained. It was thus that, by measuring many samples of various gases, each sample containing many molecules, Boyle, Charles, and Gay-Lussac described approximately the correlation of changes in volume of gas with changes in either pressure or temperature. In like manner Joule and Carnot formulated the first and second laws of thermodynamics, which describe the energic behavior of a closed physical system: the one as regards its total internal energy, which remains constant; the other as regards the portion of its internal energy available for work, which diminishes with every change initiated within the system. Not otherwise, I take it, the work of Rutherford, Planck and Bohr, and of De Broglie, Heisenberg, Schrödinger, and Dirac on sub-atomic phenomena has been accomplished, and the basic concepts of matter and energy revolutionized.[16] Such formulæ as theirs describe not structural fields, but concrete events observed (or inferred) to take place in and, so to say, give body to such fields. These statistical laws claim at most a relatively high degree of probability and approximate accuracy; but the regularities which they reveal in the flux of events, whether exact or not, are no less unmistakable than the presence also of some non-formal factor or factors which appear very plainly to differentiate an actual event from any metrical scheme.

(4) We are here face to face with the problems posed by the puzzling fact of concretion. They press upon us

most obviously when we seek to examine the units of matter, but also when we seek to describe the events in a gravitational or electromagnetic field. Even in such relatively precise description there is room for uncertainty beyond that which attaches to every human effort to perform an exact course of reasoning, as in logic or pure mathematics. No doubt mistakes in plenty have been and will be made in working out the properties even of those ideal manifolds which the highly generalized geometries describe; but in these instances the source of error and uncertainty appears to be in the observer, and not in the essential character of the situation which he is trying to define. But when we seek to describe the actual fields of our observed physical events, another sort of difficulty is involved, that prevents us in principle from ever judging with certainty whether and how precisely a given geometric schema fits a particular field. This difficulty is that measuring rods known to be perfectly rigid, in whatever way the particular problem requires, are not at hand. Measuring rods are material things or else light rays. Bars of metal, and so on, composed of moving particles like swarms of gnats, are notoriously variable in length. Material units, such as electrons, it is of course impracticable to use as measures. But supposing it could be done, even then perfect accuracy and certainty of measurement would not be had; for electrons also give signs of inner complexity, and behave now as particles, now as waves, without being clearly resoluble into either the one or the other.[17] Moreover, the impossibility of determining the precise whereabouts and limits of a particular electron, because of the uncertainty-relations described by Heisenberg, is now common knowledge. For measuring the stellar spaces, light rays are taken to move at a constant speed *c,* and to offer therefore suitable yardsticks. But supposing this velocity accepted as invariant, on theoretic grounds, still our observations of particular light rays inevitably involve the use of instruments in which perfect rigidity cannot be assumed. The direct application of metrical formulæ to physical events, therefore, cannot be effected with the accuracy and certainty exemplified, in principle, by the theoretic calculations as such.

Nevertheless, these fluid events appear to manifest organization, in the sense of unity-in-variety, wherever physical observations have been carried out, alike on the largest and on the smallest scale. If old formulæ are giving place to new, it is not because order is vanishing from the cosmos, but because order at unsuspected points has forced itself upon the notice of more acute and better equipped observers. Large-scale and small-scale "constants" are coming into view which disrupt, no doubt, familiar ways of thinking, but which hold out promise that through other ways of thinking, more complex in some respects but simpler in others, and withal more exact and comprehensive, a closer approach can be made to seeing the physical world-order as it is. It may be premature to take the fixed speed of light *c* as revealing a *"grain* of the world-structure" which is "essential and universal" [18] or to refer the gravitational constant k to a *"natural gauge"* provided by "the radius of curvature of the universe" at a given point.[19] But that these constants indicate some definite structural property of the physical world it is hard to doubt. From a different sort of observation has emerged Planck's discovery of the quantum *h* as a fixed unit, of which every discharge of energy between a body and a field is a definite multiple. These "universal constants" [20] and such special ones as the unit charge of the electron *e*

are not man-made fictions, such as hypotheses: they are
come upon as facts, that force human observers to give
them consideration. They are stubborn witnesses that
what confronts us is not chaos but a world-order.

Yet these structural unities are everywhere exemplified
in the midst of variability, and nowhere among physical
events does an instance of utter simplicity occur. Even an
electron, it would seem, on the one hand is internally
complex and furiously active, spinning like a miniature
planet, jumping into and out of unconnected orbits,
knocking about in gravitational and electromagnetic
fields, behaving now as particle and now as wave or wave-
bundle; while on the other hand it keeps, within limits,
its characteristic pattern. What is true and puzzling as to
electrons is true and more puzzling as to atomic nuclei.
Some of these are so unstable as to break up spontaneously in radioactivity; yet such explosions take place, over
a given period of time, with a high order of statistical
regularity. Some nuclei on the other hand, like that of
helium, are so stable as to survive radioactive explosions,
and to behave as projectiles and residual end-products in
sub-atomic bombardment.[21] As to atoms, their intricacies
and seeming eccentricities are such that serious question
is now being raised whether their internal behavior can be
described at all without abandoning, as regards their internal fields, the basic concepts of space-time, energy, and
gravitation which appear to hold of larger masses.[22] That
sub-atomic events display order of some sorts is plain beyond doubt; that it is associated with behavior at present
inexplicable on familiar mechanical principles is also
plain.

To make capital of the present incompleteness of our
knowledge at these and at various other points, in the

interests of uncritical piety, is plainly most unwise. On the other hand, to minimize the complexity and refractoriness of these problems by speculative dogmatism, in the interests of a naturalistic orthodoxy, is no more defensible. We seem to stand near the beginning of a new advance in physical investigation, rather than near the completion of a scientific world-view already substantially fixed. The special intractability of old-fashioned matter composed of hard pellets, caroming about in empty space, has no place in contemporary thought. The physical world is a world of happenings, rather than of rigid particles; and its particles also are at least partly fluid. Thus far, if a layman may judge, the picture of an unfinished world showing some of the characteristic marks of organization without complete fixity, of intricate order maintained in and through fluent variety, seems not out of accord with the evidence now at hand.

B. Let us turn next from physical events as such to the flux of living things and their peculiar integrations. Let us glance in turn at the nature of a highly differentiated organism, at certain factors in the production of such organisms, and at the problems posed by emergent evolution.

(1) In confronting a living individual, however primitive, one faces once more on a plane of greatly increased complexity the same problems that have arisen hitherto in respect to structured physical processes which display at once organization and unfinishedness. A living organism, to repeat a phrase used earlier, is a complex whirlpool in which detailed content perpetually changes, yet approximately stable patterns persist. In it the smaller physical units are combined and recombined into highly

complex, often chemically unstable molecules, the molecules into cells, the cells into diverse tissues and organs, and these last, along with numerous freely moving cells, fluids, and the like, into the busy community we call a living organism. In such a one as a highly developed mammal, it is convenient to distinguish anatomical from behavioral organization,[23] calling attention by the former term to factors which change more slowly, and by the latter to factors which change more swiftly, in the total life of the organism.

(*a*) In its anatomical organization, a highly developed mammal is unified or integrated in at least four important ways.[24] A jointed skeletal system of bones, muscles, and various connective elements composes a mechanical vehicle for gross movement and posture, at once resistant to strain and pliable in a large variety of positions and motions. A circulatory system keeps all parts of the organism bathed in the blood- and lymph-stream:[25] a fluid medium by means of which conditions of temperature, of chemical equilibrium as regards food supply, oxygen, carbonic acid, various hormones and other endocrine secretions, and of cellular protection against invading microorganisms, tend to be maintained within limits appropriate to each of a wide variety of changing bodily situations. A neural system of sensory receptors, and peripheral, central, and autonomic nerve tracts and ganglia, provides for the rapid passage of nervous impulses from one part of the body to another in such fashion as not only to instigate varied movements and chemical changes, certain of which are associated with conscious experience, but also to inhibit systematically such other movements and changes as would interfere with those to be performed, thus insuring for the organism as a whole within rather wide limits, integration of behavior in response to internal and external stimulation.[26] Finally, an enclosing envelope of skin and other surface membranes provides a normally unbroken and highly active and efficient protection against injury from without, and medium of interaction between organism and environment.

(*b*) The organism thus anatomically knitted together displays corresponding unification in its more fluid and shifting behavior. It is enough to mention three instances. In metabolism, food and oxygen are taken into the body, and so redistributed as to provide fuel-energy for body movement and protein and salts for the building and repair of the characteristic body tissues. In every individual animal, living through a more or less prolonged period of cell-growing and cell-destroying activity and even of repeated injury and recovery, the distinctive structure is thus established and maintained by processes whose occasional aberrations serve to remind us that they are not rigidly fixed, and whose usual regularity therefore is the more interesting.[27] At least since the days of Empedocles and Anaxagoras, these phenomena of nutrition have seemed to acute thinkers to have special importance for metaphysical inquiry; and what we are now learning of biochemistry seems rather to emphasize and clarify than to diminish their significance. Not less significant than this prolonged maintenance of characteristic form or structure in metabolism, is its transmission in reproduction. The comments just made apply here also. Chromosomes and genes are not less interesting than what Anaxagoras called *spermata,* "seeds," and their metaphysical importance is similar. Finally, besides metabolism and reproduction, we recognize complex unities in adaptive response in the way of sentiency and adaptive movement, whether to present causal impacts by way of tropismatic and simple reflex reactions, or to cue-stimuli by way of complex redintegrative responses which involve learning, and which in their totality are responses not merely to a present situation, but also to situations past or otherwise remote. Here plainly we are in the region of mind.

(2) To ask now in what manner such stable fluidities as these more complex organisms are produced, is to receive at once a familiar and probably a correct though partial answer: By evolution from simpler organisms, in accordance with the familiar concept of "natural selection," or more precisely, elimination of the less fit. For the operation of this process, two correlative sets of factors are of course required: adaptive organisms and a suitable environment. Both these terms, "adaptive" and "suitable," are to so large a degree relative to particular situations that it is not very satisfactory to try to generalize either.

Perhaps it might be said that in any organism, sensitivity, speed of reaction, toughness of integument, and other tissues, variety of available responses, and ability to learn, are likely within limits to be advantageous. But these and other factors like them add up roughly to comprise just that combination of variability and stability which we have been discussing, and it is precisely the existence of this combination that we are trying to account for. We seem now to be saying that for the production of adaptive organisms, adaptive organisms are required.

A further relevant point, however, at least helps to localize and define the problem somewhat more sharply. Factors which make for both variability and persistence in respect of a characteristic organic structure now seem clearly traceable as far back as the genes, which are the physical vehicles of heredity. "Adaptive" organisms issue, under suitable conditions, from genes whose variations Bishop Barnes speaks of as "the raw material of evolution." [28] For in them, along with the persistence of characteristic form, generation after generation, appear also the genetic variations large or small, favorable or unfavorable, from some of which new lines of descent take their rise. But why the genes behave as they do is yet unknown. Bavink suggests that they be compared with enzymes and with the "organizers" described by Spemann;[29] but until these also are better understood, the comparison again helps to define the problem rather than immediately to solve it. Plainly these entities are not themselves ultimate, but arise out of prior conditions; and their behavior, unless it be simply accepted at face value, as given, plainly calls for inquiry as to what these prior conditions may be thought to involve.

As to a "suitable" environment, one may specify briefly three general characters, each of which again involves a multitude of particular ones. First, it must be exacting, and to a considerable extent regular in its behavior: an environment in which uniformities of response can be built up without too early disaster, and in which (at the higher organic levels) learning can take place. Secondly, it must be to an extent variable: both in the way of environmental changes which it imposes on the organisms, and in the way of plasticity or modifiability by the responsive activity of the organism in return. Thirdly, as regards both concrete details of content and specific arrangements of such content, it must be relevant in a large number of ways to particular needs of things which are to live and grow. "The fitness of the environment," in the sense of Henderson's well-known discussion,[30] is what is meant here. The primary point is that for the support of life as we know or can conceive it, there is required in the environment the compresence of very numerous physical and chemical conditions which are themselves, so far as we know, not all causally linked one with another. Their presence together, therefore, is either a chance coincidence, or again an indication of some more ultimate common ground. The point here, once more, is not that, given such an environment, it is remarkable that it can sustain life; but rather, it is remarkable that the intricate combinations of apparently independent factors required to compose such an environment should have been effected in the first place. How life came to emerge and develop within it is an additional problem, already noticed; not merely a restatement of this one. Both need to be fairly dealt with.

(3) Thus to name these factors which play their parts in the process called emergent evolution is to call attention to the resemblance between certain general problems which it involves, and the problems we have already noticed in discussing physical events. There is here too the problem of accounting for the concrete conjunction (found there in physical happenings, here in organisms) of variability and stability. It has a special turn given to it at the biological level by two facts: the fact that within living organisms, chemical equilibria are maintained in the midst of reactivity and change, involving organic compounds which outside the body quickly disintegrate;[31] and the fact, seemingly established by Driesch and Spemann,[32] that the development of an individual organism into its characteristic mature form is not a fixed unrolling of a rigidly predetermined chain or clockwork, but an epigenetic process in which surprisingly wide variations can take place, and in which nevertheless there are per-

sistent tendencies to the development of the characteristic form.

But here there is also the new problem of accounting specifically for the initial emergence of distinctively organic behavior—metabolic, reproductive, adaptively responsive and sentient; in short, for the emergence of life —in the midst of an earthly environment from which we may suppose such terrestrial living things as we know were once wholly absent. This problem is especially acute in view of what appears to be the tendency of undisturbed physical systems toward disorganization of energy, according to Carnot's principle of increasing entropy. Whether or not the appearance of organisms be in conflict with that principle—and there is no evidence that it is—at any rate it is not an event which, in a physical system relaxing toward a dead level, would be anticipated as probable. The phrase "emergent evolution" is meant precisely to signalize this fact of unpredictability. But the phrase is a vivid restatement, not in any sense a solution, of the problem, as Lloyd Morgan who coined it plainly recognizes.[33]

C. Besides the flux of physical events, and that of living organisms, we confront thirdly the flux of minds and their activities, to which examination of the higher organisms has brought us once more. But we have already examined this area in the preceding chapter, and there will be a chance to say something further about it when we come, shortly, to speak of man and his place in creation.

D. Meanwhile we turn, for a moment, from the actual world to an elusive realm of possibilities which are never, as such, actual and which seem not likely ever to be completely exemplified in actual events, things, or persons.

(1) We notice first mathematical and logical forms. The number four, the group of prime numbers, the circle, the field laws referred to above: these and similar terms in mathematical discourse stand for whatever it is that the mathematician's symbols directly mean, and whatever it is to which his demonstrations directly apply. We have seen that they cannot be known to apply directly and exactly to such phenomena as we can observe. Neither is it likely that they apply merely to fictions constructed at will by human thinkers: [34] they are too intolerant of careless manipulation, and they display, when expertly employed, too much of coherence for that to be probable. Rather, they may be said to apply to systematically interrelated numbers, magnitudes, ratios, and the like, whose status is that of validity rather than actuality. So likewise with such logical terms as sameness, otherness, greatest, least, within, without; the abstract frames called "propositional functions" which express positive and negative relatedness as such; and in short, every verbal or other symbolic expression whose meaning is anything else than a particular event, thing, person, or other actual entity as particular and actual.

It is not practicable here to enter upon the vexed question of the nature and status of such mathematical forms and logical essences. The issue has already been before us at various points at which a distinction between a theoretical frame and an actual phenomenon has been remarked. [35] For even supposing an actual instance of gravitation should exemplify accurately the calculated formula, in so far as the formula purports to describe not this instance nor a given group of instances as particulars, but *any* instance of gravitation which might take place under specified conditions, it purports to refer directly to a structure or relational pattern not exhaustively definable by reference to particular actual events, though to such events it does profess to have relevance. Let us say, then, that such forms or essences as we now speak of are not events nor things nor actual particulars at all; that they constitute rather what is possible or conceivable; and that they are to be spoken of as valid, coherent, compatible or incompatible, and the like, rather than as existent or actual, though as conditions for thought they are given, objective and obdurate, and in that sense real, though not actual.[36] Given certain premises or postulates, certain consequences follow and certain others are excluded: else thinking becomes indistinguishable in principle from more or less lucky guesswork.[37]

(2) With formal possibilities or essences of this character are somehow to be numbered also ideals or unactualized values or "goods." The term good is often employed, of course, with reference to a particular thing or event: a healthy body, we say, or the pleasure of eating is a good. But we recognize also another and more general use of the term as referring to a character which may be conceived and appreciated, and which may or may not be exemplified by a particular event or thing or person. There are indeed many diverse particular goods in the former sense, we say; but all of them may fitly be called good just in so far as each of them exemplifies a certain character which is not simply identical with any nor with all of them. In so far, moreover, as each of them, in one respect or another, appears deficient in that character, and in so far as this deficiency rouses an observer to compare the present fact unfavorably with what it might be but is not, the unachieved possibility thus envisaged as what, if

actualized, would be better than the present fact, serves as an ideal. That is, it serves as a criterion for evaluative judgment and sometimes as a guide for practical action. Ideals are by this account, then, to be included among forms or essences or possibilities.[38] Like other such forms they may be exemplified or approximated in actual particulars, but never exhaustively identified with any of these. They may be supposed also, like mathematical and other logical essences, to exemplify systematic interrelatedness among themselves; though ethical theory as yet is very far from having demonstrated such interrelations among æsthetic and moral ideals, or more generally among values as such, in a manner comparable to that of the more abstract mathematical and logical theories. The distinctive note of ideals in comparison with other forms or possibles, is their ostensible claim to represent various aspects of the good as ultimate goal of thought and action, and thereby to serve as criteria for both these modes of behavior. That claim is itself in need of careful scrutiny as regards specified ideals, because of the inescapable human equation which here, even more plainly than in astronomical or microscopic observation or elaborate mathematical or logical construction, is an ever present source of probable error.[39] The only feasible precaution against it in either case is repeated critical review of premises, procedures and results.

II

We come thus by a second road to confrontation of man, as concrete product of and participant in creation. By following the line of actual events through the areas

of physical and organic processes, we came upon him as
an animal engaged in mental behavior. By following
more cursorily the lines of interconnectedness among
forms, or structural and ideal essences, we come upon him
again as an unideal and in some ways a disturbing participant in this region also. It is time to re-examine briefly
his place in our total scheme.

A. Let us say then that as product of the world-processes,
man is an animal, a world-child.

(1) He is a body-mind hierarchy in which each of the
main sorts of process we have discussed is to be found. He
exemplifies physical and chemical mechanisms which
presumably are in all essential respects like those which
the physical sciences describe elsewhere; organic integration and adaptiveness which the biological sciences can
recognize; and the distinctive mode of purposive behavior
which we have been calling mental, with which the inquiries of psychologists and students of the more complex
human activities concern themselves.

(2) Man so regarded is at all these levels intimately
interrelated with the actual world of nature which we
have, for the most part, been describing. *Continuity*
seems not too strong a word, though it is to be used with
due recognition of our uncertainty whether the physical
world is itself continuous. As regards his physical behavior, man is as deeply immersed in the currents of material and radiational transposition as any other biophys-
ical system: he too is a whirlpool, in perpetual interaction
with his physical surroundings. His mental behavior also
involves stimulus-response interaction which, however far
his symbolic ventures may range, maintains fluent contact
between him and his actual locus in space-time—what-

ever that phrase may be found to mean. And if one may step for a moment from the descriptive to the evaluative point of view and estimate the human animal in terms of worth, one sees in him the same sort of ambivalence, of good-and-badness, that one sees in any other natural fact. Man is to all appearance an authentic product of whatever world-making processes give rise to nature as we know it; and for that reason neither man and his behavior, nor the natural order within which he has emerged, nor the specific fact of his emergence therein may fairly be left out of consideration in any theory which professes to offer a serious and comprehensive account of either nature or human life.

B. On the other hand, man who is animal and world-child is also critic, creator, and worshiper. But these are rôles that can be played only by one who in some degree stands clear of his immediate environment and reacts upon it with a measure of autonomy. No being wholly immersed in the present flow of events could judge it, seek purposefully to change it, and grow acutely "home-sick," to use Chesterton's word,[40] in the midst of what alone could be to him familiar.

(1) The primary function among these three is critical judgment, which as one form of symbolic behavior involves the sort of partial emancipation from the immediate present that is basic to all such behavior. Such judgment is especially interesting when it takes the form of comparing a present fact with what is envisaged as a possible and valuable alternative not now present.

(2) Such critical comparison and evaluation is apt often to be associated with practical effort to actualize some alternative taken to be both feasible and desirable though

not yet actual. When such effort is successful, an actually
novel outcome will have been achieved. But not merely
that. Failure of an unprecedented sort would likewise
be a novel outcome. In case of success, the outcome is a
novel result which is relevant at once to the want previously felt, which it more or less fully satisfies; to the plans,
possibilities, and values envisaged, which it more or less
fully actualizes; and to the anticipatory judgment or
foresight of the worker, which it more or less fully veri-
fies.[41] With respect to critical judgment and creative
work, therefore, one may speak quite literally, I think, of
mental behavior as a medium for the directed or purposeful actualizing of imaginatively apprehended possibilities
and values.[42]

(3) The same capacity for critical judgment which
man turns upon his environment he can turn also upon
himself and his work, and often enough finds both unsatisfactory. Such judgment of the inadequacy of oneself
and one's doings in comparison with some greater good
seen, imagined, or conceived has not infrequently come
to be a primary factor in the complex experiences we call
worship: experiences of awe in the presence of something
other and greater than oneself, and of reconciliation and
self-commitment more searching and inclusive than any
less potent human experience seems to involve. The moral
and religious aspirations here referred to are taken, in the
present discussion, as not different in kind from other
human experiences, nor as entitled to privileged treatment
as theory when a question of fact is to be determined. But
as experiences of peculiar poignancy and often of excep-
tionally profound influence in human life, they are themselves facts which with all their discoverable implications
require to be given due weight.[43]

C. The wider consideration of which this last statement specifies one detail, is that man himself must be brought into just perspective as the most directly accessible clue we have to the nature of the universe, and the one with which, expressly or tacitly, every speculative theory has to set out. It is not man as an isolated phenomenon, nor man as a beneficiary of occult revelations that is meant here; but man as aspiring animal, himself a partial revealer of the universe whose critical child he is.

(1) One must take account here first of what may be called general revelation through human life as we find it, supposing man a representative member of the real world-order. The import, then, of the emergence of human mind as a creative product of evolution, and of the curious self-criticism which nature has achieved in human aspiration toward good, must be fairly assayed. Such precepts have been commonplace in theology at least since Socrates's day and doubtless will be so for a long time to come.[44]

(2) Besides the general evidential value of the fact that there have come to be men at all, what may be called special revelations may in at least one sense fairly be recognized. Any one who tries to understand human life and its relation to the world at all cannot avoid selecting among the data available; and for any such one, particular events or particular persons in which it seems to him important facts or principles are brought into sharp focus, are sure to seem of special revelatory value. To thoughtful Christians the life and death of Jesus and the consequences, good and bad, that have attended the efforts of his professed followers to live in his way and extend his influence have seemed of central significance, though by no means easy to interpret. To other thoughtful observers,

such other human facts as the tenacity of the Hebrew people and the Jewish Church under persecution, or the revolutions of 1789 and 1917,[45] or the successes and failures of non-co-operation in India, or the modern advance of the natural sciences, may seem of greater import. Whatever one's choice, the point is the same. One cannot avoid selecting, and special illumination will seem to him to be found in one place or in another.

But if there be special value in the vividness and emotional drive that can come with choice of such a "special revelation," its dangers also are obvious. And for my part, I confess that none of those named, if taken by itself, seems either intelligible or conclusive. Only by trying to see the life and death of Jesus and the ups and downs of Christianity as intimately related to the efforts of frank non-Christians to live by contrary principles; or by trying to see violent revolutions in relation to both the institutions and lives they destroy, and the goals they set out to achieve, does it seem even remotely possible to make out what these special revelations may mean. Ignore them we cannot; take any one of them in isolation as exclusively authoritative we ought not.

Rather, the principle which seems to me here again in place is the need to combine as well as one may the detailed insights and information accumulated through the processes of learning, and the sagacity of a mind open to all that may be of significance in each situation. There is much to be said for the scribe as well as for the prophet, for the patient worker with details and also for the swift synoptic genius who is the true mystic. Most of us, being neither the one nor the other, may do well to cultivate something of the virtues of both.

III

We have spoken of creatures, each after its kind. Now, of God.

A. Our concern as theologians here is two-fold: to inquire on what terms, if at all, this total world-picture may be held together in such fashion as not to violate our sober judgment as to what seems reasonable; and to discover whether in such an inquiry, there may come to light re-enforcement for belief in, and ways of thinking about, a Being at once real enough, great enough, and good enough to be called God.

(1) The mode of argument which seems to me to underlie all intellectual approaches here, excepting only Anselm's proof which I think Aquinas and Kant were right in regarding as inconclusive, is argument by analogy. Its dubious standing in courts of logic is well known, and if a better were available we should by all means prefer it. But the stricter methods of proof seem applicable only to pure forms, not to concrete systems of events; and in trying to interpret the latter, theologians share with workers in the more concrete sciences and with practical men the necessity to suppose, without being able to prove, that if two systems of events appear to be alike in certain respects thought to be essential, one may expect them to be alike in other specified respects also. That such a supposition requires to be used with acute awareness of its inconclusive character, whether one be using a machine, a protozoön, or a mind as one's analogical frame of reference, should go without saying.[46]

As to the special significance of moral judgments and religious experiences as evidence of the reality of God, we have already spoken. Neither is regarded here as offering a way to immediate certainty. Both, on the other hand, are regarded as providing data which, especially for consideration of the character of God and His relations with men, are indispensable.

(2) To account for the array of facts now before us, there seem at first sight to be at least four live hypotheses. The first is that the observed array is the outcome to date of chance combinations and permutations of ultimate physical units—call them atoms, electrons, or what not. Supposing these to have definite properties such as positive and negative electrical charges, and ability to move freely in a very large, though not infinite, space-time area, their initially random movements, impacts, and combinations in accordance with simple mechanical principles, build up the complex but wholly natural world we know. There is to my knowledge no way of disproving that this account is the correct one; and one to whom it appeals as on the whole the most acceptable now seems to have only the fact of concrete improbability, not the flaw of formal impossibility, to worry him. But besides the immense *prima facie* difficulty in supposing mental and moral behavior to be the outcome of random material combinations—as though, to use Bertrand Russell's simile, a million monkeys pounding a million typewriters should turn out, in course of time, all the books in the British Museum; or rather as though typewriters should assemble, repair, and reproduce themselves, and themselves turn out books for their own perusal, edification and improvement—there is another difficulty less commonly recognized. A theory which holds that the world is built up by association of sub-atomic units has not at present the merit, sometimes claimed for this one, of exhibiting com-

plex phenomena as describable by familiar principles; for in the present state of our physical sciences the behavior of sub-atomic units seems not yet explicable by the familiar mechanical principles of dynamics. To offer their behavior, then, as an explanation of the world experienced by men is not to explain the less familiar by treating it as a complex case of the more familiar and better understood, but rather to explain the more familiar by treating it as a complex case of what is at present not understood. This hypothesis, therefore, is logically admissible, but it has no advantage in the way of clarity and simplicity, and a considerable initial disadvantage in respect of concrete probability.

A second account seeks to lessen this apparent improbability by speaking not of chance or random movement but of natural law as explaining what has come about. This suggestion may mean either of two things. It may mean that natural law is a controlling factor which exerts constraint upon moving units, and makes them go this way rather than that. But the physical sciences know nothing of law in this sense. It is, in fact, a hybrid conception which seeks to read into the physical world such constraint as statute law may put upon human behavior, but at the same time leaves out both legislator and policeman and treats the law as somehow self-made and self-enforcing. Such naïve hypostatizing has a place in popular mythology but not in serious discourse. On the other hand the term natural law may and should mean observed or inferred regularities among phenomena, or among their more ultimate grounds, and the formulæ which describe these regularities. But if the term be used in this its proper sense, the question why events transpire as they are observed to do is still to be answered; and the answer may take the form either of supposing them to manifest the initially unguided behavior of units moving at random, or of supposing the behavior of these units to be guided in some measure by a factor or factors capable (as mathematical formulæ are not) of exercising actual control. The former of these alternatives is simply reversion to the hypothesis of random behavior; the latter plainly calls for a further account of the supposed guiding factor.

The third and fourth hypotheses deal with this further question. The third suggests that guidance is exercised by some unconscious but quasi-purposive force. Schopenhauer called it Will, Bergson *élan vital,* Marx and Engels "the dialectic." The emotional appeal of a theory of this sort is undeniable and not difficult, I think, to appreciate; but its intellectual value, like that of the formula "emergent evolution," is rather as a vivid restatement of what is to be accounted for than as a way of accounting for it. To say with the Marxists, for example, that the world is one in which advance takes place through conflict is to say what in some sense clearly is true. But to say that conflict or "negation" always and necessarily brings advance would be to say what is not true, as Engels rightly points out.[47] Advance through conflict, then, is still to be accounted for, and to call the process dialectic is merely to rename it. To rename it, moreover, with a term taken from the region of mental behavior, and to suggest thereby without expressly saying so that one may count on behavior essentially like that of mind where one at the same time denies that mind is present; somewhat as the popular concept of natural law looks for something like statutory control in nature without either legislators or executives. It is not accidental that the Marxist concept of dialectic has seemed most persuasive when applied to events within the region of human history wherein minds are admittedly operative.[48] When it has been employed to explain how, without mind, a world of moving, struggling matter or phenomena or what you will has given birth to human history at all, its success has been negligible. Some other factor than unconscious *élan* seems to be called for.

The fourth hypothesis frankly affirms that this is so, and proposes that whatever other factors may be at work —random movements, mechanical combinations, unconscious gropings, and others no doubt beyond our cognizance altogether—there seems reason to affirm that among the primary factors in the universe is such behavior as we have been calling mental, and such organizing factors therefore, or at least one such, as we have called mind. The reason is the familiar analogical one formulated in the preceding chapter. Let me repeat the briefer of the two statements there given: "If we come upon a situation which seems clearly to display intelligible or otherwise humanly appreciable or appropriable order which we have not simply read into it, and which cannot plausibly be accounted for as the outcome of known non-mental processes, it is a fair hypothesis that mental behavior in important respects like our own has helped to bring it about." [49] I take the array of observed phenomena, sketched at the beginning of this chapter, to be of that sort, and to warrant therefore preferring the fourth of these views. The point has been recently and elaborately argued by Tennant, Bavink, and Barnes,[50] in line with thinkers from Plato's time to our own; and without dwelling on it here, let us go on to inquire how such primary Mind may be thought to act.

B. We shall consider here God as Creator-Redeemer:

Living Mind at work. Athanasius and Eriugena did well, as it seems to me, in holding that nature and grace, creation and redemption, belong together.[51] *Datum* and *donum,* as Eriugena put it—the gift of being and the gift of goodness—are alike primary in divine activity. The task of world-making is a task at once of creation and redemption; or in less emotional language, a task of actualizing possibilities, thus making a world, and of actualizing values, thus making the world good. If all this were done at a stroke, then creation and redemption alike would be at once complete; but in regarding the world as unfinished, we commit ourselves to regard both world-making and world-bettering as in process. God worketh even until now, and we work. The world is not yet fully made nor wholly good; and now at least, however it may have been in the unimaginable beginning, other factors than God are at work in it too. But God is primary, central, and sovereign over them all.

Is it possible to represent to ourselves more vividly what these affirmations mean, and how our thoughts about God may take more concrete form? In particular, how if at all may God's relations with the world and with men be conceived, without too flagrant impropriety? Like Origen, I find it necessary to set out from what have seemed to me revelations,[52] and to work and rework the data so provided, by the methods which he called analogy, analysis, and synthesis.[53] Analogy is a method essentially artistic in its intent, though most of us use it with little enough artistry. It involves the concrete, conscious use of one vividly realized part of experience to illuminate another, by virtue of some apparently significant correlation of the one with the other. The worth of the analogy so used depends both upon the validity and richness of the correlation, and upon the liveliness and depth with which both terms and their relationship are apprehended and conveyed. Analysis and synthesis are, by comparison, less artistic and more critical procedures: the one employed to purge out of the analogies used and the judgments based on them such irrelevant and incongruous factors as tend to blur and falsify the impression that should be conveyed; the other—synthesis—employed to amplify the picture in systematic, coherent fashion, so far as experience and thought suggest and permit.

Let us begin each part of our argument, then, with an analogy.

(1) Suppose, first, that God's relation to the actual world were analogous with mine to my own life experience. Not to my body, merely, but to all that goes to make up my *curriculum vitae,* my "career." Moment by moment, day after day, year after year, I live in the midst of the fluid, palpitant, growing cloud of events that is my life. I am the sensitive core of it, and I am also in some measure its organizer and guide. I am moved by colors and fragrance, shame and pain, joy and hope. Yet not merely at "the core" of it: I permeate it all, and reach out beyond it in all sorts of ways. I touch things and people and am touched by them, slightly or deeply. I set my course toward distant ends, and struggle year by year toward completion of this task and that, as well as toward self-mastery and stability. "Subjectivism" as a way of life, I find, is self-defeating. One grows by giving. My children are born, and some life of mine—body, mind, and energy—goes to help make their lives, but I am not they. My "self" is nourished, a lambent fire, among other selves and things and happenings. It is like a "field of force," patterned, active, influencing and being influenced

by things that come into it and go out of it, and by other such "fields of force" that neighbor it on all sides.[54] It is, more prosaically, a growing system of partly conscious behavior, patterned and dynamic, centred about and more or less permeated and unified by an active, sentient subject or ego, which (partly but never fully revealed in its behavior) presumably is also growing.[55]

Such living as mine is never "well-done," but always incomplete and faulty. Ignorance, laziness, cowardice keep me from doing all that I could; and there are conditions given, of my body, mind, surroundings, over which I have little or no control. Even within the areas of my best work and purest devotion, the very conditions which render work and devotion possible prevent these, at the same time, from being perfect.[56] But some sort of life not devoid of good emerges, for all that; and I in the midst of it, alive to it on many levels and in many ways.

To think of God as in like manner "central" in the cold, light-flooded, shimmering immensity of all that goes on is, at first sight, both impossible and pointless. Mind cannot exist off between the stars, where no nervous systems are; and anyway, we want a God closer home. As to the first, perhaps not: we simply do not know where mind *can* exist and where not. The best we can do is to look carefully about for signs that may indicate where mind *does* exist or has existed, and whenever we find ourselves persuaded that here or there mind is or has been at work, try to frame some conception as to how that presumed fact, if it be a fact, may be thought about. Naturally there is nothing to be said for playing fast and loose with either facts or logic, nor for getting what one sees reason to believe and what one knows for certain all mixed up. We are talking here about what there seems reason to believe, and so far as I am aware it is not in conflict with what is known. More than that I have no disposition to maintain. As to the second plea, that we want a God closer home, one might answer shortly that what we want has no bearing on what is the case.[57] But I think there is a more satisfactory answer: the only God who can be close home is a God whose being ranges beyond human sight and thought. A lesser would not be God. Yet the God Who is God need not be remote.

What we have been calling "the space-time continuum" is, of course, an elaborate theoretical construct worked out on the basis of perceived data. The reality to which this construct is meant to apply—namely, the whole concourse of sensorily perceptible things and events—may or may not be spread out in linear dimensions. But in any event, it has a character such that our calculations have some definite relevance to it; and without dogmatism, let us talk of it as in fact thus extended and dynamic. Let us regard this whole perceptible concourse as occupying an extensive field of force—the gravitational field—within which other fields of force and units of electricity (matter) occur, as ripples, pulsations, whirlpools, starts and stops, which affect us in various ways.[58]

Now suppose the inclusive field—call it space-time—to be as a whole a vehicle of one Mind,[59] present and operative everywhere throughout this field at many diverse levels; somewhat as a human mind, in its far more restricted activity, runs the gamut from unconscious automatisms, through conscious reflex and habitual behavior, and through self-conscious voluntary work, critical appreciation, moral effort, and social fellowship, to rare moments of absorbing experience in which self-consciousness is transcended. How such a sovereign Mind may be

thought of in relation to other minds we shall inquire in
a moment. Let us confine ourselves here to the question
how one may think of such Mind as resident through,
active within, and transcendent beyond the space-time
order. An inquiry so full of speculative surmise can satisfy
no one, and should not be taken for more than what it is:
an effort to suggest somewhat concretely the relevance of
current thinking to our basic belief in God as sovereign
Mind. *That* is a working conviction, with roots that go
deeper than thought. This is a speculative theory, which
takes its start from analogy and proceeds by way of critical
analysis and synthesis. How far, now, can our analogy
with a human self hold? And what must analysis purge
away?

(*a*) Consider first the problems involved in thinking
of God as omniscient Knower. (i) Restrictions of at least
four sorts that beset human minds would not apply to
God. First are the limitations that hamper every one who
is bound to a particular location. Each human observer is
dependent, for sensory perception, on physical stimuli
transmitted over local pathways so as to affect his central
nervous system, which is itself located on a certain "world-
line" in space-time. For such an observer, besides the
obvious difficulties (of seeing at a distance, around corners,
and so on), there is a fixed "time-cone" which at every
moment delimits the entire range of events, past, present,
and future, which he can possibly observe.[60] For God,
no such four-dimensional barriers would hold. For Him
there would be, in space-time, no "absolute elsewhere." If
He is omnipresent throughout the whole continuum, no
event which transpires within it is physically hidden from
Him.

Next, those limitations which hem us in by reason of

the particular make of our sense organs would not apply in any similar way to God. Our sensory messages from the outside world come in as fragments, in a dozen keys: here a color, there a sound, a touch, a movement, pains, odors—enough for an exciting medley, but whether a full and perfect chorus it is hard to say. Even where we have good reason to suspect unbroken harmony, it is not directly apparent. Upon God, no such disjointed miscellany of phrases would be forced by limitations of His own. Before Him, first, the whole symphony of light would lie open, from the slow longest billows—"the Base of Heav'n's deep Organ"—of which we have no perception at all, up the pulsing scale of radiant waves, through our little octave of colors, and up through faster and faster pulsations, to the hard high treble of the cosmic rays. To us most of this is inference, well justified but indirect; and what lies at the top and at the bottom of the scale we do not know. To us these electromagnetic wave-fields, pulsing, rippling, squirming, and whirling through the ether of space-time, are mostly external. To an omnipresent God they would be objective but physically internal. To Him they would be as accessible as our breathing and heart-beats to one of us; or the trillion and one small bodily events that each of us knows in a pervasive sense of well-being. They would be, indeed, more accessible and more clear by far; since no coarse physical media and no clumsy sense organs would intervene. The very field in which the events transpired would itself be for God, as Newton suggested, a "boundless uniform *sensorium*" [61] or vehicle for immediate apprehension of such events; and every detail could make clearly its own impression. Across this inclusive field also, and the light-fields that crinkle it hither and yon, fly electrons and protons and their combinations, behaving now as corpuscles, now as tight squirming waves,[62] caught together here and there into the whirling networks we call bodies. Our knowledge of these is by far more fragmentary than our knowledge of the fields. We can neither observe the smallest units directly, nor build up out of what we now know a coherent system of inferences about their behavior and their interrelations with space-time and the known wavefields. To God, once more, these matters also lie open, so far as they are intelligible at all.[63]

Two other advantages, incalculably great, we may suppose God as Knower to have, besides those of freedom from physical localization and from dependence on sensory media as clumsy as ours. One is an infinite "timespan"[64] of apprehension, as regards all events which have transpired. We retain somehow the impressions of past events, and recall them one by one, or a group of them together. We take them up into habit-patterns, and without our being aware of them all, their after-effects condition our living. But the real time-span which we can include in a single pulse of awareness, a specious present,[65] is usually meagre; and likewise the range of concrete details which at any moment we can hold before our minds with clear apprehension of their interrelatedness. At exceptional moments and by special methods, this scope can be greatly enhanced: moments of intense "concentration" in which a great multitude of details form a luminous concrete whole;[66] methods of symbolic abstraction whereby simplified signs are made to stand for huge aggregates, so as to dispense with the effort to grasp the latter in concrete terms.[67] But by neither of these routes nor by both together can a man grasp in a moment the whole concrete coherence of things past. Let us suppose that

God can. Such time-span would then be infinite, if we suppose that actual events have been transpiring since before any event that can be specified, and that there has not been any *first* event with which the series of actual happenings began.

It may be observed that this has nothing directly to do with the space-time frame of our physical world. *That,* indeed, may well have had a beginning; and it may have been preceded by other "cosmic epochs" [68] which would not have presented themselves to us as spread out in four dimensions. What we are talking about now is not space-time but real duration, which seems to me an ultimate character of reality. Has event P transpired, or has it not? This is not a relative question, to be answered: "Yes and no: it depends on where you are." Either P has happened, or it has not, or at this very moment it is happening. The four-dimensional time-cone has a definite bearing on the precautions I should adopt before venturing an answer; but there is one and only one answer which, when I pronounce it, can be correct. Real duration I take to be intrinsically exemplified in the successive coming-to-be of events; and all the events which have come-to-be and are coming-to-be, I believe God has before Him in a single infinite time-span. When we spoke of His freedom from limitation in space-time, we affirmed His omnipresence. When we speak now of His apprehension as encompassing all that has transpired and is transpiring in an infinite time-span, we affirm His eternality. [69]

Omnipresence and eternality, *i.e.* sovereignty with respect to space-time and real duration, involve for the Divine Mind complete and clear apprehension of all the forms exemplified by events past and present. But sovereignty in these respects implies also not merely presence in and

continuance through, but transcendence beyond all that
has yet come to be. For God also, let us say, events transpire; but God sees more than the events and their forms.
He sees also all the great families of timeless forms, in
their main trunks and branches. These ramify out endlessly, through genera, species, sub-species, and forms of
individuals, beyond all that has been, is, and .will be,
through all that may or might be, and the implications of
all these, without end.[70] To say that God is conscious of
all this endless infinite, or includes all these within Himself, seems to me quite meaningless. Plato's Parmenides
was right in urging that the multitude of forms is no more
completely manageable by mind than the multitude of
events.[71] But one may fairly hold that God as determinate, not indefinite, in His Being[72] eternally has present
to Him by positive and negative implication a vast range
of possibilities not yet exemplified in what has come to
pass, including many that will never be so exemplified;[73]
and that He is conscious of such possibilities as, from
moment to moment of real duration, become relevant for
the apprehension and direction of the process of becoming. On this assumption, God would never be ignorant or
baffled, in the sense of confronting a situation which in
principle He did not clearly comprehend. There would
be for Him no learning by trial-and-error, nor confrontation with wholly unforeseen and startling events. Not because for Him all *has happened;* nor because there is no
indetermination. It is because He has access through His
own transcendent nature to the forms of all that *can* happen; He has wisdom to apprehend at every juncture the
forms that are most relevant; and He is Himself as Creator, the dominant power in bringing events to pass.[74]

(ii) God's knowing, then, approaches incomparability

with ours at least in these four ways. In this sense we think of Him as omniscient. But in two other respects, it seems to me right to suppose limitation of His knowing, strictly comparable to limitations upon our own. First, if we hold that He is determinate in nature, not indefinite or all-inclusive, this will mean specifically, as regards knowing, that He is a Subject, and occupies a distinct cognitive point of view. His thoughts are not our thoughts, nor our ways His ways. Even Eriugena, for all his monism, excluded evil from what God can know, since He is perfectly good.[75] I doubt the validity of this way of putting the matter, and prefer merely to say that whatever God knows, He knows it in *His* way and not in some other. He knoweth our thoughts afar off, and is acquainted with all our ways; and therein we may take comfort. But this again is done in His way, not in ours. We shall have more to say of this in a moment.[76]

Like us, also, God cannot know in full what has not yet come to pass. The most obvious point, which must be accepted I think on any theory, is that actual happening, the fact of coming-to-be, makes a difference for God no less than for us as regards the manner in which a thing can be truly known. What has not yet happened cannot be truly known as having happened; whereas afterwards, it can be truly and fully known not otherwise than as having happened. If besides this obvious point (which is not always treated as obvious), one believe also that in the stream of events a pervasive indeterminacy is one factor, then foreknowledge must, by so much the more, be regarded as not at any juncture complete.

Neither of these limitations, supposing that they really obtain, involves any deficiency in God. Rather, they both go with definiteness of being, in God, and real duration in the world. If some such way as Newton's of conceiving God's Mind embodied in the space-time order, though transcending it in various ways, can be entertained, then the difficulty about finding Him nearby disappears. Being omnipresent throughout the world-order, though not of it nor encompassed within it, He is everywhere near. In principle, every physical event that transpires is knowable by Him directly; though one need not suppose that He takes cognizance of them all. A definite cognitive point of view implies selection among data which in principle are all knowable; and one can hardly wish that God's Mind should be occupied impartially with relevant and irrelevant possibilities, *ad infinitum,* when there is a world in the making. The only God Who is God, and not a metaphysical abstraction, is One intent upon what needs to be done—and upon us not according to our wishes, but according to our needs.

(*b*) So far of God's omniscience as Knower. Consider now His omnipotence as Doer. The same two general characters of omnipresence and eternality, or sovereignty with respect to space-time and real duration or world-process, which so widely differentiate His knowing from ours, are basic also in His doing. Moreover, His omniscience as such is basic to His creative-redemptive activity: not as an antecedent condition but as a constituent character. He acts in wisdom and His wisdom is realized in act.[77] This is what we mean if we speak of God as purposive. Not that He sets up particular goals *ad hoc,* devises ways and means beforehand, and proceeds by intelligent experimentation. Rather this: His nature being determinative involves all possibilities, not indifferently but by definite positive and negative implication;[78] which means that God's nature being what it is, the balance is weighted in

favor of the realization of certain possibilities and the exclusion of others, when certain junctures arise. But God's
nature is such that (unlike a purblind human self) He
apprehends clearly what is the case, and His basic natural
predilection—to coin a phrase—is for Him also a conscious preference. That which His nature positively implies, His will affirms. If one try to say what, concretely,
is the object of this preference—the goal of God's purpose—one recognizes promptly that only God can know.
We can only inquire, believe, and symbolically affirm.
God's purpose, we say, is the realization of the good;
of what ought to be; of the Kingdom of God. By such
terms we denote the whole of what God's nature portends
for the world; and then try, little by little, to discover
what these terms connote in particular. Our best insights
thus far we have labelled with such words as love, justice,
truth, beauty. "The Maker and Father of all things," we
say, "is by nature generous and outgoing, not grudging.
Hence He desired that the world should be as like Himself as possible." Or we say, "God so loved the world that
He gave His only Son, that we might have eternal life." [79]
But if we are wise, we know well that by no statement
nor concept of ours can we encompass the range of God's
purpose; and that rejecting all smug supposition that we
can, Spinoza protested, in genuine piety, against our saying that God has a purpose at all.[80] With his spirit though
not with his expression, we must largely agree. God's
purpose is not one that man may comfortably define. But
unless we may think of Him as having natural predilection, it is hard to see how we can think of Him as *good*.
Here Plato's word is I think the true word: "God is
good, and the author only of good to men." And this
Spinoza also in his heart believed.[81] This indeed is, so

far as I can judge, the very crux of religious faith. The
world is great: that needs no proof. In it the sovereign
power is good: this admits no proof. But to affirm it
with all one's heart and mind is to believe in God, great
beyond our conceiving, yet not too great to be good. God
is not All, in which all things alike are one. Rather, He
acts in wisdom and with purpose, giving Himself freely
to make the world good, "as like Himself as possible."

(i) Presupposing here the examination of human work
in the third chapter,[82] we recognize quickly that the work
of a Divine Mind is unhampered by certain of our disabilities. To name them is probably enough: ignorance,
inner conflict, restrictions in space-time, and inferiority
to particular finite forces. Ignorance is excluded, if what
we have said of God's omniscience be sound. Inner
conflict is, for us, essentially bound up with ignorance,
and we gain increasing mastery over it as we grow in
wisdom. It is associated also with the discrepancy between
our desires and imaginations, on the one hand, and our
capacity for accomplishment, on the other. Seeing a
hundred careers that would be pleasant, we can pursue
but one. And in that one, whatever it be, we are torn
by contradictory impulses whenever competing particular
goods lure us (*e.g.* through conflicting loyalties) upon
divergent paths. But God is free from this sort of finitude,
and divided allegiance. With us inner conflict arises,
once more, whenever a new insight is opposed by established habit or custom. But to God we may ascribe full
vision of what, in principle and at every juncture, is the
good, toward which without ambiguity or waver[83] His
natural predilection is determined. If we should care to
speak of "habits" in His case, we should mean not behavior-patterns acquired at an earlier stage of growth

when insight is immature, which hamper the development of more adequate behavior as insight becomes more ample. We should mean, rather, enduring behavior-patterns which, through a given stage of real duration, express the fulness of God's wisdom with respect to that stage, in the light of "the good" which is His permanent goal. Such divine "habits" or behavior-patterns will not conflict with any new and "better" insight as to the good, on God's part; for His predilection with respect to the good as such[84] is fully determined, and with respect to a new juncture in the world-process, He is no more bound by the particular behavior-patterns which were appropriate only to an earlier stage than a skilled physician is bound by the memorandum he has made for the nurse at some earlier stage of a patient's illness. Like every expert who has wisdom in his calling, but with the perfect wisdom which none of them possesses, God "makes his art his law," [85] and acts without inner conflict or constraint. On this view, God's conflicts are with the world, not within Himself.[86]

But in the oppositions between His will and the world, also, God is free from disabilities that cramp our littler efforts. He is not hedged in by space-time barriers, and He is not inferior in strength or wisdom to any worldly powers. His reconciling work can be hindered, but one need not fear that it will be defeated. God is "the Allsovereign Father" (*patēr pantokratōr*) of the Church's first great creed: "All-powerful" (*pater omnipotens*) in the basic religious sense of that affirmation.[87]

(ii) On the other hand, the absolute omnipotence ascribed to Him by later Western thinkers[88] is not maintained here. In specific ways, His power is limited. First, as Origen clearly saw, by His own nature. God is not, said Origen, the indeterminate Absolute, but Perfect Spirit; and perfection necessarily involves limitation. For perfection is inner harmony and balance, not infinite, indiscriminate aggregation. God's power, thus, is limited by His wisdom and justice and mercy, as these characters in turn limit and perfect one another.[89] There are many things which God cannot do, precisely because He is God, and must be true to Himself: He cannot act unjustly, nor unwisely, nor unmercifully. Upon this basic principle the Church has never really turned its back, though from time to time strange formulæ have expressed its calculation of the balance between power, justice, and love in God.[90] This reciprocal limitation of one divine characteristic by another is what may better be maintained, I think, than what is often called the "self-limitation" of God. That implies a voluntary self-restraint, a kind of gratuitous assumption by God of ascetic manacles; as though His nature were such that without putting shackles upon His activity, the highest possible good would not be attained. By contrast, the present view regards the power of God and its exertion as limited not by quasi-artificial restraints voluntarily imposed by God upon Himself, but by the intrinsic nature of His Being, which *cannot* act otherwise than toward the fullest possible realization of good.

Besides this, God's power may be thought of as limited by various factors not within Himself. To a first group of such factors we may apply the general term *rigidities*.[91] They deserve fuller examination than any one, to my knowledge, has brought to bear upon them, and the significance of evil will be clearer when we know more about them. In themselves they are in no instance, so far as I can see, to be called bad; in every instance they contribute in some way to productive work; yet in concrete situations, the hindrances they impose bring it about that evils as well as goods result. First among them is the obvious fact that certain forms or characters are incompatible with certain others. I cannot build a fifty-foot house on a forty-foot lot; I cannot be this sort of person, and also that; and so on. Without such disjunctions, thinking would be impossible, and I suspect working also; yet they put difficulties in the way of both. Next are a whole class of rigidities which are intrinsic to various modes of extension, in space or time or both. Thus, an actual series of events is irreversible: what is done, is done beyond recall. What is remote in space-time cannot also be here now. Thirdly, that which in concrete events we call by some such name as inertia: the tendency of bodies, living things, and human minds to follow "lines of least resistance." Thus, units of matter and of energy tend to lapse from less probable to more probable random distributions, with the continual reduction of the amount of energy available for work wherever "entropy" or random distribution is actually increasing. The behavior of living things falls into stereotyped habit-patterns. Fatigue overtakes human minds and wills. Social orders develop rigidities of the sort which just now are exercising the social theorists.[92] Most if not all of these, once again, are contributory conditions for productive work in the world as we know it. Through them and by their help, mind is able to effect results that are good. Yet by them also, in diverse ways, its work is hampered and its results vitiated. For God as well as for men, I judge that such hindrances have to be overcome, and that at no actual juncture in the world-process are they completely eliminated.[93]

Into "rigidities" of the second and third sorts named, or at least into the situations which exemplify them, comes another factor for which we have, I think, no convenient name. I mean simply that factor in a *flux* which differentiates it from a form or a system of forms. One may call into service, perhaps, the obsolete term *fluence.* Or if one prefer Whitehead's term "pure creativity," [94] I think that phrase means the same thing; though there is some advantage in reserving the term creativity for description of more fully concrete process, and using a less honorific name for crude ongoingness. At any rate, this factor is manifest in the irreversible sequences of real duration, and in the behavior of all concrete things. If fluence, in this sense, involves "real contingency" or indeterminacy,[95] this will add another to the list of limitations upon God's power. No event, on this supposition, is rigorously determined until it has transpired; and in the concrete flux at every juncture there is a pervasive and strictly incalculable, but nowhere actually formless, indetermination. Like Aristotle's *hylē* ("matter") and the Neoplatonic "non-being," this factor is never found in isolation, but only within concrete events. In such events, the regularity which makes science possible is of course to be insisted on; but that this may be affirmed along with indeterminacy is now widely recognized. The picture here chosen, then, is of the sort which Plato envisaged when he wrote: "God, and with God chance and contingency, govern human affairs as a whole. It is surely reasonable to concede thirdly that scientific skill (*technē*) should go with these; as, in the contingency of stormy weather, I for one should conceive it well worth while to understand navigation." [96] In such a world, plainly, God's power though sovereign is not exclusive nor complete. Every concrete individual, from electrons and quanta upward, has a certain waywardness which makes it less than fully amenable to God's will.

Lastly, if this view of indetermination be allowed, we may without inconsistency regard finite persons as able to oppose their wills and energies to one another and to God.

(2) This brings us to a point at which a second analogy is called for; drawn this time not from individual but from social living.[97] Consider a group headed by such a one as we call an inspiring leader: a trusted general, or patriarch, or prophet. Without him, the group is a lot of mismatched individuals, each jealous of his own concerns, without common understanding and direction, and lacking in stability of morale. In such a group, individual powers are wasted; brilliant abilities go for little or nothing; and the general picture is one of futility. But let the right leader be found, and the milling individuals become a social unity of higher order than any mere crowd. Their attention is redirected, their energies canalized, their morale stiffened. Something of what the leader sees, they sense also—it may be in vague, distorted fashion, but at least in such wise as to give them a common direction. Something of the leader's devotion, courage, and calmness is mirrored in them. They do not see the goal as he sees it, but they become ready to endure hardship, disappointment, and death by reason of their faith, in him and in something—they know not what—for which he stands.

In this familiar situation, of many remarkable features the most remarkable is that which we intend when we call such a leader "inspiring." He may be personally attractive or unimpressive: Lee was the one, Grant the other. In

196

either case, it is not his "personal magnetism" nor brilliance nor social adroitness nor any quality of a purely personal kind that makes him a great leader. It is that somehow, as a kind of catalytic agent, he evokes responses from deep inside his followers, of such a sort that "a new spirit" becomes manifest in their behavior. They live "beyond themselves," under the stress of emotional impulses not ordinarily awake. We say hastily that the leader's spirit has got into them. We might better say that in the leader's presence, a spirit comparable to his own is quickened in each of them, as they confront together the stressful situation which he first has found "inspiring." They are aware of him as a personal presence; but also, rightly or wrongly, they take themselves to be aware of a compelling claim—of fatherland, of liberty, of God and His righteousness—grounded beyond and incumbent upon both their leader and themselves. In response to him and to that claim together, their lives are stirred and lifted to new planes.

How far can this throw light upon God's relations to men? The problems involved will receive further attention in the next chapter,[98] and we shall merely notice them here.

(*a*) With respect to human persons, God is transcendent, in two ways. (i) As regards His status as Subject, in knowing and in act, He is wholly other than men; as indeed each man is wholly other than his neighbor, and the leader is wholly other than each of his followers. No conscious subject can have the experience of another, nor as subject become identical with that other in any degree. On this line there is "radical transcendence."[99] There is no "invasion" of one subject by another, nor absorption of one into another. This seems to me to be true whether one call God a person or not. It applies not merely to persons, but to all subjects of experience—and perhaps also to subjects of unitary behavior (monads, or what not) which are not experients; but that need not be decided here. (ii) As regards His attributes, also, God is other than man, whom He surpasses in every namable respect, and from whom doubtless He differs also in ways of which we have no conception. In power, in knowledge, in goodness, and so on, man is here, God yonder; so that the very words by which we characterize God must be understood to have with respect to Him meanings which differ to an unknown degree from the meanings they have when we use them of ourselves. But in this case, I take it, the difference is not one of strict incommensurability. Transcendence here is relative rather than absolute. "Love" in God, however far beyond anything I know, has something in common with love in me; and so with power, justice, and the rest. A significant correlation exists, let us say, between human and divine attributes. When a gravitational equation is calculated for one frame of reference, and then for others in turn, through all these transformations run certain invariant relationships. In similar fashion we have assumed[100] that whether or no our descriptions based on phenomena directly apply to the world as it would appear to a subhuman or a superhuman observer, so far as the various sets of observations are accurately described, certain dependable correlations would run through them all. Now in like manner, it seems not unreasonable to judge that however widely in detail the attributes of God may differ from the attributes of man, significant correlations hold. And if so, we need not disavow such a word as, "Be ye merciful, even as your Father in heaven is merciful."

(*b*) This involves at once the other side of God's relation to men: communicative immanence.[101] By revelation
and inspiration, God makes Himself known to men and
quickens them into new life. How is this to be thought
of? (i) We have examined at some length the manner in
which, through causal impact and symbolic gesture, one
human self conveys its presence and character to another,
given the sort of "animal faith" or native realism that
marks healthy living.[102] We noticed especially that a real
other self becomes manifest through a combination of
dependable, unified behavior with repeated instances of
behavior unlooked-for, which may call for profound modification of one's own patterns of thought and conduct.[103]
Revelation of God involves likewise the conjunction of
observable regularity, and repeated refusal of the wish-
prompted and uncriticized categories with which men
seek to encompass Him. When one is looking for Him
too confidently in the wind, earthquake, and fire, He
speaks in a still small voice; but if one listen too complacently for the still small voice, then God speaks in
earthquake and storm. Yet, just as the unexpected, shock-
ing refusal of my friend to fit into my preconceived picture, instead of driving us farther apart can serve to bring
me closer to the real person who is my friend, so God's
refusal to be what I want Him to be can draw me
nearer to that which He is. Of these matters we shall
have more to say in the fifth chapter.

(ii) What one should think concerning inspiration as
between God and men I am far from seeing clearly. That
God as Subject does not displace nor invade nor become
infused into man as subject, I believe. As respective cen-
tres of experience and behavior, God and man are distinct.
But that between God and man a more intimate relation-

ship can hold than between man and man, I believe also.

An inspiring leader, we have said, awakens in his followers responses that have their roots deep in each man's whole self. Moreover, a great leader orients his followers, as he is himself oriented, toward a goal more ultimate and inclusive than all of them who together give themselves in devotion to it. God also, let us say, by revealing Himself to men, awakens in them responses that well up from the deeper springs within them. But these deep springs themselves have been called into being by the God who now arouses them to action. Upon the power of God, also, at every moment the believer depends for life and strength to act, as never upon a human leader. The goal, moreover, toward which a God-quickened man finds himself newly oriented may be called either the good, or God. Formally, it is the good, which God works continuously to actualize in the world; but God Himself is good, ultimately and wholly. So that though one may still distinguish between the good as formal goal, and God as Creative Mind by whom the good is concretely realized, in practice there is no disjunction. The cause toward which a human leader beckons is more than he; but the good is not more than God. He is both Ground and Goal for our striving. He is, moreover, the ever-present quickening Power to which we respond, wittingly and unwittingly. If we say then that the Spirit of God comes upon men, and that they are filled with the Holy Spirit, we should mean, I think, that by the perpetual summons of God, which comes through the whole natural and social network within which God and men are continuously side by side and face to face, men are quickened now and again to respond on new higher and deeper levels.

C. Let us now, with the cautious recklessness that is required, try to imagine a cosmopoietic myth of the sort which religion, philosophy and the sciences, not to speak of the poets and practical men, have all had occasion to use. "A likely tale," Timaeus called his account of world-making:[104] neither an irresponsible fancy, nor a proclamation of known fact, but a careful surmise which seeks to accord with what facts and principles are known or believed, and to suggest a way in which these may be thought together.

A process of redemptive world-making, then, such as our small human purview may be thought to suggest, would involve let us say three major phases. (1) The first would be establishment and maintenance of conditions suitable for the emergence, growth, and activity of beings capable of apprehending and achieving good. Apart from the presence in it of such beings, however far up or down the scale of sentiency and autonomy, one might indeed conceive a world increasing in symmetry, complexity, harmony, and like characters, in which God might perhaps be imagined to find increase of goodness. But obviously a greater variety of good can be realized in a world fit to support a variety of sentient beings,[105] and in any event that is, to an undetermined extent, the sort of world this one is.

To establish and maintain such conditions, one may surmise, is a task fraught, from the outset and at every step, with difficulties. We may think at once of three inescapable sorts, which, so far as I can now see, affect all productive work. (*a*) All work and all products of work, as we have seen, must exemplify definite formal or structural characters. But as Plato and Leibniz insisted, not all forms are "compossible," to use the latter's term.[106]

If one is to be actualized, another cannot be. There cannot, for example, be autonomy of constituent parts in a world from which contingency is excluded. But contingency, if it be admitted, in Ward's phrase, "into the heart of things," [107] brings with it other implications that cannot be avoided, and not all of them welcome. (*b*) Besides form or pattern there is in actual events what apparently is another factor or group of factors which, as we have seen, makes an actual event in some measure opaque to logical analysis.[108] Perhaps time itself—not clock time but real duration—is what makes the difference; perhaps extension of some more general sort. Perhaps energy, force, or inertia—or, more generally, "action." Perhaps qualitative particularity. In any event, if this divergence between formal and actual be ultimate, as realists believe that it is, it represents an additional source of difficulty. If, as idealists commonly hold, it is merely a symptom of our inability to discern all the formal elements that are present, then it is not different from the difficulty already noticed, but merely a particular case of formal complexity.[109] (*c*) Once actual events and things begin to interact, however, the refractoriness or inertia which each must exemplify in order to be itself at all, obviously puts a wide variety of hindrances upon further work. To incompatibilities between forms are added concrete conflicts and disharmonies between things and their several modes of behavior. The problems of the builder as regards his materials and tools are in principle the problems of any productive work such as we can at all concretely envisage.[110]

If one think then of God as effecting cosmic conditions suited to the emergence and growth of living, sentient beings, one may well think of Him as solving the sort of problems which, so far as we can judge, are intrinsic to productive work. And so long as we do not simply identify the world with God, whether we think of Him as primarily transcendent or as primarily immanent in respect to the world, the difficulties we have spoken of are in principle the same.

(2) Supposing suitable conditions established, a second major phase of such world-making would be bringing into existence such beings as may apprehend and seek to actualize values: individuals and groups capable of both learning, appreciating, and intelligent doing, who may act as local foci of organization in the world which is to be made increasingly a vehicle of varied good.

In such beings no less than in unthinking and unfeeling things, the same incompatibilities, inertias, and conflicts arise. The inertias and conflicts now take, in especial, the form of continuance into a later stage of growth, of behavior patterns established during and more appropriate to an earlier stage, in the life of the individual or in that of the group. Were it not for such persistence, no growth could take place; yet this very persistence makes growth difficult.

(3) Given sentient, intelligent beings, a third stage is to awaken in them responses that lead to the apprehension and realization of good. Such responses we have already more than once tried to describe in the first three chapters and we shall recur to them again in the fifth. Let us say here simply that they must be aroused, and made to issue in conscious co-working of intelligent creatures and God.

But at this point again difficulties are thick. For creatures brought up from simpler, less sensitive, less autonomous stages of life can hardly fail to be ignorant, slow to learn, and wayward in their behavior as the rigors of

more primitive and externally determined behavior come
to be relaxed.

It is not strange that there should be evil in the world,
if any such story as this have a measure of truth. Nor
is its presence a reason to doubt the goodness or the redemptive power of God. That He is not omnipotent in
the sense of wielding wholly unconditioned power is of
course basic to this whole account. But that in ways
which we shall try to suggest later, evil can be and is
overcome with good, and that in such events more poign-
antly than elsewhere men have found themselves persuaded of the presence, goodness and power of God, is
plain matter of fact. That such belief, moreover, is in
principle fully accordant with what is here said, I hope
will become clear as we speak more fully of the relations
between God and His creatures, and the way of life for
man.

CHAPTER FIVE

THE WAY OF LIFE

"There are three things which are too wonderful for me,
Yea, four which I know not:
The way of an eagle in the air;
The way of a serpent upon a rock;
The way of a ship in the midst of the sea;
And the way of a man with a maiden." [1]

Let us add a fifth: the way of life for mankind. It is well
to remind ourselves now and again that wisdom has not
yet been found; the more since to engage in such verbal
exercise as this sometimes obscures that unsoothing fact.
Talk may give us the illusion of accomplishment, as
though things talked of were things done; of power, because the symbols employed in talk are among the most
plastic of materials, and offer little resistance to what
seems forward movement; of insight, since words are
fairly sure to call up an assortment of familiar meanings
which we are fain at least for the moment, if in a friendly
mood, to regard as instructive, whatever be the case in
fact. From such illusions may we now, even at the cost
of some geniality and contentment, be preserved. The
legitimate values of verbal formulation and discourse
need not suffer thereby. Sometimes the products of such
formulation are really pertinent to the task of living, so
as to guide or to enrich it; and sometimes the very process
of thinking and rethinking helps to keep those who share
in it alert and alive to the world about them, provided
they do not let themselves be lulled into the delusion that
talking or listening can take the place of more inclusive

living. The way of talk is not, though it may point to, the way of life.

We began with discussion of work as a human fact and a medium of good human living. We went on, in more speculative vein, to inquire how the world may be thought of, and God whose mind and hand we think are revealed and discovered therein. Now from the remoter regions of time and space and beyond, we return once more to ourselves and our problem of living. What import can practical religion have for us, if something like what we have been talking of be thought true? On such terms as these, what can we do, and how, and what may we hope? Let us think first—remembering that we still seek, not possess, wisdom—of the way of man toward God, and then of the way of God with man.

THE WAY OF MAN TOWARD GOD

The way of man toward God is nearest to us for observation. In "the order of knowing," as Tennant would say, we must begin here, even though in "the order of being" God comes first and even though, as we have said, our own belief in God arises in the first instance not out of our thinking about the world and man, but as response more primal than thinking to impacts of unfathomable reach.

Hocking and Bennett, in their studies of the mystics, have held that the familiar dyad of work and worship marks a rhythmic alternation which is fundamental in human living.[2] Let us follow that lead, as this whole discussion from its first reference to the comparative wholeness of simple life has intended that we should. Let us think of religion from the human side as a mode of shared

living which takes the form, essentially, of worship and
co-operative work. In it, individuals and groups seek to
participate in the greatest possible good by appreciating
recognized values, discovering values not hitherto recognized, and sharing in the progressive realization of what
they take to be the best among these, in the sustaining
presence of what they believe to be God. What account
can we give now, from the human side, of such a way of
worship and of work?

I

A. The way of work involves, first of all, finding and
doing one's job.

(1) At points of detail what has already been said requires elaboration, but there is little more of a general
sort to be said here as to the first of these concerns. Indeed I know of little that can be said in general terms
about how to find a thing so individual as the task for
which a particular person is best fitted. Vocational guides
of the most clear-headed kind available,[3] rather than
such inclusive principles as those with which we are dealing here, have much to offer; and the good sense of the
individual himself will make him aware of quite personal
factors of which no one other than himself can be so
good a judge. But this at least may be said, in correction
of a too romantic individualism: not one of us has un-
restricted choice in the matter, and we may save ourselves
much frustration and waste of energy in emotional heat
by recognizing that the fact is so. Each of us must take
what he can get, or at best make his choice within limits
that are none too spacious, laid down by forces within
us and without, which we do not control. Doubtless much

can and should be done to widen these limits, by social and in due course biological reorganization of the conditions that affect our living. To that problem we shall return. But certainly for the present and probably for a very long time to come, finding one's job must be a more prosaic enterprise than we sometimes wish and fancy it might be.

This is not to say that the search and its outcome must be drab and unrewarding. Our whole argument is against that sort of pessimism. But it is to say that the search for one's proper work, no less than the doing of it, must follow the lines of fact. That means first that the only point from which, at a given moment, one can set out is the point—or rather, the whole complex present situation—in which then and there he himself stands. Dewey's insistence cannot too often be repeated, that the actual present—not a lamented past, nor a longed-for future—the actual present is the one region directly accessible to action, and therefore of the first strategic importance.[4] To wish one might start elsewhere is to wish one were not oneself, or that one were in fairyland, not here. For where else has any one, by being anxious, added a wished-for cubit to his stature, or shed the peasant and become the prince he wishes he might be? Not only is such anxiety, moreover, useless and demoralizing. Often it is almost comically uncalled-for; as one discovers when he becomes aware that his neighbor, whom he has been envying, has in turn been envying him—often for the very qualities which he has thought himself to lack. Willingness to be oneself, with all one's disabilities, is at least a beginning of wisdom.

Moreover, though in early life one's search for suitable work may well take, when possible, the form of fairly wide roaming and sampling, at least in imagination, with a view to finding just what one wants, there comes a time for each of us when the most promising procedure is not further ranging abroad, but digging in the best soil that offers, so it be tolerable soil at all. Certainly bad misfits between person and work are to be avoided or corrected whenever possible; no sane thinker nowadays can be complacent about needless waste of human powers. But the world is not yet sufficiently under control for anything like perfection to be assured now, nor in the foreseeable future; no job worth doing can yield its best rewards to a casual, transient worker with eyes roving the horizon; and given fairly decent conditions of work—which no doubt now too often are lacking—I venture, without intending dogmatism, to think a good measure of satisfaction can be had by intensive doing of any needful job that may come one's way. This is not meant to diminish in any degree what was said in the first chapter about the uniqueness of each person's contribution, the desirability of his finding suitable outlet for his capacities in the work which falls to his share, and the need for social rearrangements that will make opportunity for satisfying work more general. It is meant rather to insist on the importance of drawing our lines in the right places. We must not think, on the one hand, of inflexible and fastidious personal tastes and desires to which the world must conform. It is quite as important that persons shall grow and their tastes and desires change, as that the world shall be altered to their wishes; and such growth of persons takes place in and through labor, not in advance of it. The all-important thing is that one get somehow a foothold in genuine work, as suitable as the actual case permits; and that with such footing as actual work alone can provide, he discover progressively what his own powers and more basic interests are, and what can be done with the leverage of his own acquired competence and self-respect, in conjunction with that of other fellow-workers, to make the existing situation better than it is. On the other hand, we must not think of an inflexible and sacrosanct hierarchy of callings to which human beings must conform. In especial, there is need to attack, by word, deed, and persistent attitude, various traditions and tabus that now hedge about one or another calling with artificial prestige or dispraise. That white collars, black hats, or gold braid should be more honorable than leather aprons, or that bank accounts should rate above competence of hand and brain, is a sort of absurdity which soon or late we shall have done with, and the sooner the better. Finding one's job has difficulties enough without having the real values disguised by misleading price tags. In fine, when seeking one's place in the world and its work, whatever one's procedure in detail, one will try to achieve and as steadily as possible to maintain cognizance of relevant facts, and the ways in which they are ordered here and now, with an eye to distinguishing what is essential from what is conventional and transient—though doubtless that can never be perfectly done.

(2) As for doing one's job once it has been found, the same principle naturally holds good. The basic pattern for work, we have said, may be stated in terms of needs to be met and sound ways of meeting them in concrete situations. Into that pattern come, as we have seen, besides the exactions of what is already actual, possibilities and ideals that can be envisaged through symbolic means, and that are likely to appear in part as anticipated objectives or end-results toward which the work is directed—

results which so far as achieved will satisfy or perhaps
modify the original needs. Such end-results, and the
working as a whole and at any stage, we call good in so
far as recognizable values are exemplified therein: intelligibility, integrity, beauty, sociability, and so on. Yet
neither these specific values nor, still more, that inclusive
character *the good,* which they exemplify, can ever be
wholly mastered by any of our achievements. Always
there is a more to be attempted, a challenging better that
eludes our reach.

(*a*) The basic attitude of one who works, as we have
sought to describe work, may well combine, let us now
say, love or intense appreciation with critical realism. It
is difficult to speak of the former without offensive senti-
mentality. To speak of being "in love with one's work"
sounds affected and goody—not the kind of thing a man
in greasy overalls could stomach. The fact is our whole
vocabulary and thought about love has become so
honeyed, refined, and enfeebled that one shrinks from
using the word in public. To make matters worse, it has
also become thoroughly confused with our vocabulary of
worship, what with rapturous mystics in love with God
and rapturous lovers adoring their ladies, and a hearty
pantheist like Walt Whitman both loving and adoring
himself and all the world besides. Is it too late to un-
tangle these terms again? to clean them off and make
them fit once more for men and women to use with
power? Whitman for all his naïve extravagance and
bombast had at least the root of this matter in him. Like
Rupert Brooke and John Masefield he knew how it feels
to love and cherish material things to the health of the
soul, not its ruin—a fishing-boat, an axe, a redwood tree,
leaves of grass, sledge-hammers that "fall with joyous

clank, like a tumult of laughter." He knew also how to prize ordinary people at work, and wrote about them with transparent zeal. Now Whitman was, of course, an enthusiast, not an average man. But he was, for a poet, an uncommonly good observer and reporter of everyday facts. His people in "A Song for Occupations" and "The Song of the Exposition," "The Song of the Broad-Axe," the hospital pieces, and the amazing "Song of Myself" are real people—seen and felt, not merely fancied. That I know, having myself known unpoetic garage men to relish the touch of good metal and tools, and the hum of a sweet-running motor; carpenters who live in their lumber and ladders and nails; profane ranchmen who gentle a span of half-broken colts as though they were strong, lively children; and gardeners whose finger-tips know the feel of good earth and the roots of healthy growing things.

Such natural, sensual love as this a workman needs if his work is to be more than a dead routine. Such love for people, too, and deep satisfaction in working with them. Pure altruism, divine disinterestedness, has its place as an ideal, beyond the reach of human animals; but this other —this love for things and people that has roots among the fibres and corpuscles of our bodies no less than branches reaching out toward "the sun and the other stars"—can be a mighty power here and now, which modern religion and morality have too long snubbed into disrepute, and left for irreligion and immorality to exploit. No doubt, as Plato said, it is daimonic, not tranquilly divine;[5] capable alike of exaltation and disaster. But how shall we justify ourselves if we fail at least to try to enlist its aid against those other daimonic powers—hate, blind rage, inertia—whose whole trend is toward chaos? How shall we justify what preachers like us have done to eviscerate such love in the name of piety, to bleed it pale and put a halo on it, and set it among the angels, until no average man is likely to recognize it nor be moved by it for either bad or good? Some would justify such enervation, doubtless, in two ways. First, the damage love does in its wild state requires that it be unfitted for doing harm. Secondly, the danger of idolatry is always close at hand when love is too strong. Both the harm and the danger are facts, but not sufficient reasons for what thin-blooded piety and stern ascetic zeal between them have done to human life. Our need is to distinguish between love, which is a fitting response to creatures high or low, and worship which is more than love, rightly offered only to God; and to refuse both the way of the idolater who can see nothing greater and higher than things or people, and the way of the ascetic who dare not trust himself to love frankly and deeply this world and his fellow-men. This is dangerous doctrine now, and always has been. But when religion grows too weak to endure it and thrive by it, the powers of hate, egotism, and sham, petty malice, cruelty, and greed have an easy time making headway. These are not foes to be met with fine-spun amities and pietisms. They call for the robust delight and wrath of men and women who, like God on the sixth day, see that the world is very good, but because they love the world and worship God alone, cannot rest from seeking that this good world be made better.

Herein comes the need for that critical realism of which we have spoken. Partly it will devote itself to questions of fact: what needs to be done, how best to do it. But also it must be perpetually concerned with questions of worth, and the discrepancy between what might be and what is. A competent workman is the last to be satisfied with his own work. The most appreciative friend is one from whom cheap eulogy is impossible. It is no compliment to oneself or to another to have unfavorable criticism tacitly suppressed, because one or the other cannot bear it well. One of the surest signs of decadence, I venture, is inability to give and take appraising judgment, and unwillingness to risk it from either side. It may be that we preachers and teachers, as some have said, are in especial danger of growing soft at this point, protected as we are, for the most part, from any but admiring comments; though I surmise that this failing is fairly general among all sorts of comfortable folk, and not wholly lacking wherever self-esteem still exists. For the good of our souls, in any case, let us read and hear what the tough-minded children of this world have to say about us, encourage one another in greater frankness by showing ourselves ready to welcome it, and cherish with peculiar gratitude a candid friend who puts truth above rubies and does us the honor to suppose that we do also. Such criticism must be, in part, severe since we men are still raw, unlicked cubs in a dangerous world, and can inflict egregious damage on one another by our failures. But in part it may well take the gentler form of humor, which does not forget how near we are to the dust, and how great are the burdens under which we are trying to rise.

(*b*) This brings us to a closely related point. In all our doing, a place should be made for play; though just what place I doubt that theologians are as yet very well prepared to judge. The question deserves a chapter by itself, but two or three comments must be included here, even though they are incompletely thought out, and more than a little likely to be misleading. We have spoken of play as activity in which present rather than future satisfaction

214

primarily is sought. We may sometimes recognize in it also, as compared with work, a lessening of strain, which favors recuperation from fatigue and refreshment of morale, without cessation of activity.⁶ Plainly, on these terms no clear objective line is to be drawn among activities as such, separating play from work. What one man at one time finds presently enjoyable and refreshing, another man or the same one at a different time, under other conditions, may find wearisome: we can make play of our work, and drudgery of what we call play. But if the difference thus be one of attitude—of physiological and mental set—rather than of overt act, it is none the less real and important.

As to the possibility of bringing more of the play spirit into our work, what can be said briefly is too obvious to need saying. Some day, when jobs, men, and traditions of work have all been altered, more of it will be possible than our present highly self-conscious industrial and social order makes place for. In proportion as one's working attitude includes such love as that just spoken of, for the things and the persons with which and among whom one works, the fusion of the working and playing attitudes is likely to be effected. The more of such illumination and suffusion of present exertion with present enjoyment, the better. In great artistry this fusion is most complete, and as already said, no higher plane of living seems possible for human creatures.

Meanwhile, most of us are not great artists and never will be. For us play is likely to come, for the most part, through avocations, rather than out of work itself. At this point the Puritan doctrine of vocation, whatever its pertinence to a particular historic juncture, went sadly astray as a formula for whole living. In theory—though

actual Puritans in practice could live with immense gusto
—it condemned both present enjoyment and relaxation
of strain, except as one might find both in worship and
meditation on the Sabbath day. Yet this very theological
anti-hedonism helped, as we have seen, to produce an
economy of growing abundance which, at first for a few,
then for a larger number, and in time perhaps for all,
makes ascetic rigorism at once more difficult and less appropriate. With the currents of taste and thought, however, running so strongly against the claims of disciplined
living as, in our own part of the world, they have done
since the War, one must hesitate before seeming to side
with their recommendations of unrestraint. That hedonism as a basic philosophy seems to me indefensible, this
world and mankind being what they are, the whole foregoing argument has intended to make plain. Life on its
active side, we have said, is to be conceived primarily in
terms of work, not play; of remote, complex, and difficult,
not present and easy satisfaction. But the same regard for
facts which leads to that emphasis as basic, leads not less
clearly to the recognition that human sanity requires also
times of irresponsibility and release—what James called,
perhaps too picturesquely, "moral holidays" [7]—in which
present enjoyment has a central place, and the pressure
of exacting work can be for awhile unfelt. How diverse
such intervals of escape from routine must be if they are
to serve their purpose for diverse individuals, it is needless to point out. To regiment play is more absurd, if
possible, than to mechanize work. But one general ex-
action, at least, such avocations may be required to fulfill:
namely, that they shall be capable of integration into the
actual fabric of life, individual and social, of which they
are proposed as parts, without too grievous damage to the

basic pattern. Dissolute day-dreaming, as we have seen, can wreck one's power to work. Carefree drinking does not integrate with the need to manage high-speed machinery. The gigantic moral holidays called wars grow less and less assimilable as cultures grow more complex and interdependent. These incompatibilities are not matters of taste nor opinion but matters of fact, empirically discoverable; and intelligent play, no less than intelligent work, must come to terms with them as best it can. On the other hand, as in the case of work, traditional tabus now make it difficult to judge avocations on their merits, and these tabus require to be thoroughly overhauled, in the interests of moral realism and sound idealism alike. Perhaps in this area, if the promise of increased leisure for the rank and file of workers be fulfilled, one of our most important tasks of theoretic and practical appraisal will soon have to be performed. Simple inherited stereotypes will not serve any longer.

B. Thus far we have spoken of work and play as they may go on within an existing natural and social order. Love for things and people, a keen eye to facts, a sense of reality as regards both facts and values, and a readiness to engage alike in vigorous criticism, strenuous work, and light-hearted play are more basic than any particular economic or social order. One's theology and ethics, I take it, are not or should not be dependent on one's political affiliations, nor tied to the fortunes of any social institution or movement. On this point, the Barthians seem to me eternally right. But on the other hand, such a theology and ethic as that implied in this book is by no means indifferent to the ordering of social affairs. We have come, again and again, to the judgment that the

pursuit of vocations as herein conceived is hampered un-
duly by this or that factor in the existing social order,
which ought therefore to be changed. It is time now to
inquire more closely how such alteration may come about,
and what attitude toward it may be most consistent with
this doctrine of vocation.

(1) One may notice first the widespread and readily
understandable attitude of those who in effect oppose
change, either by active resistance or by passive acquies-
cence in the existing state of affairs. The convinced conservative opposes change because he believes in the per-
manence of the existing culture and the advisability of
staying with it, or in its worthiness to be permanent, or
at least in the expediency of keeping it substantially intact
until a later day. The merely habitual conservative clings
to what is familiar and blindly resists novelty, without
weighing either facts or values. The academic skeptic sees
faults in every proposal for change, dislikes active exertion,
and prefers to let things take their course, whatever that
may turn out to be. How each of these modes of behavior
may be judged from the present point of view I trust has
been made sufficiently clear. No actual order is permanent, nor ought to be permanent; and the order now existing has convincingly shown its need to be changed, not
simply restored nor maintained as it is. One may like and
respect an honest conservative or an honest skeptic, and
steadily dissent from the attitudes of both.

(2) A second familiar attitude is that which affirms the
desirability of change, but puts its trust in high ideals and
superhuman powers, and endeavors by enlightenment
and persuasion alone to move men toward what is better.
This mode of thought and action, which may be characterized as the practice of non-resistance, also may be passed

with only a word; not in disrespect, for very noble spirits have taken this way—some without doubt among the noblest of all. When such idealism is not easy-going verbalism, but a martyr's passion for good that masters and molds his whole life, its worth is in the strictest sense incalculable. The world is not and will never be worthy of that which these men and women see and live by, whom the world does not understand and cannot overcome.

But genuine martyrs are few, and most of those who in words recommend pure idealism untainted with force or coercion are themselves not unwilling beneficiaries, as we are often reminded, of social orders which are maintained in large part by force, and can hardly be changed in their main framework or major functions without its use. The fact is that people do not respond whole-heartedly to appeals worded in terms of pure altruism, service, and the like; and that such appeals not infrequently, by reason of their unreality both to him who makes them and to those to whom they are made, obscure and falsify the behavior patterns according to which both really act. A first principle of workmanship is violated thereby; as though a builder should try to lay up walls out of blue-prints instead of brick and oak. Noble dreams may guide, and persuasive words may quicken those who are already able to understand and respond to the language used; but no symbols can long fill the place of facts and their inter-relations, and the facts at present are such that major social enterprises cannot be conducted by enlightenment and persuasion alone.[8] The brick and oak of human nature are powerful basic "drives" partly ordered into native and acquired behavior-patterns; and it is by expert balancing of these, one with another, to make their diverse stresses and strains work together in concrete, dynamic (not abstract) harmony, that social architects and builders must do their work. Among these basic behavior-patterns, love is indispensable for the builder's task. No version of separative self-interest, however enlightened, can take its place. But it must be actual, not verbal or theoretical love; and actual powerful love is never abstract nor free from complexity, however high a degree of integration it may attain and help to effect. For man, "the mixed life" [9] is the best attainable.

In and for such life, the vision of the martyrs provides a strain of perpetual challenge and hope without which men would cease to be men. Where there is not this vision, the people perish.

(3) The third major attitude is that of active proponents of change who are prepared to use coercive measures to bring it about. But there are essential differences among them, as regards both the kind of change they desire, and the methods they are prepared to employ. Excluding simple political *insurrectos,* who desire only to supplant one party or faction by another, without any important social and economic change, it is convenient to name three main types of active opposition: revolutionaries, moderates, and contra-revolutionaries. (*a*) The contra-revolutionaries of our day are likely to be fascists of some sort, with a program of political and economic centralization under a dictator. Their ranks are likely to fill up with ruined or frightened "lower middle class" folk—small farmers and shopkeepers, white collar workers, impoverished professional men, students, unemployed, and hard-pressed people of many sorts. Their funds are contributed, sooner or later, by the owners of industry. Their aim (whether the rank and file know it or not) is to salvage and perpet-

uate the old order, unchanged as regards the seat of control, under the façade of what appears to be a new one. Basic social and economic realignment, which is the essential thing in a genuinely new order, fascism is designed to prevent.

The other two groups agree in desiring to bring about such realignment, transferring control of industry and finance into the hands of a new rising class. Both intend, also, to use the machinery of government to that end. But the moderates hope to attain control and thereafter to exercise it by legal and constitutional measures; whereas the revolutionaries intend, when the time seems ripe, to resort to civil war. The leaders and "intellectuals" of either group may be drawn from any social stratum; but their respective followings show, in the mass, fairly definite lines of cleavage. (b) The rank and file of moderates come typically from social strata within the range or on the edge of "privilege"; have been reared in some refinement; and are averse to both the risks and the brutalities of civil war. They are prepared to take the slow road of building up legislative majorities, for the sake of getting the basic changes made by law with a minimum of wreckage. They are prepared also to use strikes as well as ballots, but they compromise freely with the *status quo* and its defenders, and they do not deliberately plan to use armed violence.

(c) The revolutionary extremists differ widely among themselves, but their main strength is drawn from social strata further removed from privilege and gentle culture; and since they have less to lose through destruction, and more experience of toughening hardship, they have less aversion to armed conflict. They also engage in propaganda, political campaigning, labor organizing, and educational activities. But it is their conviction that the possessors of power will never yield it up peacefully, even to a legislative majority. The only way in which ultimately the transfer of power can come about is through demoralization of the old ruling group in a time of general crisis, and the forcible seizure of power by a determined minority, prepared to defend itself thereafter against counter-revolution. To insure the survival of the new order during the perilous transition period, a temporary "dictatorship of the proletariat" must be established, and maintained with ruthless resolution. When all danger of counter-revolution has passed, and economic inequalities have been wiped out, the dictatorship will give way peacefully to the free self-government of a new classless society.[10]

The flush of Utopianism in this last notion is evident, and it may fairly raise for a critical mind the question how far sober realism has dictated the whole argument for the use of violence. To that point we shall return shortly. On the other hand, in their estimate of the essential character and significance of work, socialism and communism show themselves far more straightforward and realistic than competing views. Underlying both of them is the presupposition of technical progress as pushing steadily toward inevitable readjustment. Involved in both, moreover, is the presumption that enlistment of the rapidly growing company of technical experts on the side of the revolutionary program is indispensable to its success. Both, in short, insist (as regards theory) that we think of industry in terms of production rates rather than price; in terms of essential knowledge and skills rather than net profits; and in terms of human needs rather than credit ratings. Which clearly is putting the primary emphasis back where it belongs: on basic (not artificial) demand,

and on goods and services and the problems of supplying them plentifully, rather than on what one can get for them. So long as the stresses fall where they do now, in the various current theories of social economy, there seems to me no doubt that there is, in principle, closer correlation between our doctrine of calling and the general conception of work in these two left-wing theories, than there is between our doctrine and any similar concept in either fascism or the existing phase of capitalism. This does not mean, needless to say, that affirming this concept of vocation commits one to a certain political creed among those now prevalent. None of them, nor any political theory, can serve as a satisfactory theology. But it does mean that, as we have seen, the concept of vocation is definitely in conflict with various phases of the existing order; and that so far as socialistic and communistic theories reaffirm certain of the basic requirements for sound work and social health, they are thus far to be preferred to any theory which fails to keep the basic pattern of work and the conditions for meaningful life clearly in view.

With respect to the soundness of advocating violent seizure of power and maintenance of despotic control in the name of social justice, on the other hand, I am very dubious. The usual arguments for it are not difficult to understand, nor to recognize as having much force. Whether or not it be certainly true that no privileged class has ever relinquished its predominance without resort to violence by the rising class, there is no doubt that usually such has been the case. I am quite aware, moreover, that my own strong reaction against deliberate planning for civil war as a major factor in revolutionary policy is conditioned in part by concern for the safety and freedom of myself and of others for whom I care greatly, and that this may

fairly enough be interpreted as concern for the maintenance of a personal privilege which the great majority of
folk do not now share. How far such narrowly personal
interest or timidity is crucial in determining one's judgment in this area, one cannot be sure. Be that as it may,
there seem to me convincing reasons against the advocacy
of violent revolution and dictatorship, even as temporary
expedients; and these reasons seem to me valid for any
one concerned for social justice and good life, whatever
his own place in the present order. They have been widely
debated and incisively summarized by others,[11] and there
is no need to dwell on them here.

It is worth while, however, to note the distinction (not
always observed) between irresponsible terrorism and intelligent revolutionism, and to make clear that my conviction of the unsoundness of violent tactics applies primarily to the former but ultimately to both. The former, if
conceived and employed as a way of bringing about a
desired revolution, has nothing to be said for it. None
but such "infantile leftists" as Lenin excoriated will waste
energy in sporadic terrorism that, in the absence of a general crisis climaxing a long process of attrition, has no
chance of important success and is sure to provoke ruthless counter-attacks. A dominant group can be overthrown
by violence and the victory successfully exploited only
when the ruling group has finally lost, and the revolutionary leaders can win, the confidence (or at least the acquies-
cence) of a preponderant share of the populace who are in
a position to count effectively for one side or the other.
In particular, the connivance of the army is indispensable.
But undisciplined terrorism is as poor a way as possible to
bid for the neutrality of the army and the support of
ordinary citizens. Intelligent revolutionary leaders know

this,[12] and plan to use violence only at a suitable crisis to seize control of the government, and later as need arises, for defense of the new government against counter-revolution.

But even this far less romantic, far more responsible and effective program seems to me still unacceptable as a coherent working procedure for social reconstruction, so far as it depends on violent seizure and despotic use of power. In its more familiar form,[13] it proposes, in effect, a "war to end war": an armed rebellion and dictatorship of the proletariat, to usher in a free classless society. For such a program, it is well known, difficulties centre about two points: it is necessary first to win the war, and after that to win the peace. The latter may prove to be the more difficult. Even an exhilarating war can have a disillusioning aftermath.

At any rate, the first thing needed is to win the war, if this be the method one chooses. Before deciding on destructive force, not as a Quixotic gesture nor just for exhilaration but to clear the way for a better social order, one must weigh coldly the chances that the proper group will get into power. Chivalry and blind desperation aside, violence is not an appropriate method unless one has a fair prospect of coming out on top. Until now, after nearly a century of trying, the record shows only one major success for proletarian revolutionism. Russia in 1917, but newly embarked on developing a modern industrial system, with an army and people sick and tired of foreign war, and a thoroughly discredited feudal ruling class, offered a real chance for revolution from the left; and when the moderates fumbled, Lenin seized upon it successfully and emerged as a leader of extraordinary ability. His capacious intelligence, disciplined will, and rare perceptiveness and resource in dealing with swiftly changing situations held for him the confidence both of his own party and of the urban masses. Elsewhere, no such combination of factors has offered; and nowhere else has proletarian revolutionism come out on top. In more highly industrialized countries, with far more real power centralized in the hands of a more modern ruling class, and more people having—or thinking they had—a stake in the existing order, violence has profited none but ruthless contra-revolutionary groups.

But supposing that a revolutionary party were successful in seizing the reins of power in a complex industrial state. Having won the war, could it go on to establish a just peace, and fulfill the promises for which the war was fought?

(i) The immediate destructiveness of civil war in a complex industrial state would be far greater than it was in Russia, where most of the people lived on the land. A serious break in the working, say, of our industrial and commercial machine would mean deaths by starvation and disease more numerous, one may presume, than deaths at the barricades either before or after a successful *coup d'etat*. If the fighting were long drawn out, it is problematic how long it would be before the machine could be got going again. A victorious proletarian dictatorship would have to begin its program of reconstruction not where the Soviets began, but with both material and human resources more seriously depleted—how seriously we have no way of knowing. It is urged in reply that a successful revolutionary party would have on its side a sufficient proportion of the country's technicians and skilled workers—railway men, and the like—to keep the machines going and the people fed. But if that were so, it

is hard to see why a general strike could not serve as well
as a civil war, with far less destruction; whether before
or after the seizure of political power. The fact is that to
count in advance upon keeping destruction within moderate bounds, in the event of open class war, is to show
unwarranted optimism.

(ii) Moreover, it is an essential part of violent revolutionary policy to stamp out the nucleus of any effective
opposition, as promptly and thoroughly as possible. To
the destruction wrought by actual open fighting must be
added the destruction of human resources involved in a
follow-up policy of extermination. Such "liquidation" of
critics and opponents, actual, potential, or suspect, is directed by an inclusive system of *espionage,* and carried
through with the fanatical, inhumane thoroughness that
so often has characterized the operation of powerful,
quasi-primitive religious zeal. At this point, the line
marking off disciplined revolution from irresponsible
terrorism is broken through, and indiscriminate killing,
torture, and exile are indulged, in the name of revolutionary necessity. What Robespierre called "the despotism of
liberty against tyranny" [14] reappears in "the dictatorship
of the proletariat."

The latter is to be really the last such unhappy time,
leading directly to the classless society. As soon as the
danger of counter-revolution is past, the dictatorship will
give place to complete and genuine democracy.

(iii) But the dictatorship is composed of human persons, made of much the same stuff that appears in other
ruling groups. Economic privilege is not the only form
of privilege, nor the most dangerous to human sanity. The
most dangerous form of privilege is dictatorial power.
Economic wealth is, for many who devote their lives to

acquiring it, mainly an instrument for the exercise of power, which for them is the primary thing. To suppose that men, though high-minded and devoted, who have seized dictatorial powers by violence are likely to escape the delusions of grandeur which play such havoc with poor human judgment, is to abandon realism. Why, having seized power as a temporary expedient, are they more likely than other rulers have been, to welcome or even to recognize the time for laying it down? Seventeen years after its establishment, the Soviet government still finds need for terrorism; still sees danger of counter-revolution. When is that danger likely to end? And why should there not be—as Trotsky maintains that there is —need for yet another revolution, to unseat a recreant communist oligarchy? another war to end war?

Violence, as we suggested earlier, seems a regression to primitive behavior which can serve only for destruction. Begun by a disciplined revolutionary minority, it grows by what it feeds on, and in the form of undiscriminating terrorism, destroys resources, provokes deep-seated hatred, and prepares the ground for further outbursts of vindictive rebellion. We are hearing in these days with respect to class war what some of us once believed, but can no longer believe, about international war: that such struggles may be fought through without vindictiveness, and without essential damage to good will, which after the struggle is won may be counted on to bind up wounds and establish a better life. We who call ourselves realists now should re-examine such belief with great care. The fact is, I think, that revolutionists who permit themselves to indulge in good will toward the enemy will not bear the brunt of any such struggle. Not that they may not take a heroic and noble part in it: happily for the human race, even war cannot prevent some men from being decent. But the heavy end of the fighting will be done by less squeamish folk. Any one who has had even a little of bayonet drill should be free from illusions here. It is so much easier to regress to simpler political and cultural behavior, than to labor toward a more complex and self-disciplined mode of behavior, that to advocate the former as a means to the latter seems to me a dubious course, for champions of social justice and good life.

(4) Without having any systematic theory to offer in place of these, I think a way of conceiving social reconstruction may be sketched roughly in terms of everyday work. To a convinced theorist it must seem, no doubt, merely eclectic and futile, with no rallying cry in it anywhere. That may well be so. Rallying cries are good rather for war than for work, and I find it easier to get some sense of reality about problems of reconstruction by thinking of them as work than by trying to see them in terms of war. I have no thought of denying nor of ignoring the reality of the class struggle. It is an obvious fact, though a more complex one than the literature of revolt might lead one to believe. By insisting on its basic importance for hard-headed social thinking and action, Marxist thinkers have made it impossible to content ourselves any longer with general appeals to human brotherhood and the common welfare. Both those concepts stand for goals which Communism and Christianity both acknowledge; but they are goals to be approached, not possessions to be guarded. The present fact is that we are still immersed in struggle, one against another, class against class, group against group of every size and complexion. But to recognize war as a fact is one thing: to advocate war as a way to end war is quite another. Instead of war,

it seems to me better to begin thinking in terms of work.

What needs, in a given area, are not being properly met? And why not? What hindrances stand in the way of meeting them? Wherein, as precisely as possible, is the existing order at fault? What changes are called for, and how can they best be made? Such questions as these will guide men who come at social reconstruction as a job of work.

Basic methods of reconstruction must go directly to such basic problems as population control, both quantitative and qualitative; conservation, utilization, and enhancement of natural physical resources; and development of more adequate provision for public health (physical and mental) and for public education, including adult education. Far too little is yet known about any of these problems. The needed research is only well begun. But even now much is known which cannot at present be put into practice. For in a complex society political and economic habit-patterns become stereotyped, and block the way for needed basic changes. To bring about conditions more favorable to such basic reconstruction, political and economic methods must be employed.

These methods too must be specific, not panacean; adapted to profit by whatever advantage a specific situation may offer to the insurgent group. Sometimes negotiation is possible and promising; and whether promising or not, should be sincerely tried, for the sake of making clear the justice of one's grievance and the need for whatever further measures may be required. Sometimes a political campaign or a series of them, and the skilful use of advantages thus gained, whether in the form of elections to office or in the way of a hearing for aggressive and intelligent opposition, may have substantial value. Such campaigns fall into line, on the one hand, with more general programs for education, discussion, and widespread publicizing of abuses and proffered remedies. But on the other hand, if they are to be more than sporadic gestures, they involve also the development of strong, determined, enduring organizations to carry on between campaigns, without interruption. Such organizations—radical parties, labor unions, co-operatives of farmers and consumers —may when needful use other methods than those of persuasion and political campaigning. Direct coercion through strikes and boycotts may at times be effective; and, it goes without saying, the wider and stronger the organization, the more effective such pressure can be made.

Non-violent coercion of still more extreme type, to be used in more extreme emergency, implies a still higher level of discipline and devotion by insurgent groups: the active non-co-operation with the existing régime which Gandhi and his followers have used. How effective, in a given situation, it may be I presume can scarcely be judged without more extensive experiment. Certainly it is no method to be casually employed by undisciplined insurgents. But given courage, devotion, and self-control among the protesting minority, and an ordinary measure of human vulnerability in those called upon to beat down their non-violent resistance, plainly it may win where counter-violence would surely lose.[15] Moreover, such a method, with its entailed spiritual discipline, would leave those who employed it not worse but far better qualified to become participants in whatever organized social life might emerge as the outcome. It would not essentially negate, as the using of knives, guns, and torches must if they are to be immediately effective, a steady good-will

231

toward one's opponents that may break down barriers in them, and prepare the way for a more inclusive social wholeness which can include them also, as unleashed violence does not. And it is a method which can serve as a last line of defense in support of any of the other specific measures noticed in the preceding paragraph—provided fit leadership, preparation, and discipline can be brought to bear.

How difficult this must be, especially in a Western society steeped in traditions of violent attack and counter-attack, I am well aware. A long process of reconditioning of thought and behavior, at first probably among small volunteer groups, must open the way. But plainly it is a way about which we sorely need to know more; and it may prove a powerful weapon against barbarism in whatever modern guise: the more powerful in that it stands opposed to barbarism in oneself as well as in one's enemies.

Meanwhile, it is needful to recognize that determined use of any of the methods noticed above, by an insurgent minority, is likely often to provoke violence on the part of those defending the *status quo,* and to be accompanied also by violence among those working toward a change. So long as the basic policy of the rising group is to stand by non-violent coercion, sporadic outbreaks by some of its members need not, and should not, lead to withdrawal of support from its effort to rise; while the employment of lawless violence by either side can be steadily opposed. On the other hand, a revolutionary policy in which wholesale destruction of opponents, non-sympathizers, critics, and suspected persons is deliberately projected, now seems to me essentially wrong. To hold such a policy even for that crucial moment when an outworn order is supposed to be tottering and the time at hand to kill or be killed wholesale seems to me wrong: for the expectation of such a moment is all too likely to help precipitate an otherwise needless slaughter. And if such slaughter can be justified at all, to minds not squeamish but not gullible, it must be on the basis of far better evidence than our best actual dictatorships have supplied. Lacking such evidence, I now find it necessary to hold by a view more experimental and less dogmatically assured.

(5) Two objections to any such view may be noticed. (*a*) It can easily be charged with inconsistency, both by advocates of pure non-resistance and by advocates of a policy of violence. To the former, an admission that specific situations demand coercive methods may seem an abandonment of allegiance to love and rational persuasion. To the latter, it seems hypocritical that beneficiaries of a social order which employs violence should deplore its use by insurgents. The answer to both is in principle the same: controlled coercion and irresponsible violence are different in both intrinsic character and social effect. The former is necessary to the conduct of social living, at present; the latter is not. Coercion as such is not incompatible with love and reason, as any one who has lived in a normal household must surely be aware. One may without inconsistency approve and participate in what seem to him disciplined, reasonable, and controllable measures of coercion requisite to there being social order, and needed social change; and at the same time disapprove and oppose irresponsible violence, whether committed by professed opponents or by professed representatives and defenders of the existing order.

To lump coercion and wholesale violence together, and demand that we either accept or reject both, is on the one

hand to generalize the threadbare, fallacious equation of
police duty and war; or on the other hand, to make no
distinction between responsible and reckless insurgency.
With such confusions it is important that we decline to
associate ourselves. To approve police duty, even when
it involves unavoidable violence, does not commit one to
approval of either international or civil war. Police duty
implies responsible and reasonably discriminating behavior on the part of a peace officer, who is expected to
distinguish between good citizens and enemies of the
commonwealth, and not to treat one as though he were
the other. The competent policeman, moreover, prefers
peaceful means when such can be used;[16] and when it
becomes necessary to kill in defense of peaceable citizens,
such extreme penalty need fall, and in theory is meant to
fall, only upon murderous outlaws. Violence offered to
non-violent picket-lines or paraders is no proper part of
police duty, whether committed by men in uniform or
not. It is itself lawless denial of that orderly social life
which a genuine peace officer helps to maintain, not violate; and it is quite as indefensible as any other breach
of public trust. To appreciate and approve the arduous
and often dangerous work of real guardians of the peace,
and to recognize it as indispensable in any social order, is
not to associate oneself with needless brutality of men
wearing police uniforms or deputies' badges.

Conversely, there is no inconsistency in supporting an
insurgent movement which gives evidence of its sobriety
and responsibleness by using centrally the methods of
disciplined protest, even though sporadic violence attends
its efforts; and refusing to support a movement, either
revolutionary or reactionary, which plans to use terrorism
as a deliberate and major resource. The former gives

ground for confidence in its capacity for self-government and discriminating use of authority if it should come into power. The latter gives ground, rather, for serious question as to its fitness to govern either itself or others. Against the violent tactics of any such group, revolutionary or reactionary, a proponent of the views here maintained will stand committed, though he accept frankly the need for non-violent coercion by an insurgent movement, and the likelihood of sporadic violence also.

(*b*) The advocate of violent revolution, however, is less interested in logic than in results; and the proposed approach to social change he regards as hardly less feeble and unrealistic than the abstract idealism to which it professes to be an alternative. In the long run, says he, violence cannot be avoided, and the realist will not waste time in trying to avoid it. In the past, possessing groups have yielded only to violent dispossession, and the sooner it is done, the sooner we can get on. This raises for the religious realist the whole question of the basis on which he rests his faith in non-violent procedure, and what realism in fact requires of him.

We have seen that he objects to violence primarily because its practice involves distintegration and regression which, in given circumstances, are more likely to retard than to hasten social betterment. What reason can he give for supposing that there is, however, any real hope of getting ahead without risking such regression? Briefly, he finds ground for hope through his faith in the ability of man to learn, however slowly; and in the supremacy of God. Neither the one sort of faith nor the other blinds him to what has actually transpired in the world and what probably will continue to happen in it for a long while to come: namely, a bewildering mixture of advance and regression, of better and worse, of rational behavior and blind animalism. But his faith in man and in God leads him to work steadily for what seems to him the better way, and to refuse to be stampeded into either advocacy of what seems to him subversive of good life, or despair when the forces of disintegration seem in the ascendant. Let us see more concretely what this means.

Faith in the teachability of man means in essence faith in the increasing scope of concrete processes of learning, by which long, painful, and dangerous processes of trial and error can be short-circuited. In such learning or short-circuiting the essential difference between human and subhuman behavior comes most clearly into view. Applied to our present problem, this is to say that blundering again and again through the mire of actual violence is in essence subhuman behavior, though it be practiced by intelligent men. On the other hand, such overt plunges into anarchic or mechanical violence can be short-circuited, if enough men can be brought to foresee and fear its consequences, and act to relieve the conditions which if unaltered are liable to bring it about. One may, without foolishly looking for such concrete rationality to become general overnight, give one's best efforts to increasing its range and opposing the forces which make against it. And when those anti-rational forces become ascendant, as in varying degrees of course they do, and will continue to do, one may still hold fast what seems to him good, and refuse to surrender to either disintegrative opportunism or despair.

This presupposes faith in God. Whatever men may do or fail to do, there have already been revealed to us resources in the world which were operative before we appeared and which extend beyond all that we have yet

imagined. Good is not bounded by what we want or
know or hope. It comes, indeed, often in other forms than
those planned and worked for: not seldom in sequence to
frustration and partial disaster. It is not foolish, therefore,
to do what seems to one, in the light of all that one knows
and believes, to be right. Civilizations must change, our
own with others. It seems best that they change without
too great damage to the pattern of rational working and
living. But if they change also by way of disaster, the
world's resources are not thereby exhausted, nor God's
sovereignty disproved; since out of wreckage again and
again has come new life.

II

We are brought thus to the other side of man's way
toward God: the way of worship. Let us note briefly its
familiar occasions, its character, and its relation to work.

A. The most poignant occasion of worship is a time of
human extremity, when man's work clogs or crashes about
him, and he is acutely aware of the presence of powers
mightier than he. It may be individual frustration, failure,
or loss. It may be social disaster. In any case, human
prowess is brought to a halt. If now, out of such an
impasse a person or a group find unsuspected ways opening, and fresh access of endurance, insight, and tranquillity
emerging in the midst of the ruin, each participant may
come thus to his first living apprehension of such Reality
as grown men can worship. Of peculiar power and significance among such experiences of release, for individuals and groups, are those involved in repentance and
moral regeneration. Then, not merely is one thwarted,

but one recognizes that "the source of dislocation" is in oneself, and that the thwarting is not only deserved but is to be welcomed. One acknowledges a good violated by oneself, alone or with others, and one reacts, it may be with profound disturbance of habitual thought and behavior patterns, against such violation. One welcomes being brought to a halt; and in the struggle for better orientation, sometimes there will come new perspective, power, and conviction of the reality and mercy of God, who can requite repentance of sin with enlargement of life. The consequences of sin cannot be annulled, but they can be worked into new life patterns, in the midst of the complex interworking of natural, social, and divers other factors that make up man and his total environment, in such fashion that the outcome is positively though never perfectly good. And one who becomes acutely aware that this is so not by merit nor prowess of his own, but by grace of powers beyond his own, may find himself irresistibly persuaded of the living presence of God.

Other occasions correlative to these may come as what have been called "experiences of consummation." [17] Not failure transcended but success achieved, or joy discovered, is here the vehicle of revelation. To the complete egoist, naturally, no revelation will come. For him the achievement, the joy, is his doing and his alone. But for one able to look beyond the confines of his privacy, it will be plain that his success is won, his joy attained in co-relation with a world whose ultimate order is not of his devising; yet which it appears can welcome his best effort, and which offers him freely such beauties and wonders as he is able to receive. This demands openness on his part, of the sort we have been calling sagacity: alertness to present stimuli which an obtuse or preoccupied observer would miss. It demands also venturesomeness that breaks beyond the bounds of what is given. Appreciation of an instance of beauty as given is good; but worship is more than appreciation. It is venture and self-commitment also. Worship can be, only for one who is able to worship; and not seldom the shock of failure and loss is needed before one is able.

B. The character of such experience defies analysis and record, but words may suggest something of it to one who already knows by acquaintance what it is. In adoration one stands face to face with that which moves him to the "noble fear," *Ehrfurcht,* which we call awe. It is like one's response to the sublime, but more inclusive and profound. Burke thought it characteristic of the sublime to awaken fear; Bradley, more penetrating, said not fear, but a more complex reaction in which the impulse to flee is swallowed up, though not cancelled, in a stronger impulse to stay.[18] Mountain peaks, the desert, the interstellar spaces are sublime, some would say; a twisted pine high up, above timberline; a wild thing dead in defending its young; a coast guard crew going out through icy breakers; the still face of one whom death did not frighten; a man nailed to a cross between thieves; a man saying, "Why callest thou *me* good?" If we are sensitive or timid, we shrink from the pain of these things, and may never learn to face them with eyes fully open.

But if they take hold on us until we cannot turn aside, it may come that beyond them all we discern "as in a mirror, dimly," a Ground that is greater than they, from which we also have our being. It may come that we welcome being alive in such a world; not because it is all good, but because through it, good and bad together, we discern the presence of God, and into His hands commit our living. That I take to be worship.

But such commitment does not stop with contemplation. It seeks issue in work. For the God discovered thus is a God at work, reconciling the world to Himself. And those who worship in spirit and truth find themselves called to a ministry of reconciliation. A world unfinished and broken is to be made whole. Ultimately it is God, not we, who must heal it, but in our small measure, we may be co-laborers with God. That is our calling. Worship sends us out to work. But work in turn, through frustration or consummation, may continually tend again toward worship, wherein illumination and renewal are to be found. Such, in part, is man's way toward God.

THE WAY OF GOD WITH MAN

But herein already we have found ourselves speaking of the way of God with man, which includes, shall we say, communication, co-working, and transcendent sovereignty. There is no correct point at which to begin discussion of these matters, for each involves all the rest and so much more, so intimately, that every sentence uttered has a flagrant kind of impertinence, unless the inadequacy of all human words here be constantly borne in mind. Whoever speaks of God must remember that he is not defining God for his hearers, who thereupon will know Him without further ado, as one may know a circle from its definition. St. Anselm and Spinoza, by taking for granted more depth and width of insight than many of their readers exercise, have unwittingly done us a disservice here; since we have read their pregnant formulæ as having in fact the sterile geometric clarity which they profess, and have been encouraged to try our hands also at framing definitions, like theirs—in all but vision. What they so well knew and so constantly presupposed that they could write, without self-consciousness, as though quite unaware of it, we need continually to reiterate to ourselves and one another: that words may point toward God, but cannot make Him known. He must make Himself known; and only to one who has come to believe himself confronted by God, in the concrete rise and fall of his own living, can such words be more than counters in a mental exercise.

We have said we believe in God as Mind, Spirit, Holy Will at work within and beyond our half-made actual world; a Creator-Redeemer God bringing order out of chaos. Not mere chaos and not perfect order; but concrete stuff (matter, energy, flux, whatever it be) in process of being shaped into more complex and meaningful parts and wholes. God, we have said, is transcendent beyond the actual world of any specified epoch, even while operative within it as effective organizing power; effecting change in the current world-situation, while extending beyond it in time-span, in cognitive range, and in mode of being.

Men are not parts of God, nor one with God, nor gods in their own right. They are creatures, in the sense that for their existence they are utterly dependent upon powers beyond themselves; and in the further sense that their goodness and their powers to achieve good are likewise derived, and when compared with even such good as men themselves can clearly envisage, and far more when compared with what one may dimly suppose God to be, must seem humiliatingly small. Yet men, for Christian faith, are likewise such that they may become "sons of

God" and "co-laborers with God." Co-laborers to share in
the task of reconciliation, which is healing, whole-mak-
ing; and sons of God to reflect in their small, faulty, but
germinal lives something of the will—the justice and the
mercy—of their Father. Such inheritance they are at once
free and bound to claim. Herein is the ultimate ground
and meaning of each man's vocation: not that he is an
isolated object of divine solicitude, prompting, and salvage, but that he is called to be a contributing participant
in a shared task and a common life—a task shared and a
life in communion with his fellow creatures and with
God. The call is not coercive, and each man's response
must be his own. But the initiative is first and forever
from God's side.

I

"God speaks." Aye, and with what voice? (1) Ordinarily we men communicate, one with another, by
perceptible signals—gestures, sounds, written symbols, and
the like—which need to be interpreted by the observer, if
the intent of the sender is to be revealed. Something comparable to this is, perhaps, to be seen as Berkeley thought
in the order of nature and of human life, so far as these
appear significant and intelligible.[19] "The whole choir of
heaven and furniture of earth" will then indeed appear as
media of communication between God and man—"a
divine visual language" which, like any other but on a
vaster scale, needs to be laboriously studied out, interpreted, decoded by the human observer who desires to
enter more and more fully into an understanding, or at
least a recognition, of God's will. Through patient deciphering of the webs of natural and of human events,

one may come like Kepler to feel that in some small measure one may think God's thoughts after Him.[20]

Not all of such data, needless to say, stand on the same level of meaningfulness and value as revelation; and not one kind of skill alone, on the observers' side, will help to find their meanings. A man is of more value than a sheep, for the seeker after God's will; and some among human lives—a prophet's life, a martyr's, a savior's—will shine with peculiar clarity as luminous foci through which immense ranges of meaning are made plain. Through "the starry heavens above and the moral law within" comes general revelation; through illuminating crises, apparently slashing across but in fact carrying forward eruptively the stream of events, come special revelations. Scientists, men of affairs, poets, plain folk look out upon all these signs. To some, keen and powerful grasp of facts and logic is given; to some, sensitive feeling and subtle imagination; to some, inarticulate steadfastness and patient desire. Men and women of all these groups will add their special contributions to our understanding of ourselves, the world, and God.

Jesus' life and death has brought into focus, for many, what otherwise would be a blurred and disheartening turmoil. Among "special revelations" it has a central place. But the meaning of it, too, needs to be discovered and apprehended through patient, penetrating study. It is not self-explanatory. For many besides the Jews and the Greeks of St. Paul's day, the cross has been a stumbling-block and an absurdity. Only to those who by faith, insight, devotion, have penetrated beyond the obvious, brutal denial of human decency and human hope in such a tragedy can it serve to reveal "the power of God and the wisdom of God."

By such communication as this, one may surmise, must come detailed divine "guidance" for men; which needs to be deciphered, year after year, generation after generation, by individuals employing all their powers of sensitive observation and appreciation, and critical judgment, always at the risk of error but not without hope of increasing insight.

(2) Besides this more usual mode of communication through detailed, intentional signals, there is a rarer sort of communication between human persons, especially between those who know each other well through long life together. It is by no means confined to such long associations, and it need not be thought to involve other media than those ordinarily employed; but whatever the means, the outcome is of uncommon worth for living. There are clairvoyant moments when, without a word spoken or a conscious gesture made, the presence of another self comes home to one with vivid reality. One's friend, one's child, one's mate emerges from the fragmentary and often perfunctory contacts of routine association into galvanic aliveness and "immediacy." With such experiences, I venture to think, the visions of the mystics are to be compared; not the hallucinatory phenomena of sights and sounds which the great mystics have themselves disparaged as mere adjuncts or even distractions, but the central conviction of the overwhelming presence of God.

Such experiences are not everyday occurrences as between human friends, even the most intimate; and I doubt that they should be expected as routine happenings in man's quest for communion with God. Doubtless one may become more sensitive, and in some sense more fit for such experience, through discipline. But I suspect it must be a much more inclusive discipline than simple

devotional exercise; and I suspect too that seeking the
experience directly and frequently, as an everyday guide
to living, is not without danger that one may mistake a
less significant but more readily exploitable sort of experience for the greater and rarer vision, and cultivate the
less instead of seeking the greater. In any event, no impact less moving than the sort of human contact here
referred to can well be taken as conveying in any lively
way the real presence of God. And it is my strong persuasion now, mistaken or not, that in the true height of
communion or confrontation, what is likely to be com-
municated is not some specific instruction for details of
conduct, but such an unspoken word as "Fear not, I am
with thee," or "Give in, and know that I am God!" Not
one's stock of information, but stability of morale, joy of
living, or basic direction of will, is primarily affected by
the vividly felt presence of one's friend or of one's Maker.

In sum, if this way of conceiving the matter have any
validity, one may hope by patient deciphering of the laws
of nature and of human life to discover what details may
be discernible of God's will as revealed through the media
of actual events. To such interpretation both the acumen
of scientists, the vision of poets, the vigor of men of action, and the patient fortitude of plain folk must all
contribute. To this end we read our Scriptures and our
newspapers, we search the stars and the shop and street-
corner, with what wisdom we may. And as we search,
the air may brighten and the heart lift from time to time,
and we go on, still groping but of good cheer.

II

Of God as co-working with men, little more need be
said. The phrase must not, of course, be taken to suggest

anything like parity of man with God, nor the substitution of human for divine ends. But it does quite frankly affirm, against extreme doctrines of the discontinuity of God and the world, that so far as men wittingly or unwittingly align themselves with the divine order, God Himself sustains and furthers what they do. "And establish thou the work of our hands upon us" becomes otherwise an idle word, and religious insight suffers at a crucial point.

"The God of heaven, He will prosper us; therefore we His servants will arise and build." Here is no suggestion of rigid determinism nor of human futility. Here rather is the word of a vigorous human will, in the grip of firm conviction that God is a very present help in time of stress, and that *therefore* it is needful that men shall do with their might what their hands find to do. Divine support is no ground for human slacking. But neither does it leave room for human pride and self-satisfaction. "Except the Lord build the house, they labor in vain that build it"; and no thoughtful worker who is aware of God needs to be reminded that this is so.

To think of God as co-working with man seems to me to involve two affirmations, both touched in the preceding chapter. First, the environing conditions of human life result continuously from God's creative ordering of the extra-human world. The world-order which thus continuously issues into being is not God, nor wholly the work of God, but at every point is the resultant of God's working *and* other factors, material, formal, and dynamic. Of no single event can one say, "This is God's doing alone," nor of another, "From this God's hand is wholly absent." Rather, every event showeth His handiwork, yet in every event rigid forms, continuous flux, and the stresses and strains exerted by other agents and actual events are involved also. Neither in heaven nor in Sheol can one escape His presence, yet neither in Sheol nor in heaven can one say: "Here is nothing other than God." The actual world is one world, not "split off with an axe," one part from another;[21] but in it many factors are at work, now in harmony, now in conflict, and the issue at no present moment is rigorously fixed. There is dependable order, as we have tediously insisted, present wherever our minds have probed; and in establishing and maintaining the particular ordering that obtains in actuality, God assures man of a fit environment for life, growth, and creative struggle. But also there is process, change, surprise, and one may suspect "real indeterminacy"; not concentrated into certain gaps, as it were—certain vacua from which order is absent—but present everywhere in all actual events as correlate to order, so that every resultant case of actual orderedness comes to be as it is contingently, rather than necessarily, as an event which up to the moment of its occurrence might not have come about as it does. To take any of these terms—order, process, contingency—as directly descriptive of God in His ultimate being is to go beyond what either experience or thought can warrant. But to regard them all as exemplified in the continuously created world is to imply that their compresence involves real problems for God as well as for man. And this our present view does believe to be so. Nature as man's environment is in process of being brought into accord with the demands of "what ought to be"—in process of being "reconciled"—rather than already exemplifying perfectly the will of God. In its progressive ordering God, men, and other agents may work together.

Secondly, the same correlation of order and contingent

process appears also in the lives of men and women, and that in all their details. For this reason, human persons can sin, in real rebellion against God, and be saved through God's persuasive grace. If God works with men in that He effects within their environment such ordering as fits it for human life, growth, and learning through meaningful work, He works with men also in that He calls them to work and to communion with one another and with Himself. Man in waywardness and folly is able, since his conduct shares the indeterminacy of all actual events, to act in conflict rather than in harmony with God's will to bring about what ought to be. He may act thus in ignorance of God and of his own obliquity; or he may act thus in deliberate rebellion. In either event God is with him—"the Hound of Heaven"—patiently, silently turning him back from satisfaction craved but wrongly sought; silently urging upon him, by signs within him and without, the need to repent, to orient himself anew. By the suffering he brings upon others and upon himself; by the failures and the unnourishing successes he achieves; by the love of those who love him, and the pain of those he may love; by the inward gnawings of whatever repugnance he may have for cowardice, cruelty, sham, and by the outward and upward pull of whatever may be his measure of response to beauty, truth, and right: by all these ways, epitomized in confrontation with Christ crucified, God works with him to his own salvation. Silently: yet speaking. For these are ways of such communication as we have been examining, and through them God persuades man of His presence, power, and love. "All things betray thee, who betrayest me," He says: and when man hears and begins to respond, his salvation is begun.

III

A final word concerning God as sovereign Ground and Goal, and the need for what has often been called negative theology. In speaking of God as Living Mind, we have meant in no wise to suggest that nothing more need be said, nor that now the nature of God is well within our grasp. Rather, Spinoza said in principle the fitting thing when of infinitely numerous attributes of God, he conceded man knowledge of no more than two. God then is Mind, and more.

He is Ground of being, we say sometimes, and Goal of the world-stream. Mind in a sense is both. It is a medium by which possibilities become actualized; and it is a concrete culmination of simpler stages of growth. But other factors than mind must be looked for both at the beginning and at the end. Some of them we know or suspect: some we cannot now even conceive. How much of them all is God, moreover, we cannot tell. That not all are God the realist is convinced. That God is neither sole ground nor all-absorbing goal he must believe. But that God is great beyond our knowing and our desiring he would affirm no less. We tell our stories of Him as best we can, and know when we have done that silence is better.

NOTES

NOTES

CHAPTER ONE

1. Karl Barth: *Dogmatik,* I (1927), 326: "That the Word of God is *God's* Word—this is not distinct from *what* it tells us, as form from content; this is itself content, the very plenitude of content." Cf. *Das Wort Gottes und die Theologie* (1925), 194: "That *God* bears witness to Himself in the Holy Scripture —this was to our fathers emphatically not mere 'form'; nay rather, not 'form' at all, but content, most present, most vital, most complete . . . the one thing known: GOD speaks!"

2. For a succinct, well-documented sketch of the development of this usage from St. Paul to Luther, see Karl Holl, "Die Geschichte des Wortes Beruf," in his *Gesammelte Aufsätze zur Kirchengeschichte* (1928), III, 189–219. In general it is his view, with certain rather important exceptions, that I am following here.

One needed correction is supplied by Troeltsch's judgment (*Die Soziallehren der christlichen Kirchen und Gruppen,* 1912, 311 ff.) that "die Berufsidee," in the sense of a concept of the individual's labor as contributive to an organic whole, had an important place in the Thomistic system; and that, conversely, St. Thomas effected a significant advance in the understanding of the value of work. So far Troeltsch is in accord with the earlier judgments of Maurenbrecher and Paulus (see Holl: *op. cit.* 202, for references), and with the recent statement of R. Linhardt: *Die Sozialprinzipien des hl. Thomas von Aquin* (1932), 162–164. This view calls attention to important facts which Holl dismisses too brusquely: the new place of the guildsmen in thirteenth-century society, and its importance for ethical and religious thought; the more genuinely organic character of St. Thomas's social theory as compared with those of his chief predecessors; and his clearer recognition of positive worth in the providentially ordered array of occupations, which serve not merely the higher orders but the common weal (*ad perfectionem multitudinis, ad necessaria multitudini,* etc.). These traits are perhaps still more evident in the work of the ardent Thomist, St. Antoninus of Florence (1389–1459), whom Troeltsch apparently had not read (cf. *Soziallehren,* 313, note 136).

But so far as I can discover, St. Thomas never applied to the doing of *opus manuale* (secular labor in its widest sense) the distinctive terms *vocare, vocatio;* nor did he ever grant to those engaged in such work a level (*gradus*) of life comparable to that of the orders set apart to engage in *opera spiritualia.* On this latter point, the tract *De perfectione vitæ spiritualis* (listed as *Opusculum* 17 by M. Grabmann: *Die Werke des hl. Thomas von Aquin,* 2d ed. 1931, 293) is decisive.

An important step beyond his view was taken by Eckardt and Tauler, and after them by various mystics, preachers, and moralists (Holl: *op. cit.* 204–208. Cf. Max Weber: *The Protestant Ethic,* tr. Parsons, 207–208 n. 3, 212 n. 8). They associated the concept of the divine call (*Ruf*) with an experience which not only monks and clerics but farmers or housewives might have, viz., the *visio Dei;* and Tauler expressly applied the term *Ruf* also to the earthly task to which each has been "called." But the further affirmation that there is no generic superiority in the monastic or clerical life, and no special merit in following the *consilia evangelica* (of Matt. 19:21, and similar passages), seems first to have been ventured by the Reformers, as Weber and Holl insist, and Linhardt disapprovingly concedes (Weber, 80–81; Holl, 206, 210–213, 216–217; Linhardt, 164).

Since this last step is basic for the development attempted in this book, of a positive conception of the religious significance of ordinary life and work, the view presented herein professes to spring directly from the Protestant tradition. Its broader grounding, however, is in what may be called the Judæo-Christian as distinguished from the classical pagan conception of work; and at many points its affinities are closer with philosophical Catholic theology than with the more stringent Biblicism of the Reformers.

3. The regular term for "calling" in the New Testament is

κλῆσις, a summons (to court), or an invitation (to a feast). An ἐκκλησία is an assembly made up of ἐκκλητοί, those who have been summoned.

4. Which has, indeed, the look of an *obiter dictum,* especially in view of its absence from vs. 24. In any event, it affords a most meagre basis in Scripture for the later doctrine.

5. It was used also, in similar fashion, with reference to the priestly and episcopal status; as in St. Thomas Aquinas: *De perfectione vitæ spiritualis.* The development of this usage I do not find anywhere fully described.

6. So Eckardt, Seuse, and Tauler (quoted by Holl, *op. cit.* 205, notes 5 and 6).

7. The works of Gerson may provide exceptions. Certainly he approached in his Latin diction the equivalent of Tauler's German usage. But the few passages quoted by Holl (207–208) do not offer any clear-cut instance of the use of *vocatio* as equivalent to *officium* or *ministerium* (task or occupation), nor even to *status* (condition of life); though the statement is expressly made that one is "called" by God to one's own task: "impleat ipse tantum fideliter ministerium suum ad quod deus vocavit et satis est." I have not been able to examine Gerson's works for other instances than the three in Holl's note. His own comment is: "Luther is our witness that in his day, the word 'Ruf' already was commonly used in the sense of status (*Stand*). On the other hand, a corresponding instance for the Latin *vocatio* is not forthcoming before the Reformation, except—in Luther himself." (208–9.)

8. As in *Confessio Augustana* (Th. Kolde, ed.: *Die älteste Redaktion der Augsburger Konfession,* 1906), Part I, articles 6, 13, 15; Part II, the sections *"von der priester ee"* and *"von den kloster gelübden."* Cf. Weber's note, *The Protestant Ethic,* 206 n. 2. Similarly Calvin: *Institutio* (editions of 1543–5, and 1550–54), IV, 11–13 (in *Opera Omnia,* 1:444–5); repeated in the definitive edition of 1559, at IV, xiii, 10–12 (*Opera,* 2:932–4), in which the exaltation of the monastic life above "all divine callings" (*omnibus Dei vocationibus*) is excoriated.

9. Above all, in his great declaration of independence, *Von der Freiheit eines Christenmenschen* (in *Sämmtliche Werke,*

Erlangen ed., 27:173–199; translated in Wace and Buchheim:
Luther's Primary Works, 1883, 104–137).

10. *Inst. Christ.*, editions of 1539–1554, VI, 37 (*Opera,*
1:1151–2). This section stood in these editions as the concluding paragraph of the entire work, which ended with these
words: "Thence will arise also rare consolation, since there
will be no work so base and mean but, if only thou follow thy
vocation, it may shine and be accounted very precious before
God." In the definitive edition of 1559, this passage was re-
tained, but removed to a comparatively inconspicuous place,
at III, x, 6 (*Opera,* 2:532).

11. The dominant note in all his dealing with this matter
is the need for humility and contentment, and the maintenance of due order, under God. This note is struck again and
again, both in his doctrinal writings, his commentaries, and his
sermons. It is central in the passage cited from the *Institutes*
in the preceding note; and when in the edition of 1559 that
passage is removed from its emphatic place, it is to make room
for a longer and stronger declaration of the need for political
obedience. In a sermon on *Deut.* 31 (*Opera,* 28:605), he urges:
Let every man attend to his own task, "and not attempt anything more than what God has bidden, but simply follow his
vocation" (*mais suyvre simplement leur vocation*). In a sermon on *Eph.* 3–4 (*Opera,* 51:510–514), he interprets such obedience and manifest contentment with one's lot as a way of
showing by one's life the gratitude one feels toward God for
His gracious calling.

A partial exception, with implications more far-reaching
than Calvin would have welcomed, is his comment to *I Cor.*
7:20 ("Let each abide in his calling"), in the *Commentary* of
1546 (*Opera,* 49:415): " 'Calling' (*vocatio*) in Scripture means
a lawful way of life; for it has reference to God as 'calling'
(*ad Deum vocantem, i.e.,* summoning, commanding). Let no
one misuse this saying to perpetuate modes of life which
plainly are impious and immoral." Moreover, St. Paul did not
mean, by the saying in question, that one may not change his
occupation, but that one is not to be forever discontented, nor
change "without good reason" (*sine justa causa*).

12. And as Weber himself held. See *The Protestant Ethic,*
tr. Parsons, 183, concluding words.

13. Centring about what Troeltsch calls *"Neucalvinismus"*
(in *Soziallehren,* 733 ff.), which verged toward and frequently
became a non-conforming, democratic, puritanical Protestantism of the sectarian type. Ultimately, through assimilative contacts with liberal rationalism and with the spiritual heirs of
Anabaptism, it developed with these into the familiar poly-
morphous "ascetic Protestantism" of our time (*ibid.,* 762–773,
792–794).

14. Harold Laski, an observer not predisposed to give religion more than its due, said recently of Russian Communism: "I have used the analogy of the Society of Jesus. Perhaps even more just, from another angle, is that of Cromwell's
Ironsides, with the emphasis that it was the depth of their
religious conviction which made of them such splendid soldiers. . . . Men who can await the future with complete certainty as to its character can go forward with a confidence
denied to men who see only as through a glass darkly." (*The
Nation,* 139:71, July 18, 1934.) Cf. C. H. Firth: *Cromwell's
Army* (2d ed., 1912), 349, 351, 409–22; cf. 144.

15. Edward Dowden: *Puritan and Anglican* (1900), 275–6.
Cited by both Weber and Troeltsch.

16. It is for his leading part in this effort, indeed, that
Schleiermacher is now denounced as a heresiarch by leading
"dialectical theologians." The basic statement is that of Emil
Brunner: *Die Mystik und das Wort* (1924). For a more general survey, cf. W. Bartelheimer: *Schleiermacher und die
gegenwärtige Schleiermacherkritik* (1931).

17. Max Weber, *The Protestant Ethic,* 181, 182.

18. Witness Calvin's tirade against the Libertines who
mocked at this doctrine in his day (*Opera,* 7:211–2); Shake-
speare's Falstaffian banter in *I Henry IV,* Act I, Scene 2; or
Butler's insults in *Hudibras,* Part I, canto 3, and Part III,
canto 1. These early scoffers left little for moderns to add.
For example, in *Hudibras,* III, i, the devil admiringly questions the Presbyterian hero, and receives his answers:

"Why didst thou chuse that cursed Sin,
Hypocrisie, to set up in?
Because it is the thriving'st Calling,
The only Saints-Bell that rings all in,
In which all Churches are concerned,
And is the easiest to be learn'd. . . .

What makes a Knave a Child of God,
And one of us?—A Livelihood. . . .

What makes all Doctrines plain and clear?
About two hundred pounds a year."

Or this from the same, I, iii, on the Puritan lay elder:
"This Zelot
Is of a mungrel, divers kind,
Clerick before, and *Lay* behind,
A Lawless *Linsy-Woolsy Brother,*
Half of one Order, half another;
A Creature of amphibious nature,
On Land a Beast, a Fish in Water;
That always preys on Grace, or Sin;
A Sheep without, a Wolf within."

19. How loosely the terms "atheist" and "unbeliever" were bandied about in the sixteenth century, and how mild were many of the views denounced as atheism, is made clear by F. von Bezold, in *Historische Zeitschrift* 113:295–315 (1914). Professor R. H. Bainton directed me to this article.

20. Stuart Chase, in *Current History* 39:130 (Nov., 1933). These figures, based on a Federal Reserve report, are in general accord with the elaborate calculations of Frederick C. Mills: *Economic Tendencies in the United States* (1932).

21. The terms *Beruf, Berufung,* and the like, are seldom used by these theologians in the sense of earthly calling. The passage in Karl Barth's fine pamphlet, *Theologische Existenz heute!*, pp. 3–7, written "am Abend des kritischen 24. Juni 1933," is an exception well calculated to prove the rule. With Barth himself, the terms are not of frequent occurrence, particularly in the earlier works. *Der Römerbrief* in its comment on *Romans* 11:29 is almost perfunctory. In *Das Wort Gottes*

und die Theologie (1925), the first edition of *Dogmatik, I*
(1927), and *Suchet Gott, so werdet ihr leben* (with Thurney-
sen, 1928), I find by somewhat cursory inspection almost no
occurrences, and none of importance. In the second edition
of *Dogmatik, I, i* (1932), however, *Berufung* occurs with
noticeable frequency, usually in the sense of *Offenbarung,*
"revelation." Thus, it is the prophet's message (59–60), or the
theologian's (303); the Word of God addressed to man (153,
155, 407); the Word of God to each individual, to which he
must respond and wherein is his "crisis" for better, for worse
(165–6, 349–350). The passage last cited is especially clear and
emphatic in its rejection of any such concept of vocation as
that defended in this book: "It is *not* any human disposition.
Berufung is an inexplicable (*unableitbares*) fact, or one to be
accounted for only by divine election. Prophets and apostles
are such, not as men raised in their full humanhood to some
heroic status, but rather as prophets and apostles fallen so to
say from heaven, as much to their own astonishment as to that
of their neighbors, in a rôle (*Amt*) that cannot be explained
by their human circumstances; bearers of a 'burden' which
they have not taken upon themselves, but which is laid upon
their shoulders." With much that this statement implies, I
of course warmly agree; but fundamentally the viewpoint of
this book would not be acceptable to Barth. Cf. above, pp.
54–71.

Emil Brunner employs the term *Berufung* likewise to refer
to the "calling" of the prophet, of Jesus Christ, or of the
human individual to his providentially allotted task. Thus,
e.g., Die Mystik und das Wort (1924), 224–5: "die Berufung
auf das, was einzig und allein in Gottes Willen beruht." The
term *Beruf* he uses in a different and highly interesting sense,
to denote the evocation of the human individual from animality into ethical selfhood, by a summons (*Anspruch, Aufgebot*)
that comes to him from beyond the natural order, from God
(*ibid.,* 343–4, 159–160). With this latter usage, cf. F. Gogarten:
Ich glaube an den dreieinigen Gott (1926), 68–70. Brunner's
keen philosophic interest and insight give to his development
of this conception a pertinency to our problem which Barth's

more severe Biblicism does not have. But even in Brunner I find no inclination to seek God through the common life of ordinary men.

22. As Barth also insists: "Galvanised ancestral piety is emphatically *not* what we need. That which has been comes not again, and should not come again." (*Das Wort Gottes,* 193.) His demand is for a faith that responds to a "contemporaneous" (because eternal) Word of God; but this is to be found "nowhere else in all the world than, new each day, in the Holy Scripture, the Old and New Testaments." (*Theologische Existenz heute!,* pp. 4–5.)

23. Plato: *Phædrus* 266b, 5–7.

24. For an ancient analysis of the two extremes, see Plato: *Parmenides* 137–166, with the exposition in J. Burnet: *Greek Philosophy, Part I* (1914), 260–272; and for a modern critique of the intermediate position which Plato preferred, see F. H. Bradley: *Appearance and Reality* (2d ed., 1897), ch. ii and iii. Bradley's argument is essentially Eleatic or Megaric in character; and against it, no concrete world-view is logically impregnable (including, of course, Bradley's own). Plato's own conception of sound method is suggested in *Philebus* 16b–17a, and elsewhere, in terms which frankly recognize that what we experience is not wholly amenable to logic. See above, p. 195; cf. 156–7, etc.

25. On this whole matter, see W. H. Sheldon: *The Strife of Systems and the Productive Dualism* (1918), 407 ff.

26. See J. B. Bury: *The Idea of Progress* (1920), and the literature, Spenglerian and other, of historical pessimism.

27. Another term to which Weber's and Troeltsch's critics have taken exception. I use the word here deliberately in the loose, wide sense of Weber's initial essay. See *The Protestant Ethic,* 26, 117–120, etc., and cf. Weber's "Antikritisches Schlusswort" in *Archiv für Sozialwissenschaft,* 31:589–591.

28. As Augustine in the Pelagian and Semi-Pelagian controversies, and Luther in his passage at arms with Erasmus.

29. On this development, see B. Geyer: *F. Ueberwegs Grundriss der Geschichte der Philosophie,* Bd. II (1928), 625, and more generally, 583–636.

30. See, for example, the *Compendium Theologiæ (Opusc.
2)*, sections 123–5, 131–5. This was among St. Thomas's latest
works, left uncompleted at his death (M. Grabmann: *Die
Werke des hl. Th. von Aquin*, 286).

31. *Compend. Theol.*, sections 124–5, 127–9.

32. *Quodlib.* VII, 17: "primo ex divina providentia, . . . ;
secundo etiam ex causis naturalibus, ex quibus contingit quod
in diversis hominibus sunt diversæ inclinationes ad diversa
officia vel ad diversos modos vivendi." Cf. the similar passages at *Sum. cont. Gent.* III, 134, 136. Note that these "inclinations" do not have the binding force of divine decrees:
"ex tali inclinatione non obligatur quilibet homo per modum
præcepti" (quoted by Linhardt: *Die Sozialprinzipien des hl.
Th. von Aquin*, 163 n. 5, from the *Commentary on the Sen-
tences*, 26:1, 2). Thus also *Compend. Theol.* 128: ". . . per
passiones voluntas ad aliquid inclinatur. sed quia voluntas pas-
sionibus non subditur, ut earum impetum ex necessitate sequa-
tur, sed magis in potestate sua habet reprimere passiones per
judicium rationis," etc.

33. In especial, that which later was called "the principle of
sufficient reason." See above, pp. 145–147; and see R. L. Pat-
terson: *The Conception of God in the Philosophy of Aquinas*
(1933) for an extended discussion of the point.

34. Cf. W. Gass: *Geschichte der christlichen Ethik*, 2 v.
(1881, 1886), I, 392–402.

35. As St. Augustine had done in combating the ethical
atomism in Pelagian doctrine. Cf. B. B. Warfield's introduc-
tion, *Nicene and Post-Nicene Fathers*, 1st series, Vol. 5, pp.
xiv–xvii.

36. J. T. McNeill: *Unitive Protestantism* (1930).

37. Cf. Troeltsch: *Soziallehren*, 622–4 and note 320.

38. For evidence which on the whole I find convincing, see
G. G. Coulton: *Five Centuries of Religion*, 2 v. (1923, 1927).
Father Herbert Thurston's small compendium, *Some Inexacti-
tudes of Mr. G. G. Coulton* (1927), is keen, skilful debating
which clearly gets inside Coulton's guard; but it is confined
to a few matters, mostly of minor importance.

39. Troeltsch: *Soziallehren*, 500–506; 661–666.

40. A comment of Professor Bainton's.

41. See above, pp. 41–43, 46 ff.

42. E. Bernstein: *Die Internationale der Arbeiterklasse und der europäische Krieg* (1915), 4, 20–21, 53–54. K. Kautsky: *Die Internationalität und der Krieg* (1915), 29 ff. Here is the familiar picture of high sentiments enlisted into the support of a dominant nationalistic furor, with the pious hope that the interests of the working class at large will thus be furthered. This sort of "opportunism" called forth Lenin's stinging pamphlet, *The Proletarian Revolution and the Renegade Kautsky.* Cf. his remark: "just as the Christians, after Christianity had attained the position of a State religion, 'forgot' the *naïveté* of primitive Christianity with its democratic revolutionary spirit." (*The Paris Commune,* 1931, p. 30.)

43. With this and the following sections, cf. C. Ilgner: *Die volkswirtschaftlichen Anschauungen Antonins von Florenz* (1904), 17–23. I was not acquainted with this study at the time these paragraphs were written, nor with St. Antoninus' *Summa theologiæ moralis;* of which Part III deals in great detail with the various "stations" (*statūs*) in which men live, and their respective duties and rewards. Part III, title viii, on commerce and the crafts, has as its theme the Vulgate text of *Psalms* 104:23 (103:23 in Vulg.): *"Exibit homo ad opus suum et ad operationes suas, usque ad vesperam."* Man is prompted to virtuous deeds by God, and to wrongdoing by the devil, but to ordinary labor by his own native endowment. "For the various other animals, Nature provides food, raiment, and weapons of defense, without work on their part. But to man she gave reason, whereby as he proceeds through discourse to reflection and investigation, he can provide for himself food, clothing, and defense, through physical labor of divers sorts; and to this end nearly all man's physical labor is ordained." (*Sum. theol. mor.,* III, viii, introd.)

All such human activity should exhibit three notes: rectitude, suitability, and persistence (*bona conscientia, convenientia, permanentia*). As to the second: "A man's work may be called *his* when it suits him by reason of an inclination and natural aptitude for it. 'Pleasure,' said Aristotle, 'makes work perfect' (*delectatio secundum philosophum perficit opus*). When, therefore, any one inclines naturally to a permissible task (*ad unum opus non malum*), let him work in accord with nature pleasurably by devoting himself to that pursuit (*exercitium*). Such practice makes perfect." (*op. cit.*, III, viii, 2.)

Man's work, moreover, should be communal in intent. Like the members of one body are the members of a society, "who, in diverse occupations aiming at the interchange of reciprocal services, ought in all cases (*uniformiter*) to aim at the common weal." (*op. cit.*, IV, iii, 2.)

44. In Calvinistic theology, a view of this general character was first approached by Möyse Amyraut (d. 1664) and Claude Pajon (d. 1685), a century after Calvin. Their views were rejected by the French Calvinist Churches as out of accord with the Canons of Dort. See Herzog-Hauck: *Realencyklopädie*, 1:476–481; 14:553–55.

45. The basic discussion is in Marx: *Das Kapital*, parts IV–VII (Eng. tr. from the fourth German ed. by Eden and Cedar Paul, 1929, pp. 325–789). The theory of crises is summarized by Julian Borchardt, in K. Marx: *Capital* (Modern Library ed., 1932), 302–314. This viewpoint has been widely publicized by such books as Max Eastman: *Marx, Lenin, and the Science of Revolution* (1926); Scott Nearing: *Must We Starve?* (1932); Sidney Hook: *Toward the Understanding of Karl Marx* (1933); John Strachey: *The Coming Struggle for Power* (1933); and Lewis Corey: *The Decline of American Capitalism* (1934).

46. Succinctly resumed by George Soule: *The Coming American Revolution* (1934), 81–149.

47. See M. Leven, H. G. Moulton, and C. Warburton: *America's Capacity to Consume* (1934), 115–133, and *passim*. This and the companion study by E. G. Nourse and others: *America's Capacity to Produce* (1934), both publications of the Brookings Institution, are of fundamental importance for discussion of the points here at issue.

48. O. W. Riegel: *Mobilizing for Chaos* (1934).

49. R. R. Kuczynski: *The Balance of Births and Deaths*, 2 v. (1928, 1931). Another Brookings publication. Covers

the countries of Europe. For a general summary statement by the same author, see "The World's Future Population," in *Population* (Chicago, 1930), 283–302. These are statistical studies. In the more speculative theoretical discussions, based on the projected working of certain selected factors (biological, agricultural, etc.), widely variant conclusions are reached.

50. See p. 64 and note 46.

51. W. N. Polakov: *The Power Age* (1933), 179–197. Cf. Thorstein Veblen: *The Engineers and the Price System* (1921), ch. i, on "sabotage."

52. A term used in conversation by Prof. A. D. H. Kaplan, in the sense set forth in detail by such books as *America's Capacity to Consume* (see note 47), Gove Hambidge: *Your Meals and Your Money* (1934), etc. It has since been used by Secretary Wallace in the title of his recent book, *New Frontiers* (1934).

53. Cf. Norman Thomas: *Human Exploitation* (1934).

54. So J. M. Keynes: *Essays in Persuasion* (1931), pp. viii, 358–373.

CHAPTER TWO

1. See above, pp. 132–3, 146–8.

2. F. von Hügel: *The Mystical Element of Religion* (1908), I, 79.

3. The word here referred to was that of O. G. Villard, in *The Nation*, 138:293 (Mar. 14, 1934). The same note is sounded repeatedly in current reporting: *e.g.,* B. S. Alper and G. E. Lodgen in *The Survey*, 70:285–6 (Sept. 1934), G. Springer in the same journal, 70:342–4 (Nov. 1934), Edith Abbott in *The Nation*, 140:41 (Jan. 9, 1935): ". . . good news to all who understand the unmerited sufferings of the unemployed and their eagerness for work."

4. C. Lloyd Morgan: *Emergent Evolution* (1923), 4, 7, 8, 36, and elsewhere, uses the phrase "natural piety" in the sense of unprotesting acceptance; and refers the phrase, in turn, to S. Alexander.

5. On the Greek Cynics, the most familiar account is that of Diogenes Laertius: *Lives,* Bk. VI. The unsatisfactoriness of this late compilation is well known. The excellent brief article by Robert Eisler, in *Encyclopedia of the Social Sciences,* 4:680–684, gives a vivid though somewhat over-imaginative picture. The Cynic temper is strikingly represented in some of the letters attributed to Diogenes of Sinope (in R. Hercher, ėd.: *Epistolographi Græci,* 1873); among which may be mentioned especially *Ep.* 28 (whose author, though not Diogenes, was "verus et sincerus Cynicus"—W. Capelle: *De cynicorum epistulis,* 1896, p. 28), 29 (perhaps by the same author), 35, 40, 44. Cf. Jonathan Swift: *Gulliver's Travels* (ed. Temple Scott, 1899), Part II, ch. vi, p. 136; *Poems* (ed. W. E. Browning, 1910), I, 165, 193–211, etc. Carlyle's temper is, of course, far different. His *Table Talk* needs to be corrected by *Sartor Resartus* and *Heroes and Hero Worship.* The heartening thunders of these last are still missing from the work of our modern cynics.

6. Plato: *Phædo,* 98c–99a.

7. Nietzsche seems to have no authentic successors. His
Zarathustrian contempt for Man is vulgarized into the contempt for *some* men, to wit, those not of one's own race, nation, class, that appears in the writings referred to in the next
note. The Barthian anti-humanism is in theory far more thoroughgoing; but how in practice this also may be given the same
all-too-human twist, Gogarten's defection to the Aryanizing
"German Christians" bears witness.

8. B. Mussolini: *Scritti e Discorsi* (1934, 8 v. issued), II,
307–22, 327–337 (speeches at Udine, 20 Sept., and Milan, 4
Oct., 1922); III, 77–79 (article on "Coercion and Consent"),
233–9 (speech at Perugia, 30 Oct., 1923); etc. (The Milan
speech is translated, under date of 6 Oct., 1922, in *Mussolini
as Revealed in his Political Speeches* (1923), 161–170.) E.
Boepple, ed.: *Adolf Hitlers Reden* (1934, speeches delivered
1922–24). A. Hitler: *Mein Kampf* (1926–7), I, 300–350; II,
80–90; etc. H. Goering: *Germany Reborn* (1934). A. Rosen-
berg: *Der Mythus des 20. Jahrhunderts* (1934), *passim*. The
keynote of this group of fascist dicta is struck by O. Spengler:
Jahre der Entscheidung (1933), 69: "Die Demokratie des 19.
Jahrhunderts ist bereits Bolschewismus."

But the genuine Bolshevist is no less scornful and bitter
toward "democracy," from the opposite pole: "What ridicule
Engels would have heaped upon the head of that vulgar
petty-bourgeois, the 'Social-Democrat' (in the French sense of
the forties of last century, and in the European sense of 1914–
18), who would have talked about 'pure democracy' in relation to a society divided into classes!" On the contrary, the
Soviet Republic is "a *proletarian* democracy, a democracy *for
the poor,* and not a democracy for the rich, as is the case with
every bourgeois democracy, even the best." (V. I. Lenin: *The
Paris Commune,* Eng. tr. of speeches, articles, and excerpts,
pub. 1931, pp. 46, 48.) I cannot read materials which are available only in Russian, but in the brief articles and excerpts
translated as "The Little Lenin Library," there is ample evidence of Lenin's vindictive rejection of all that savors of
"bourgeois democracy"; *e.g., The Tasks of the Proletariat in
our Revolution,* 10–24, 28–31; *On Religion,* 14–15, 38–41, 49–56:

"We deny all morality taken from superhuman or non-class conceptions. . . . We say that our morality is wholly subordinated to the interests of the class struggle of the proletariat."

9. Stalin's recent reprisals after the assassination of Kirov (see *New York Times,* Dec. 6, 16, 18, 22, 23, 1934), visited not merely on "counter-revolutionists" but on left-wing members of his own party (Zinoviev, Kamenev), strongly suggest that a communist dictatorship is not essentially different at this point from other dictatorships. See below, pp. 227–228.

10. The sort of romanticism urged some years ago by Count de Gobineau, and popularized by Madison Grant: *The Passing of the Great Race* (1916), and W. McDougall: *The Group Mind* (1920), and *Is America Safe for Democracy?* (1921), has now, of course, been applied in bloody earnest by the Nazi adventurers. As against all this, I take it the critical sobriety of F. H. Hankins: *The Racial Basis of Civilization* (1926) is on solider ground. O. Klineberg: *A Study of Psychological Differences between "Racial" and National Groups in Europe* (1931), in *Archives of Psychology,* No. 132, gives support to this view; and Paul Radin: *The Racial Myth* (1934) summarizes it in pungent terms.

11. See above, note 51, Chap. I. A more widely read statement of the same sort is Stuart Chase's *The Economy of Abundance* (1934).

12. Not, be it said, the wickedness of a few individuals, but the ingrained habits of whole groups; including the relatively comfortable and complacent "middle class," to which the writer and most readers of this book belong.

13. Cf. E. C. Lindemann: *The Meaning of Adult Education* (1926). Ruth Kotinsky: *Adult Education and the Social Scene* (1933). At this point I owe a special debt to conversations with Professor Hugh Hartshorne, and his richly suggestive book, *Character in Human Relations* (1933).

14. Cf. Scott Nearing: *Education in Soviet Russia* (1926); A. P. Pinkevich: *The New Education in the Soviet Republic* (tr. N. Perlmutter, introd. by G. S. Counts, 1929).

15. This point, I believe, will be more fully discussed in a forthcoming book by John C. Bennett: *Social Salvation* (1935).

16. James C. Rorty: *Our Master's Voice* (1934), and the various publications sponsored by Consumers' Research are convenient surveys. Cf. Stuart Chase and F. J. Schlink: *Your Money's Worth* (1927); Arthur Kallet and F. J. Schlink: *100,000,000 Guinea Pigs* (1932); M. C. Phillips: *Skin Deep* (1934). These are polemical works, and their emotional bias is evident; but a critical reading of the advertisements carried, in recent years, by current periodicals—not excluding certain of the liberal weeklies—gives strong support to their indictment. Reports of the Federal Trade Commission, technical journals such as the *Journal of the American Medical Association,* and trade journals such as *Advertising Age* and *Printer's Ink,* supply a background of information for judging the integrity of particular advertisements.

17. See above, note 48, Chap. I.

18. George Seldes: *The Truth behind the News* (1929); *Can These Things Be!* (1931).

CHAPTER THREE

1. *E.g.*, F. M. Cornford: *From Religion to Philosophy*, ch. 1–3; Karl Joël: *Geschichte der antike Philosophie*, I (1921), 246–254. One need not adopt a more highly specialized theory, for example that of R. Eisler: *Weltenmantel und Himmelszelt* (1910), II, 647 ff., to recognize the general plausibility of this view, which the great ability and influence of Zeller and Burnet have too successfully obscured.

2. Anaxagoras, fr. 11–12 (H. Diels: *Fragmente der Vorsokratiker*, 3d ed., 46B; tr. in J. Burnet: *Early Greek Philosophy*, 3d ed., 1920, 259–260). For a clear and consistent interpretation see A. L. Peck, "Anaxagoras and Predication as a Problem in Physics," in *Classical Quarterly* (1931), 25:27–37, 112–120.

3. Plato: *Cratylus,* 399e–400b; *Phædrus,* 245c ff.; *Sophist,* 248e–249c; *Philebus,* 28a–30d; *Laws,* 893a–899d; etc.

4. *E.g. de Anima,* 415b, 7–28; 416b, 32–418a, 6; 467a, 9–38; 468a, 26–43.

5. Plotinus: *Enneads* (tr. MacKenna, 1924–1930), IV, ii, 2; iii, 3; vii, 6. Augustine: *De Trinitate* X, xi, 18; XIII, xx, 26. I. Kant: *Kritik der reinen Vernunft,* 1st ed., 1781, pp. 98–110, 115–130 (Prussian Acad. ed., 1903, 4:77–83, 86–95).

6. W. James: *Principles of Psychology* (1890), I, 225–7, 330–340. Pierre Janet: *L'automatisme psychologique* (1889), 483–488; *Les obsessions et la psychasthénie* (1903), I, 495 ff. H. Head: *Aphasia and Kindred Disorders of Speech* (1926), I, 535–545.

7. *E.g.* H. Lotze: *Microcosmus* (tr. Hamilton and Jones, 1885), 152–167, 531–562. J. Royce: *The World and the Individual* (1889), I, 385–398; II, 243–331. B. Bosanquet: *The Principle of Individuality and Value* (1912), 31–81 and *passim.*

8. H. L. Hollingworth: *Psychology, its Facts and Principles* (1928), vii, 6, 47–48, 49, and *passim.* G. H. Mead, *Mind, Self, and Society* (1934), 121, 125, 133, offers a similar but narrower

definition, restricting the term "mind" to human social behavior involving the use of language-symbols.

9. Raymond Dodge: *Conditions and Consequences of Human Variability* (1931), 158–9.

10. What is meant here is not logical nor statistical probability, for which very often the requisite conditions cannot be known to be present in a given concrete situation to which inquiry is directed. What is meant here is simply plausibility to a careful, critical, and tolerably well-informed observer. See F. R. Tennant: *Philosophical Theology* (1928, 1930), I, 288–9.

11. James: *Principles of Psychology,* I, 609, etc. Cf. P. Janet: *L'automatisme psychologique,* 484.

12. K. Dunlap: *Scientific Psychology* (1922), 26.

13. *Kritik der reinen Vernunft,* 1st ed., 98–110. Cf. Augustine: *de Trinitate,* XIII, xx, 26.

14. *Principles of Psychology,* I, 363.

15. *Ibid.* 337–342. James is quite aware of difficulties (341 n.), and leaves the way open to affirm a "non-phenomenal Thinker" if there should seem reason to do so.

16. Such, for example, as E. B. Holt, E. C. Tolman, and Clark L. Hull. One may refer to E. B. Holt: *Animal Drive and the Learning Process,* vol. I (1931); E. C. Tolman: *Purposive Behavior in Animals and Men* (1932); and the suggestive papers by C. L. Hull in *Psychological Review,* 37: 511–525; 38:487–506; 39:25–43; 41:33–52, 134–152.

17. I hope to say something more on these points in a paper on "Knowing and the Knower."

18. Compare Hollingworth's vivid account, *op. cit.,* 136–139, and the experimental reports quoted, 393–396.

19. *E.g. L'automatisme psychologique,* 460–488; *Les névroses* (1909), 383–394. Cf. J. M. Montmasson: *Invention and the Unconscious* (tr. H. S. Hatfield, 1932).

20. Hollingworth: *op. cit.,* 466–70; cf. James: *op. cit.,* II, 340 ff.

21. For a brief, clear approach to the view here intended, see B. A. G. Fuller: *History of Greek Philosophy* (1931), II, 311–315. If one desire a full, detailed exposition, there is C. Ritter: *Platon* (1923), II, 3–428. Or, for very pure revelation

and brilliant description, G. Santayana: *The Realm of Essence* (1927).

22. *Statesman,* 293a-297a.

23. James P. Kelley: *Workmanship in Words* (1917).

24. Above, pp. 211-213; cf. 58, 95, etc.

25. See above, pp. 57 f., 100 ff., 137 f., 244. Cf. W. E. Hocking: *Human Nature and its Remaking* (1918), 280-284.

26. See above, pp. 43-4.

27. Cf. G. H. Mead: *The Definition of the Psychical* (in *Chicago Decennial Publications,* 1st ser., vol. 3, 1903), 106-7. The theme was a favorite one with D. H. Lawrence, who treated it often (as in *Sons and Lovers, The Rainbow, Women in Love*) with painful intensity, and sometimes with fine clarity.

28. After G. Santayana: *Skepticism and Animal Faith* (1923).

29. W. H. R. Rivers: *Instinct and the Unconscious* (2d ed., 1922), 22-51 and *passim.* This view presupposes the neurological work of H. Head and his associates, reported mainly in *Brain,* as indicated in Rivers's footnotes, and again, with replies to the criticisms of Trotter and Davies, von Frey, and Boring, in H. Head: *Studies in Neurology,* 2 v. (1920). Head, in turn, both in this general field and in his studies of aphasia (see above n. 6, Chap. III) is developing the profound general and special theories suggested by J. Hughlings Jackson, in *The Evolution and Dissolution of the Nervous System* (The Croonian Lectures, reported in *Lancet,* 1884, vol. I, pp. 555, 649, 739) and his papers on aphasia, reprinted in *Brain,* 38:1-190 (1915). I find, perhaps too fancifully, a close correlation between this view and A. N. Whitehead: *Symbolism, its Meaning and Effect* (1927), 43, 44 and *passim.*

30. Cf. above, pp. 58 f., 79, 90-93, 99, 237 ff.

31. *Treatise of Human Nature,* Bk. I, Part iv, sect. 7 (*Collected Works,* Edinb., 1854, I, 331-4; Selby-Bigge's ed., 1896, 269-271).

32. P. Janet: *Les obsessions et la psychasthénie,* I, 431-439.

33. H. R. Niebuhr's translation of Paul Tillich's phrase, "gläubiger Realismus." See Tillich: *Die religiöse Lage der*

Gegenwart (1926), 48, etc. Cf. Niebuhr, tr.: *The Religious Situation* (1932), pp. ix-xv; and Tillich: *Religiöse Verwirklichung* (1930), 65-87. Cf. also E. Von Hartmann: *Das Grundproblem der Erkenntnistheorie* (1889), 125: "Der transcendentale Realismus ist ein Postulat des instinktiven sinnlichen Bewusstseins."

34. Pp. 127-130.

35. A. N. Whitehead: *Symbolism, its Meaning and Effect*, 50-51.

36. On this whole question, cf. W. W. Spencer: *Our Knowledge of Other Minds* (1930). This view goes back through Berkeley and the Schoolmen at least to Augustine: *De Trin.*, VIII, vi, 9.

37. *E.g. Phædo*, 100d, *Sophist*, 250b, 251e, 252d, etc. He applied the term not directly to interpersonal communication, but it was out of such communication that the term had arisen. See Liddell and Scott: *Greek-English Lexicon*, 1930, s. v. κοινωνέω.

38. S. Alexander: *Space, Time and Deity* (1920); cf. A. N. Whitehead: *Process and Reality* (1929), 53: "extensiveness becomes, but becoming is not itself extensive."

39. R. A. Millikan, "Present Status of Theory and Experiment as to Atomic Disintegration and Atomic Synthesis," in *Annual Report of the Smithsonian Institution for 1931* (1932), 284-5; *Electrons* (+ and −), *Protons, Photons, Neutrons, and Cosmic Rays* (1934), 354-9, 398-9; but cf. 177-181, and more generally, 158-181.

40. There seems no longer any doubt that atoms of high atomic number break down, under given circumstances, into atoms of lower atomic number. The reverse process has not, I think, been demonstrated but it is held probable that hydrogen nuclei and electrons may be regarded as "building blocks" out of which all atoms are composed. Cf. E. W. Barnes: *Scientific Theory and Religion* (1933), 207-214; R. A. Millikan: *Electrons* (+ and −), *Protons, Photons, Neutrons, and Cosmic Rays*, 450-451.

41. L. J. Henderson: *The Fitness of the Environment* (1913).

42. P. Kropotkin: *Mutual Aid a Factor of Evolution* (1902);
R. Briffault: *The Mothers* (1927), I, 85-194; cf. E. W. Barnes:
op. cit., 521.

43. L. T. Hobhouse: *Development and Purpose* (2d ed.,
1927), pp. xviii, xxii–xxv, xxxiii ff.

44. B Bosanquet: *The Principle of Individuality and Value.*

45. *Soph.,* 248e–249c; *Phileb.,* 28a–30e; *Laws,* 893a–899d, etc.

CHAPTER FOUR

1. J. Rickaby, S. J., tr.: *Of God and His Creatures* (1905); an abridged and annotated version of *Summa contra Gentiles*, of which the complete English version was made by the English Dominican fathers, and published 1923-29.

2. G. W. Leibniz: *Monadology*, §§32, 36 (tr. R. Latta, 1898, 235, 237; cf. 62 ff.); cf. *Essais de Theodicée*, §44: "principe . . . de la raison determinante" (*Philosophische Schriften*, ed. Gerhardt, 1885, 6:127).

3. Kant: *Nova dilucidatio*, 1755, sect. 2 (Prussian Acad. ed., 1902, I, 391-410; tr. in F. E. England: *Kant's Conception of God*, 1929, 220-244). A. Schopenhauer: *Ueber die vierfache Wurzel des Satzes von zureichenden Grunde* (*Werke*, ed. Brasch, 1891, I, 59-193).

4. F. R. Tennant: *Philosophical Theology*, I, 247; II, 253. Cf. B. Bavink: *The Natural Sciences* (tr. from 4th German ed. by H. S. Hatfield, 1932), 228-247.

5. See above, pp. 131-136.

6. Santayana, a leading figure in the group of American "critical realists," draws directly upon the Schoolmen. E. von Hartmann: *Das Grundproblem der Erkenntnistheorie*, defends on Kantian grounds "transcendental realism" against "naïve realism" and "transcendental idealism": cf. note 33, Chap. III, above. Von Hartmann is called by Bavink (*The Natural Sciences*, 243) "the real founder of modern critical realism." See also von Hartmann's *Kritische Grundlegung des transcendentalischen Realismus* (1875).

7. *Summa Theologica*, Part I, Q. 1. Kant: *Religion Within the Limits of Reason Alone* (tr. Greene and Hudson, 1934), pref. to 1st ed., pp. 8-10.

8. Cf. F. R. Tennant: *Philosophical Theology*, 2 v. (1928, 1930); E. W. Barnes: *Scientific Theory and Religion* (1933); C. Lloyd Morgan: *Emergent Evolution* (1923); L. T. Hobhouse: *Development and Purpose* (2d ed., 1927); B. Bavink:

The Natural Sciences (4th ed., tr. 1932); F. von Hügel: *The Mystical Element of Religion*, 2 v. (1908); A. N. Whitehead: *Process and Reality* (1929). Naturally the views suggested in this book differ, by way of both variation and defect, from those of any of the authors named; and naturally I have learned also from others than these. But the general temper, method, and outlook involved in a steady effort to keep faith and reason, "revealed theology" and "natural theology" together, and refusal to permit either to be impoverished by separation from the other, is that which seems to me sound. Many of the ideas which appear in this chapter have been discussed repeatedly with Professor Herman A. Brautigam, and my thinking has profited much from his acute insights.

9. A. D'Abro: *The Evolution of Scientific Thought from Newton to Einstein* (1927), 126, 436. Bavink: *op. cit.*, 111–116. Sir J. J. Thomson, in *James Clerk Maxwell* (commemorative volume, 1931), 26 ff.

10. D'Abro: *op. cit.*, 362–3; cf. 41–44, 37–38, etc. For a vivid thumbnail characterization of the three "classical spaces," see W. de Sitter: *Kosmos* (1932), 116 ff.; and for an equally vivid elementary discussion of some of the general principles involved, see E. T. Bell: *The Queen of the Sciences* (1931), 20–46. Brief discussions for readers trained in mathematical theory may be found in A. N. Whitehead: *The Axioms of Projective Geometry* (1906), and *The Axioms of Descriptive Geometry* (1907), of which the opening chapters are intelligible also to an ordinary reader.

11. D'Abro: *op. cit.*, 360 ff.; Bavink: *op. cit.*, 163. The new generalization referred to is described in H. Weyl: *Raum-Zeit-Materie* (4th ed., 1921), 110–131, and its possible application to the problems of physical cosmology in the same work, 248 ff. (English tr., by Brose: *Space, Time, Matter*, 1922.)

12. W. de Sitter: *op. cit.*, 112; M. Planck: *The Universe in the Light of Modern Physics* (tr. Johnston, 1931), 20; cf. Barnes: *op. cit.*, 189

13. The theory is not bound to a "closed" (Riemannian) space-time (see D'Abro: *op. cit.*, 469). Indeed it appears that Einstein himself now inclines to another view, formerly held

by de Sitter; viz., that the Gaussian curvature of space-time is not positive but negative. If this be the case, space-time is "open" or "infinite," and Lobachevski's, not Riemann's equations describe it best. De Sitter had clearly maintained that any of the three types of curvature—positive, negative, or zero —may, "for aught we can say at present," be exemplified by our space-time order (*Kosmos*, 117-129).

14. Barnes: *op. cit.*, 193-4. D'Abro: *op. cit.*, 126-9.
15. H. Weyl: *Raum-Zeit-Materie*, 258-9, 269; and more generally, 256-282. Cf. D'Abro: *op. cit.*, 360 ff., 472-3; Bavink: *op. cit.*, 163.
16. Bavink: *op. cit.*, 173-192. Barnes: *op. cit.*, 199 f., 213-224, 261 f., 275-284. Hans Reichenbach: *Atom and Cosmos* (tr. E. S. Allen, 1933), 213-264.
17. Barnes, 198 f., 278-281. Reichenbach, 251-8.
18. A. S. Eddington: *The Nature of the Physical World* (1929), 56.
19. D'Abro, 364 ff.; cf. Eddington: *The Expanding Universe* (1933), 139-144, 30-35.
20. Planck: *The Universe in the Light of Modern Physics*, 23.
21. See note 17, Chap. IV.
22. Bavink, 287; Barnes, 217, 223, 225, 281-4; Reichenbach, 263-4.
23. If for these two relatively, but not radically, different modes of organization the familiar biological terms *structural* and *functional* should be used, it must be clearly and constantly recognized that this is a different use of the term structure from that metaphysical use which is basic in this discussion as a whole, and for the sake of clarity it will be avoided here. A bone is no more exclusively structure, in the basic sense of form or pattern, than is a heart-beat or a headache: in all of these, as in every concrete event or cluster of events known to us, both structure and process are to be found. We shall prefer at this point, therefore, to speak of anatomical and behavioral organization, including under the latter term all that are commonly called physiological and psycho-physiological processes.

24. This way of putting the matter was suggested to me by a lecture of Dr. E. R. Hilgard.

25. L. J. Henderson: *Blood* (1928), 22-38, 371-2, etc.

26. *E.g.* C. S. Sherrington: *The Integrative Action of the Nervous System* (1906).

27. More illuminating than the spontaneous anomalies of ontogenesis, from which their work set out, are the artificially induced abnormalities studied by Hans Spemann, and his associates in experimental embryology. For a summary of striking recent results, see H. Spemann, "Neueste Ergebnisse entwickelungsphysiologischer Forschung," published as a pamphlet in 1934 by the Freiburger Wissenschaftliche Gesellschaft; and more generally, H. Spemann and others: *Abhandlungen zur Theorie der organischen Entwicklung* (1926).

28. Barnes, 515, 518, 519, 523.

29. Bavink, 389.

30. See note 41, Chap. III.

31. *E.g.* W. H. Howell: *A Text-Book of Physiology* (8th ed., 1922), 460-465.

32. Hans Driesch: *The Science and Philosophy of the Organism* (1908), 59-149; H. Spemann: *op. cit.* It is not necessary to accept Driesch's special theory of *entelechy*. His experimental findings and those of Spemann are thought by the latter in any case to establish epigenesis, however this is further to be interpreted. It may well be that mechanistic hypothesis will prove here again the most fruitful line to pursue. Cf. Spemann, "Neueste Ergebnisse," p. 3; B. Fischer: *Vitalismus und Pathologie* (1924); Bavink: *op. cit.*, 387-403.

33. *Emergent Evolution*, 8-9. The term "emergent" was used by Lloyd Morgan in *Instinct and Experience* (1912), after G. H. Lewes: *Problems of Life and Mind* (1874-5), II, 412; and taken from Lloyd Morgan by S. Alexander: *Space, Time and Deity*, II, 14, n. 2. See *Emergent Evolution*, 2-3.

34. For a brief discussion of some of the issues involved here, by a philosophically able mathematician, see Hermann Weyl: *The Open World* (1932), 68-82, and more generally, 57-84. The problems are treated at full length from the standpoint of mathematical theory in D. Hilbert and P.

Bernays: *Grundlagen der Mathematik,* Bd. I (1934); and, with much fuller recognition of the philosophical problem as such, in the phenomenological work of O. Becker: *Mathematische Existenz* (1927), and in L. Fischer: *Die Grundlagen der Philosophie und der Mathematik* (1933).

35. *E.g.* pp. 155–157.

36. G. Santayana: *The Realm of Essence,* 18–25, and *passim.*

37. Plato: *Parmenides,* 135bc; *Theætetus,* 170d–171c. This holds good even for the most abstract, "positivistic" logic or mathematics, so far as I can see. Hilbert's chess-game analogy (Weyl: *The Open World,* 75–77; Bell: *The Queen of the Sciences,* 21–27), and "the postulational method" which gives point to it, presuppose the strictest possible observance of "the rules of the game," which themselves presuppose the "principle of contradiction" (Bell, 27). The view, in short, is wholly in accord with Plato's account of such procedure: *Republic,* 533b–d, 511bc; *Phædo,* 99e–101e; etc.

38. Whether as "qualities" or as "relations," or otherwise, I do not clearly see.

39. Cf. Plato: *Euthyphro,* 7b–d.

40. G. K. Chesterton, "The House of Christmas," in *Collected Poems* (1932).

41. It is this, in part, that Bosanquet means by saying "There is more in the mind than is before it" (*The Value and Destiny of the Individual,* ch. on "The Miracle of Will.").

42. J. Dewey: *A Common Faith* (1934). G. H. Mead: *The Definition of the Psychical* (*Chicago Decennial Publications,* 1903); *Mind, Self, and Society* (1934), 201–204, 215–218. Cf. Plato: *Philebus,* 23d, 5–8; 30de; etc.

43. It seems to me that Dr. Tennant's finely conceived and impressively argued *Philosophical Theology* does not give these facts due weight. I concur in his criticisms, in vol. I, ch. 12; but I cannot see why experiences of regeneration and of worship should not have found room, along with æsthetic and moral experience, in vol. II, ch. 4.

44. The inadequacy of Protagoras' dictum: "Man is the measure of all things," should not blind one to its hold on a profound truth. Plato was not blind to it; cf. *Philebus,* 28c–30c.

45. Lenin is said to have found such illumination in the Paris Commune of 1871. Cf. the closing paragraphs of his article "In Memory of the Commune," in V. I. Lenin: *The Paris Commune* (1931), 16–17.

46. Cf. David Hume: *Enquiry,* sect. 4 (*Works,* Edinb., 1854, 4:41–43). On the meaning of analogy as used here, cf. Berkeley: *Alciphron,* IV, 21 (*Works,* ed. Fraser, 1871, 2:167–8).

47. F. Engels: *Herrn Eugen Dühring's Umwälzung der Wissenschaft* (3d ed., 1894), 144–5.

48. The instrumentalistic interpreters of Marx, *e.g.* Max Eastman and Sidney Hook (cf. note 45, Ch. I), throw into especially clear relief the importance of mind in social change.

49. See above, p. 113.

50. See note 8, Chap. IV.

51. Athanasius: *Contra Arianos,* II, 64, 4–50 (Migne: *Patrologia Græca,* 26:284), and more generally, II, 62–64 (*PG,* 26:277–284). Eriugena: *De divisione naturæ,* III, 3 (Migne: *Patrol. Latina,* 122:631a-d); but cf. V, 23 (*PL,* 122:904a–905b). Like ps.–Dionysius Areopagita: *De cælesti hierarchia,* cp. 1 (*PL,* 122:1037c), Eriugena appeals to the Vulgate text of *James* 1:17, "*Omne datum optimum, et omne donum perfectum, desursum est, descendens a Patre luminum.*"

52. See above, pp. 199, 242–5.

53. Origen: *Contra Celsum,* I, 2; VII, 42, 44–46 (Migne: *PG,* 11: 1480–89). Notice then how in Origen's own effort to set forth a doctrine about God, all these methods are used: *de Principiis,* I, i, 1–9 (though how close Rufinus' text here is to what Origen wrote, one cannot be sure).

54. J. E. Boodin: *Cosmic Evolution* (1925), 210 ff., 218 ff.; *A Realistic Universe* (2d ed., 1931), 123.

55. See above, pp. 117–122.

56. Both "hereditary" and "environmental" conditions of all sorts are intended here. Cf. pp. 29–31, 82–4, 90–3, 101–6, etc.

57. Cf. W. E. Hocking: *Human Nature and its Remaking* (1918), 402–3.

58. See above, pp. 153 ff.

59. Somewhat as the Stoics and Spinoza held; but with the basic affirmation also (which the former did not share, and

the latter obscured by his mode of statement) of the transcendence of God, no less than His immanence. This is, up to a point, the familiar view of Neoplatonic philosophy and Christian philosophical theology.

60. So far as we know, there is no faster physical messenger than light, whose speed apparently is invariant. Hence, at a given locus in space-time, no events can possibly be observed other than those which are happening at that locus (here-now), or which have happened near enough by and long enough ago for light to have traversed the interval from where the event then-and-there transpired, to where the observer is here-and-now. All that happens outside those space-time limits is necessarily closed to him. See Eddington: *The Nature of the Physical World,* 47 ff.; Weyl: *The Open World,* 12–16. The theoretical grounds for this conception are worked out in H. Weyl: *Raum-Zeit-Materie,* 156–161.

61. Sir Isaac Newton: *Opticks* (4th ed., 1730), 379.

62. W. P. Montague's brilliant paper, "A Possible Interpretation of the Quantum," in *The Scientific Monthly,* 38:343–360 (Apr., 1934), proposes a new hypothetical construction devised to throw light on this as yet unsolved problem. I am unable to estimate its theoretic value. It has the advantage (for the layman) of picturesque, non-technical statement and is suggestive at many points; yet its basic concept—of a *self-reversing* "squirm" or spiral wave—seems to do hardly less violence to accustomed physical categories than the wave-particle phenomenon it is meant to interpret.

63. Cf. what is said above, pp. 155–159, 195–196, 246–248, on "real contingency."

64. Royce: *The World and the Individual,* II, 142, 122 ff. It may be observed that whereas Royce includes "past," "present," *and "future"* in the Absolute *totum simul,* the view here maintained is that only events which have actually transpired or are transpiring, and forms (but not events) other than those hitherto actualized, can be included within God's purview.

65. See above, pp. 117–120.

66. E.g. Royce: *The Spirit of Modern Philosophy* (1892),

456-7. H. Bergson: *L'energie spirituelle* (4th ed., 1920), 16–18; cf. *Time and Free Will* (tr. Pogson, 1910), 170, etc.; *Creative Evolution* (tr. Mitchell, 1911), 359–362. C. A. Bennett: *A Philosophical Study of Mysticism* (1923), 93–102.

67. The manner in which mathematical formulæ are used to summarize immensely complex physical relations is familiar, and we have had occasion to notice the persistence of mathematicians in seeking to develop symbolic systems of increasing generality (see above, pp. 151 ff.). A similar development is in progress in the closely associated field of logical theory. Modern symbolic logic is a generalization beyond the limits of Aristotelian logic, somewhat as modern geometry is a complex generalization beyond Euclidean geometry. And the symbolic logic of Russell and Whitehead's *Principia Mathematica* is now further generalized in the new theory of W. V. Quine: *A System of Logistic* (1934), which expounds a method of dealing with theorems about relations among *n* terms—that is, among *any* number of terms, the number being unspecified. This advance Whitehead judges to be "a landmark in the history of the subject" (*op. cit.*, p. ix).

68. Whitehead: *Process and Reality*, 139–141, etc.

69. An awkward term, but the more familiar "eternity" would be misleading. Cf. note 64, Chap. IV.

70. Santayana in *The Realm of Essence, e.g.* 82 ff., denies that among forms as such there are "families," and maintains that every essence is entirely separate from every other. He holds, in short, the view indicated in Plato: *Sophist*, 251c. But does he not, then, become liable to the consequences noticed in *Sophist*, 252a–c? Descartes got into similar difficulties with his "clear and distinct ideas." The position here taken is that of *Sophist*, 252e.

71. *Parm.*, 132ab. The same point is urged by F. H. Bradley: *Appearance and Reality* (2d ed., 25–34); and his Absolute is not "thought" or "mind" but "sentient experience" (146–7) more like feeling than like thinking. His later affirmations (482, etc.) that "the universe as a whole may be called intelligible" are not made good by argument. As A. K. Rogers points out, in *English and American Philosophy since*

1800 (1922), 251, he does not expose his own conclusions to the full force of his Eleatic dialectic.

72. We go here with Origen: *c. Celsum*, III, 70 (*PG*, 11: 1012–13); V, 23–24 (*PG*, 11:1216–7); *de Principiis*, II, ix, 1. The last, a fragment of the Greek text preserved in a letter of Justinian to Mennas, gives an especially clear expression to Origen's thought here (see *Origenes Werke*, Bd. V, 164, in *Griech. christl. Schriftsteller*, 1913).

73. Cf. Whitehead: *Process and Reality,* on "the primordial nature of God," and on "positive" and "negative prehension."

74. I am far from satisfied with the foregoing analysis, though in principle it seems to me defensible. There is much that I do not clearly see, in the direction indicated by H. F. Hallett's *Æternitas* (1930), a most suggestive study of Spinoza, which applies with almost equal relevance to the philosophy of Plotinus. But in contrast with these views, I am not able to regard all that is, has been, will, may, or might be as *All-Eine*.

75. Eriugena: *De divisione naturæ*, II, 28 (Migne: *PL,* 122: 596a–c). The doctrine appears to go back at least to Philo.

76. See pp. 197 ff.

77. Partly realized: (*a*) incompletely as to extent, and (*b*) imperfectly as to character.

78. See note 70, Chap. IV.

79. Plato: *Timæus,* 29e (on which see A. E. Taylor: *A Commentary on Plato's Timæus*, 1928, 75–79). *Gospel of John*, 3:16.

80. E.g., *Cogitata metaphysica*, II, viii, 1–3; *Korte Verhandeling van God*, etc., ch. vii (*Opera*, ed. Van Vloten and Land, 1895, 3:31–33); *Ethica*, Part I, appendix; cf. Part V, prop. xix. For his general attitude, cf. *Ep.* 75 to his friend Oldenburg (*Opera*, 2:414 f.): "But on the other hand, let me ask whether we manikins (*homunciones*) know so much about Nature that we can determine how far its power and potency extends, and what exceeds its power?"

81. Plato: *Republic,* 379–380; Spinoza: *Ethics,* Part V, prop. xxxvi, corollary and note.

82. See above, pp. 123–127, etc.

83. Cf. *Republic,* 381.

84. *Republic*, 508–9; cf. *Timæus*, 27e–31a.
85. Plato: *Statesman*, 297a, 295c–e. Cf. the suggestion of E. Boutroux: *De la contingence des lois de la nature* (1874), and the comment of H. Poincaré, "L'evolution des lois," in *Scientia*, 1911, 9:275–292.
86. Cf. for an opposing view, E. S. Brightman: *The Problem of God* (1930).
87. The Old Roman Symbol (R) of the second century on which see, *e.g.* A. C. McGiffert: *The Apostles' Creed* (1902).
88. *E.g.* by Augustine, Eriugena, Aquinas, Duns Scotus, Zwingli, Calvin.
89. See n. 72, Chap. IV.
90. See, *e.g.* pp. 43–53, above.
91. Plato's word is ἀνάγκη, "necessity". (*Timæus*, 47e–48a, etc.; cf. *Republic*, 616c–617e, and *Laws* 818a–d, for contrasted uses of the term). I have commented briefly on this problem in Plato's thought, in *Religious Realism* (ed. D. C. Macintosh, 1931), 245–247.
92. See above, pp. 64 ff.
93. See above, pp. 75–76.
94. *Process and Reality*, 11, 31, etc.
95. I mean more than, *e.g.* James Ward: *The Realm of Ends* (1911), 454–5, was ready to mean by contingency. The issue here is one over which judgments will perhaps always differ; as now the judgments of Heisenberg, Born, Reichenbach differ from those of Planck and Einstein. The matter is not, so far as I can see, susceptible of decision by any "crucial experiment."
96. *Laws*, 709bc.
97. No dichotomy, needless to say, is here intended. Cf. above, pp. 127, 138–9.
98. See pp. 240–249.
99. See pp. 131, 139, and 349; and cf. J. Oman: *Grace and Personality* (1919), and R. S. Franks: *The Atonement* (1934).
100. See pp. 146–148, and notes 4, 6, Chap. IV.
101. See p. 139.
102. See pp. 130–136, and notes 32, 33, Chap. III.
103. See p. 131.

104. Plato: *Timæus*, 29d.

105. Plotinus: *Enneads*, VI, vii, 13-15; Origen: *de Principiis*, II, ix; ps.-Dionysius: *De divinis nominibus*, iv (*PL*, 122:1132b-1135b); Eriugena: *De divisione naturæ*, III, 3 (*PL*, 122:630a-631d); cf. Peter Lombard: *Sententiæ*, II, i, D-H; Thomas Aquinas: *Sum. theol.*, I, xix, 2.

106. Leibniz, Letter to Bourguet (*Phil. Schriften*, ed. Gerhardt, 3:572-3). Cf. Plato: *Phædo*, 102; *Soph.*, 252e, etc.

107. J. Ward: *Naturalism and Agnosticism* (4th ed., 1915), 570.

108. See pp. 155 ff., 194 ff.

109. Cf. A. E. Taylor: *A Commentary on Plato's Timæus*, 300-301.

110. Cf. pp. 115-116.

CHAPTER FIVE

1. *Proverbs,* 30:18–19.
2. W. E. Hocking: *The Meaning of God in Human Experience* (1912), 405–427. C. A. Bennett: *A Philosophical Study of Mysticism* (1923), 127–151.
3. *E.g.* A. B. Crawford and S. H. Clement: *The Choice of an Occupation* (1932). M. S. Viteles: *Industrial Psychology* (1932); *The Science of Work* (1934).
4. *E.g. Human Nature and Conduct* (1922), 265–9.
5. *Symposium,* 202de.
6. The physiological basis of this difference may be conceivable in terms of removal of inhibiting innervations, as Professor C. L. Hull suggests.
7. *Pragmatism* (1907), 74.
8. Reinhold Niebuhr's service to the cause of truth at this point, especially through his *Moral Man and Immoral Society* (1933), cannot easily be over-emphasized.
9. *Philebus,* 22a–e.
10. K. Marx: *Misére de la philosophie,* ch. II, §5 end *(Gesamtausgabe,* Abth. I, Bd. 6 (1932), 227–8).
11. *E.g.* by Harold Laski: in *Current History* (Oct., 1928).
12. Cf. V. I. Lenin: *"Left Wing" Communism, an infantile disorder* (1920?). L. Trotsky: *The Strategy of the World Revolution* (1930), 13–15, 66–7.
13. Besides this familiar form of revolutionary doctrine there is another, framed on the presupposition of "permanent revolution." This, I believe, is Trotsky's view. Some such view seems more nearly in accord with the main current of Marx's theory of the dialectic, if that be interpreted realistically and not romantically, than Marx's own hope for a classless society. It seems also to be suggested on empirical grounds by such a study as L. P. Edwards: *The Natural History of Revolution* (1927), as representing the most probable outlook for our society for "generations to come," unless something very

different from the Russian revolution is achieved (*op. cit.,* 213 ff.).

14. Quoted by Alfred Meusel, "Revolution and Counter-revolution," in *Encyclopedia of the Social Sciences,* 13:375a.

15. C. M. Case: *Non-violent Coercion* (1923); R. B. Gregg: *The Power of Non-violence* (1934). Cf. the interesting comment in Lenin: *The Revolution of 1905* (1931), 33, on "converting the troops."

16. For a striking instance, see reports of the conduct of police duty by Brig.-Gen. Pelham D. Glassford in Washington, D. C., during the summer of 1932.

17. Harold I. Rugg: *Culture and Education in America* (1931). Cf. John Dewey: *Art as Experience* (1934).

18. A. C. Bradley: *Oxford Lectures on Poetry* (1909), ch. ii.

19. G. Berkeley: *Alciphron,* IV, 7–15 (*Works,* ed. Fraser, 1871, II, 146–159); cf. *New Theory of Vision,* §§147–8 (*Works,* I, 103–4).

20. The familiar words, *"denkt deine Gedanken dir nach,"* are from Herder's translation, in *Adrastea,* Bd. III, Stück 2, of the hymn with which Kepler concluded his *Mysterium cosmographicum.* See J. G. von Herder: *Sämmtliche Werke* (ed. Suphan, 1877–1913), 23:556. The translation is a very free one, and no words corresponding to the quoted phrase are to be found in the original; but the thought occurs more than once in Kepler's works. Cf. *Mysterium cosmographicum,* dedication (in *Opera omnia,* ed. Frisch, 1868, 1:98); *Harmonices mundi,* V, ix (*Opera,* 5:323).

21. Anaxagoras, fr. 8.

I. INDEX OF PERSONS

II. GENERAL INDEX

I. INDEX OF PERSONS

Index of Persons

Faraday, 149.
v. Faulhaber, 33.
Firth, 257.
Fischer, B., 277.
Fischer, L., 278.
Franks, 283.
Fuller, 270.

Galilei, 146, 153.
Gandhi, 14, 231.
Gass, 261.
Gay-Lussac, 155.
Gerson, 255.
Geyer, 260.
Glassford, 286.
de Gobineau, 266.
Goering, 266.
Gogarten, 259, 266.
Grabmann, 254, 261.
Grant, M., 266.
Grant, U. S., 196.
Gregg, 286.

Hallett, 282.
Hambidge, 264.
Hankins, 267.
v. Hartmann, 272, 274.
Hartshorne, 267.
Head, 269, 271.
Heisenberg, 155, 156, 283.
Hemingway, 97.
Henderson, 141, 162, 272, 277.
v. Herder, 286.
Hesiod, 12, 15.
Hilbert, 277, 278.
Hilgard, 277.
Hitler, 266.
Hobhouse, 142, 148, 273, 274.
Hocking, 206, 271, 279, 285.
Holl, 253, 254, 255.
Hollingworth, 112, 122, 269, 270.
Holt, 270.
Hook, 263, 279.
Howell, 277.
v. Hügel, 148, 265, 275.
Hull, 270, 285.
Hume, 133, 279.
Huxley, A., 27, 97.

Ilgner, 262.

Jackson, 271.
James, 111, 119, 120, 122, 269, 270.
Janet, 111, 121, 269, 270, 271.

Jesus Christ, 7, 12, 51, 172, 183, 243, 248, 259.
Joël, 269.
Joule, 155.

Kallet, 268.
Kant, 111, 118, 119, 148, 174, 269, 274.
Kaplan, 264.
Kautsky, 262.
Kelley, 271.
Kepler, 243, 286.
Keynes, 264.
Klineberg, 267.
Kotinsky, 267.
Kropotkin, 142, 273.
Krutch, 97.
Kuczynski, 263.

Laski, 257, 285.
Lawrence, 271.
Lee, R. E., 196.
Leibniz, 145, 201, 274, 284.
Lenin, 9, 224, 225, 262, 266, 279, 285, 286.
Leven, 263.
Lewes, 277.
Lewis, Sinclair, 25.
Lindemann, 267.
Linhardt, 253, 254.
Lobachevski, 151, 276.
Locke, 146.
Lodgen, 265.
Lombard, Peter, 284.
Lotze, 269.
Luther, 4, 17, 19, 20, 21, 22, 26, 28, 31, 32, 40, 41, 44, 50, 253, 255, 260.

McDougall, 267.
McGiffert, 283.
McNeill, 261.
Marx, 64, 177, 263, 279, 285.
Masefield, 211.
Maxwell, Clerk, 154.
Mead, 269, 271, 278.
Mencken, 25.
Meusel, 286.
Millikan, 272.
Mills, 258.
Montague, 280.
Montmasson, 270.
Morgan, Lloyd, 85, 148, 165, 265, 274, 277.

290

Index of Persons

II. GENERAL INDEX

(Page numbers in italics refer in each case to a passage in which a given subject is treated with some attention to detail.)

General Index

In other selves, 131-3, 136, 147.
In God, 3, 28-9, 76, 174 ff., 183, 191, 206, 241.
See also *Faith, Presence, Realism.*
Beruf, Berufung, 20, 31, 253, 258-9.
Bible, 16, 31.
See also *Scriptures.*
Cited, 17, 18, 19, 254, 255, 256, 282, 285.
Quoted, 6, 15, 18, 48, 98, 188, 190, 198, 205, 239, 243, 245, 246, 262, 279.
Biblical, Biblicism, 16, 18, 254, 260.
Buying power, 65, 67-8, 102-5.

Calling, 200, 240, 248.
"General calling," 47, 54, 56.
"Special calling," 54, 56, 58.
"Effectual calling," 40, 47.
See also *Vocation*, etc.
Calvinism, Calvinist, 21-3, *39-53*, 55, 57, 255, 256 f., 263.
See also *Neocalvinism, Puritan*, etc.
Capitalism, 23, 26-7, 39, *61-71*, 101-7, 218, 223.
Catholic, Catholicism, 18-19, 32, 33, 40-44, 45, 48, 51, 145 ff., 253-5, 261, 262-3, 274.
Cause, causal, 42, 51 f., 133-5, 146, 162, 164.
Cells, 160, 161.
Chance, 143, 164, 175, 195.
Chaos, 82, 153, 158, 212, 241.
Christ crucified, 7, 8, 172-3, 239, 243, 248.
Christian, Christianity, 17, 29, 41, 48, 50, 92, 96, 172-3, 229, 240, 241 f., 242-3, 248, 254, 262.
Church, churches, 76.
Christian, 17, 18, 23, 32, 46, 48.
Roman Catholic, 25, 33, 42-3, 45-6, 48.
Protestant, 22, 33, 40, 263.
Jewish, 173.
Civilization, 56, 83.
Simple, 12, 59, 66, 225.
Complex, 13 ff., 22 ff., 65-6, 226.
Class struggle, 23-4, 26, 223, 229, 235, 267.

Coercion, 63, 136-7, 219, 220 **ff.**, 233 ff.
Non-violent, 231-5, 286.
Violent, 99 ff., *221-9*, 232, 266-7, 285-6.
Coherence, rational, 37 ff., 49, 150, 152, 166, 180, 185.
Collectivism, 99-101.
See also *Communal life, Contributive living, Communism, Fascism.*
Common life, 3.
Everyday life, 12, 17, 19, 20, 28, 53, 212, 254.
Communal life, 14, 45-7, 59-60, 66-7, 70-72, 242, 253-4, 263.
Communication:
Among men, 115, *127-136*, 138, 196-7, 200.
Between men and God, 199-200, *242-245*, 248.
Communicative immanence, 139, 199-200, 244-5, 247-8; cf. 10.
Communism, 17, 91, 99 ff., 222, 223, 228, 229, 257.
Companionship, 127, 130-31, 133-6, 137-8, 182.
Competition, 54-5, *60-72*, 87-8, 91, 100, 102-3, 104-7.
Complacency, 28, 83, 190, 199, 246.
Compromise, 22, 25 ff., 221, 262.
Concretion, 76, 155 ff.
See also *Actualization.*
Conditions:
Of life in general, 163-4, 201-2.
Of human life and growth, 37, 67, 70, 83, *102-5*, 181, 201-4, 208 f., 230, 246-7.
Formal, of thought, 167.
Of productive work, 116, 123-6, 193 ff., 201 ff.
Confessions:
Old Roman Symbol, 192, 283.
Nicene Creed, 28, 29.
Augsburg Confession, 255.
Conflict, 45, 50, 177-8, 191, 192, 202 f., 247, 248.
Conservative, conservatism, 9, 21, 32, 52 f., 218.
Constants:
Geometrical, 151, 152.
Physical, 153, 157-8, 276, 280.
Consummation, 238-9, 240.

293

General Index

Contempt, depreciation, 32, 48, 91–2, 136.
Contingent, contingency, 42, 52, 161, 247.
  "Real contingency," 57, 195, 202, 247, 283.
  See also *Flux, Indeterminacy,* etc.
Continuity, 169.
Contra-revolution, 220–21, 222, 224, 226, 227–8, 234.
Contributive living, 46, *59–72,* 80, 84–5, 89–90, 104, 242, 253–4.
Co-operation, 61, 62, 63, 65, 70, 80, 136–8, 207.
  See also *Co-working.*
Correlation:
  Metrical, 153, 198.
  Qualitative, 179–180, 198.
  Factual, 61, 125, 129, 162 f., 182, 223, 238, 247.
"Cosmic epochs," 186, 241.
Co-working, 247.
  Among men, 60, 61, 63, 80.
  Of man with God, 51, 203, 240, 242.
  Of God with man, *245–248.*
Creation, 168, 187, 201–4, 247.
Creatures, 22, 51, 77, 145, *148–173,* 174, 200, 203, 213, 241.
Creeds, see *Confessions.*
Crisis:
  Of individual living, 44, 76, 243.
  Social crises, 62, 64–5, 222, 224–5, 232 f., 243.
  "Crisis theology," see *Barthianism.*
Criteria:
  Of sound theory, *33–8.*
  For thought and action, 168.
Critical realism, see *Realism.*
Criticism, 75, 96, 97, 148, 170 f., 180, 182, 214.
Cue-stimuli, 112, 114, 122, 129, 132, 135–6, 162.
Culture, 21–3, 56, 77, 101.
Curvature:
  Of abstract "spaces," 150, 151, 152.
  Of physical space-time, 140, 153, 157, 276.
  In fields of force, 153, 154.
Cynic, cynicism, 87, 88, 91, 96 ff., 265.

Daimonic powers, 212–13.
Day-dreaming, 121–2, 217.
Definite, definiteness, 187, 188–9.
Deformity, 84, 90, 101–2.
Dehumanization, 101–3, 136–7.
Democracy, 22, 227.
  Political, 23, 39.
  Social, 99 ff., 266.
Despair, 88, 104, 236.
Determinism, 40 ff., 164, 246.
Devotion, 58, 95, 196, 200, 243.
Dialectic, 145.
  "Dialectical theology," see *Barthianism.*
  "Dialectical materialism," 9, 72, 177–8, 285.
  See also *Marxism.*
Dictatorship, 220–21, 223, 227–8, 233.
  See also *Anti-democracy, Proletariat.*
Direction, human need of, 5, 10, 32, 39, 196, 245.
Discipline, 16, 29, 44, 55, 58 f., 67, 80, 89, 132, 229, 231–2, 244.
Discontinuity, 35, 246.
Discrimination, rational, 37 f., 78, 82, 132–3, 136, 148, 180, 234–5, 244.
Disillusion, 4, 6, 9 f., 87–8, 91–2, 143, 225.
Disintegration, 46–7, 50, 61, 62–3, 82–3, 88, 97, 122, 140 f., 165, 235 f.
Disobedience, 248.
Dispositions, working, 84–90, 126, 211–14.
Distribution, 68, 102–3.
Division of labor, 46, 57–8, 59–60, 62, 253–4, 263.
Dogma, dogmatism, 4, 16, 53, 100, 159, 209.
"Drives," psychophysical, 16, 98, 100, 117, 219.
Drudgery, 54–5, 71, 79, 101, 215.
Duration, real, 186, 188–9, 192, 194, 195, 202.

"Economy of abundance," 68, 70, 102–3, 105, 216.
"Economy of scarcity," 102.
Education, 103–4, 230, 231.
Ego:
  Subject, 118, 180.
  "Other ego," "thou," 131, 199.

General Index

Egotism, 28, 70, 79, 80 f., 86–7, 93, 98–9, 213, 214.
Eleatic criticism, 110, 260, 282.
Electromagnetism, 149, 154.
See also *Physical fields.*
Electrons, 140, 154, 156 f., 158, 175, 184 f., 196, 272.
Emergence, 141, 143, 164, 165, 170, 172, 201–4.
Emergent evolution, 143, 148, 159, 164 f.
Energy, 202.
  Physical, 69, 141, 155, 157, 158, 165, 194.
  Vital, 80, 196.
  Moral, 15 f., 76–7, 79, 83, 89–90.
Enjoyment, 49, 215 f.
Enslavement, 29–30, 62–3, 88.
Entropy, 140, 155, 165, 194.
Environment, 47 ff., 79–80, 124, 141, 165, 170.
  "Fitness of," 143, 162, 163–4, 238–9, 247.
Epicurean, 83.
  See also *Hedonism.*
Epigenesis, 161, 164, 277.
Equilibrium, 160, 164.
Essences, 166–8, 281.
Events, 117, 134, 149, 150, 155, 159, 167, 174, 180, 185 f., 189, 202, 246 f.
Evil, 76, 101–3, 105–7, 181, 188, 193–5, 204, 212, 213, 248.
Evolution, 8, 139–142, 162–5.
  See also *Emergent evolution, Progress,* etc.
Expansion, social, 61 ff., 65.
Exploitation, 14, 28, 53, 62, 87–8, 91, 245.
Extension, 182, 194, 202.

Fact, 8, 9, 16, 37, 38, 49, 55, 158, 181, 213, 217.
Faith, 4, 16, 20, 32, 40, 42, 44, 49, 51, 95, 126, 136, 145, 148, 191, 196, 235–7, 243, 246.
  See also *Belief.*
Fascism, fascist, 14, 99 ff., 220–21, 223, 266.
Fatigue, 82, 194, 215.
Feeling, 26, 119, 129, 134, 136, 281.
Feudal, feudalism, 20, 25, 39, 44, 45, 62–3, 100.

Fictions, 113, 158, 166.
Field of awareness, 111, 117–120, 121.
  See also *Attention, "Specious present."*
"Fields of force," 149, 180–81, 182.
  See also *Physical fields.*
Finding one's job, 207–10.
Fluence, 195.
Flux, change, 148–9.
  In the physical world, 140, 149, 154–9.
  In living organisms, 141, 149, 159–65.
  In conscious experience, 120–21, 149, 165 (and Chap. III, *passim*), 180 f.
  In human history, 3–5, 21–7, 39, 105, 217 ff., 222.
  As factor in productive work, including world-making, 195–6, 201–4, 241, 246–8.
Foreknowledge, foresight, 120.
  In human work, 171.
  Divine, 188–9.
Forms, 75–6, 152, 174, 194.
  Pure possibilities, 115, 124–5, 165–8, 171, 187, 189, 281.
  Ideals, 49, 73, 107, 124, 167–8, 218.
  Structural factors embodied in actual things and events, 64, 66, 99, 124, 141, 153 ff., 157–8, 163, 187, 246.
  See also *Pattern, Structure.*
Frame:
  Logical, 166.
  Metrical, 149–153, 186.
  "Frame of reference," 118, 153, 174, 198.
Freedom:
  Social, political, 29.
  Metaphysical, 57, 170 f., 192, 196, 203–4.
"Friends of God," 18, 19.
Frontier:
  Wilderness, 26, 59–60, 69.
  Economic "frontiers," 69 ff., 264.
  See also *"Over-production."*
Frustration, 68, 73, 85, 88, 196, 207.
  Overcome, 80, 237–8, 240.

Genes, 162–3.
Geodesic lines, 151, 153.

General Index

Geometries:
  Euclidean, 150 f., 153, 281.
  Non-Euclidean, 151–3, 156, 275–6, 281.
German clergy, 33.
Goals:
  Of human work, 123–4, 200, 210–11, 229, 262.
  Of God's working, 190 f., 192, 200, 245, 249.
God, 3–53, 71–2, 93–5, 144–8, 171, 174–204, 211–13, 236–249.
  Existence of God, 3, 145–8, 174–8.
  God as Living Mind, 179–204, 241–8, 249.
  Being: As Subject, 181, 197 f., 199.
  Characters: Omniscience, 183–9, 191.
    Omnipresence, 182–5, 189.
    Eternality, 185–6, 189.
    Omnipotence, 189–196, 204.
    Transcendence, 21–2, 31, 51 f., 183, 187, 188, 197–8, 241, 249.
    Immanence, 183 ff., 199–200, 241.
    Goodness, 76, 188, 190–91, 200.
  Working: Creation, 179, 187, 189, 201–4, 246–7.
    Redemption, 179, 189, 191, 201–4, 240, 247–8.
    Revelation, 199, 242–5, 248.
    Inspiration, 199–200.
  Relations: To Nature, 7–8, 10, 180–196.
    To men, 6–10, 197–200, 241.
  God as Sovereign Ground and Goal, 200, 249.
  See also Belief, Co-working, Justice, Mercy, Will, Wisdom, Word.
Good, goodness, 58, 76, 90, 99, 167–8, 171, 181, 190, 191, 193, 198, 201, 203 f., 211, 213, 219, 237, 238, 241.
  The Good, 90, 168, 191–2, 200, 207, 211.
  See also God, Value.

Good life for men, 54, 58, 67, 74, 101 ff., 206, 220, 224, 229.
"Good works," 18, 19, 20, 22, 43.
Grace, 40, 46–7, 51, 179, 238, 248.
gradus, 45, 254.
Gravitation, 149, 157, 158, 166, 198.
  See also Physical fields.
Ground:
  Of observed behavior, 146–7, 164.
  God as Ground of the world-order, 147, 239, 249.
"Group mind," 100.
Growth, personal, see Selfhood, Conditions, etc.
Guidance, 6, 39, 53, 79, 116, 177 f., 187, 207.
"Guidance," divine, 57, 244, 245.

Habits, 64, 103, 185, 191–2, 219–20.
Harmony, 184, 193, 201, 247.
Health, healthy, 49, 58, 97–8, 122 f., 133, 167, 199, 211, 223, 230.
Hedonism, 48, 216.
History, human, 3–5, 37–9, 142–3, 178, 242 ff.
Hope, 10, 58, 85, 88, 95, 126, 136, 220, 235.
Hormones, 82, 160.
Humanism, Humanist, 98.
  Literary connoisseurship, 22, 42, 49.
  Humanitarianism, 6, 47, 92.
  Anti-theism, 4, 6, 29, 81, 93.
Humility, 32, 171, 246, 256.
Humor, 214.
Hypothesis, 113, 158, 183.
  Cosmological hypotheses, 175–8.

Ideal (vs. actual), 73, 75, 76, 166 ff., 210–11.
Idealism:
  Moral, 32, 79 ff., 97–8, 126, 217, 219, 235.
  Metaphysical, 8, 9, 112, 118, 202.
  Epistemological, 118, 274.
Ideals, see Forms.
Idolatry, 22, 92 f., 213.
Ignorance, 92, 181, 183, 184, 185, 187, 191, 203, 248.
Imagination, 5, 61, 63, 92, 118, 121–2, 171, 191, 209, 243.
Immaturity, 73, 90–91, 191–2.

General Index

Imperialism, 26, 65.
Impiety, 9, 33, 81, 93 f.
Improbable, improbability, **175-6**.
  See also *Probable*.
Impulse, 119, 191, 197.
Inclination, 42, 52, 261, 262-3.
Incompatible, incompatibility, 167, 194, 201-3, 217.
Indeterminacy, 187, 188, 195, 247, 248.
  See also *Contingency, Uncertainty relations*.
Individual, individuality, 56 ff., **71**, 100, 127, 131, 180, 195, 209, 216.
Individualism, 23, 25-6, 46-7, **62**, 70, 100, 196, 207.
Industrial Revolution, 26, 59.
Industry, modern, 23, 61 ff., **226-7**.
Inertia, 82, 194, 202 f.
Infinite, infinity, 150, 151, 175, 185-6, 187, 193, 276.
Information, conveyance of, 61, 66, *127-130*, 242-4 (cf. 245).
Inspiration, 196-7.
Insurgency, 21, 32, 52 f., 221 ff., 223, 230 ff., 234.
Integration, 111-112, 121-3, 141, 161, 169, 216-17, 220.
Integrity, 59, 79, 89 f., 211.
Intelligence, 9, 61, 71, 79, 111, 203.
Intelligible, intelligibility, 55, 99, 113, 145, 185, 211, 242.
Interrelatedness, 34-5, 49, 71, 104, 117, 121, 166, 168, 169 f., 185, 238.
Intuition, 36, 145, 184-5, 243.

Justice, 190, 193, 223, 224, 226, 229, 242, 248.

Kantian thought, 16, 111, **118-19**, 147-8.
Kingdom of God, 32, 190.
Knowledge, 181.
  General character of, 145-8, etc.
  Basic to work, 89-90, 125-6.
  Of other selves, 131-6.
  Of God, 145-8, 174-5, 240-41.
  Divine knowledge, 183-9, 198.

Laissez faire, 53, 61-2.
Law:
  Human, 63, 176, 221.

Natural, 42, **55**, **62**, 176-7, **245**.
  Divine, 19, 44, 50 f.
Leadership, 196-7, 200, 225-6.
Learning, 55-6, 58 f., 79 f., 99, 103-4, 112, 122, 126, 129 f., 162, 163, 173, 187, 203, 235-6.
Leisure, 83, 103-4, 217.
Lethargy, 82-3, 91, 181.
Liberal, liberalism, 4, 6-9, 92.
Light, 153, 154, 156-7, 184, 280.
Limitations:
  Upon man, 57, 77, 116, 183-4, 185, 191, 192.
  Upon God's activity, 188-9, 192-6, 201-4.
Location, locus, 169, 183, 185, 280.
Logic, 8, 35, 42, 76, 133, 136, 145, 147-8, 156, 166 f., 174, 176, 181, 202, 235, 278, 281.
Logos, 135.
Loss:
  Economic, 64.
  Personal, 239.
Love, 18, 46, 50 f., 53, 89-90, 92-3, 95, 96-8, 126, 136, 190, 193, *211-13*, 215, 220.
Loyalty, 45, 63, 70, 191.
Lutheran, Lutheranism, **21-22**, **39**, 49.

Machines, 30 f., *61-6*, *101-5*, **217**.
Man:
  Animal, world-child, 97-8, **100**, 101, 132, 169-170, 212.
  Knower, 117-123.
  Critic, 54, 97, 170.
  Worker, 54 ff., 123-7, *170*-**71**.
  Social being, 59, *127-139*.
  Worshiper, 171, *237-240*.
  Clue to world-order, 172-3.
  See also *Anthropic viewpoint*.
Martyrs, 58, 219, 220, 243.
Marxian, Marxism, 6, 8-10, 29, **53**, 93, 177-8, 229, 285.
Mathematics, mathematical, **156**, **166** f., 277, 278, 281.
  See also *Geometries*.
Matter:
  Physical, 140, 153, 154-6, **182**, 194, 241.
  Abstract (*hylē*), 195.
Measuring rods, 152, 153, **156-7**.

General Index

Organization:
Of materials, 113–16, 124 ff.
Of individual experience, 117–123.
Of persons in society, 63, 136–8, 196–7.
Of the cosmos, 139–144, 201–4, and Chap. IV, *passim.*
See also *Mind, World-order, Flux, Forms, Work.*
Organizations for social change, 231 f.
Orientation, 3, 11, 73, 79, 200, 238, 248.
Otherness, 51, 131, 132–3, 136, 197–8, 199.
"Ought to be," 50, 73, 74, 75, 94, 190, 218, 247, 248.
"Over-production," 30 f., 64–5, 104–5.

Paradox, 49, 50 ff., 58, 73, 94, 203.
Participation, 60, 63, 71, 80, 104, 137–8, 139, 168, 207, 231, 242.
Pattern, 114, 118, 121, 149, 153, 159, 167, 181.
See also *Form, Structure.*
Perceptible events, 128, 145, 150, 153, 166, 178, 182.
Perception, 110 f., 118, 121, 243–4.
See also *Apprehension, Sentiency,* etc.
Perfection, 94, 193.
"Counsels of," 18, 19, 254.
"Life of," 18, 19, 46, 50.
Persuasion, 116, 137, 218, 219, 231, 248.
Pessimism, 88.
Regarding man, *96–101,* 265, 266 f.
Regarding the world, 75.
Physical fields, 149, 153, 155, 158.
Gravitational, 153, 154, 182.
Electromagnetic, 120, 154, 182, 184–5.
See also *Fields of force.*
Piety, 12, 15 ff., 26, 54, 94, 158, 190, 213.
Plasticity:
Of materials, 116. 205.
Of environment, 79, 163.
Of growing things, 79–80.
Platonism, 35, 148, 195, 260.
Play, 54–5, 103, 116, 137, *214–17.*
Competitive sport, 54–5, 87.

Pleasure, 49, 55, 56, 167, 262.
Pluralism, plurality, 8, 34, 247.
Poets, poetry, 39, 201, 211–12, 243, 245.
Police duty, 234, 286.
Population growth, 65–7, 230, 263–4.
Positivism, 41, 119, 132, 146, 278.
Possibilities, see *Forms.*
Postulates, 150–52.
"Postulational method," 275 n. 10, 278.
Power, 193, 198, 204, 227–8, 243.
Predestination, 17, 40, 46–7, 50–53, 55, 57.
Presence:
Of another self, 131 ff., 147, 197, 244, 245.
Of God, 171, 207, 238, 239–40, 244–5, 248.
Prestige, 55, 56, 210.
Pretense, pretentiousness, 80, 86–7, 91, 94.
Primitive life, 11, 13 f., 60.
See also *Civilization, Wholeness, Barbarism.*
Privacy, 50, 128, 130–31, 138–9, 238.
Probable, probability, 155, 165, 176, 194, 270.
Production, economic, 30 f., 49–50, 62 ff.
Profit, 55, 56, 67–9.
Progress, 9, 37, 38, 49, 56, 61, 62, 140, 142.
"Projection," 133.
See also *"Wishful thinking."*
Proletariat, 99, 225, 226, 266–7.
"Dictatorship of," 99 f., 222, 225, 226, 227.
Propaganda, deceptive, 106, 263 n. 48.
Prophet, prophetic, 4, 12, 14, 173, 243.
Protestant, Protestantism, 15–28, 31, 32, 36, 39 f., 42–53.
Protons, 140, 154, 184 f.
Providence, 40 ff., 55, 261.
Providential order, 20, 43, 49, 50 ff., 253.
Psychasthenia, 133.
Public life, 50, 130–31, 138–9.
Public sentiment, 61, 66.
Puritan, Puritanism, 16, 23–4, 26, 29, 30, 215–16, 257.

General Index

Purpose, purposive action:
  Human, 58, 120, 169, 170, 180, 182.
  Divine, *189–192.*
  "Unconscious purpose," 143, 177–8.

Quietism, 22, 95–6, 246.

Race, 81, 99, 100, 268.
Radical transcendence, 139, 197 f.
Random movement, 175–7, 178, 194.
Realism, 53–4, 78, 98, 217, 235.
  Native, animal, 132, 199, 274.
  Critical, 126, 132–3, 146–8, 199, 211, 213–14, 271–2, 274.
  Metaphysical, 8, 202, 249.
  Religious, theological, 4, 22, 29, 38, *74–8,* 81, 101, 235.
  "Bread-and-butter realism," 54, 92, 94.
  See also *Complacency.*
Reason, 42, 43, 56, 145, 233, 236, 262.
Reconciliation, 171, 191, 192, 240, 242, 247.
Reconstruction, social, 21, 77, 207–8, 209, *217–237.*
Redintegration, 112, 162.
Reformation, Protestant, 20–22, 45.
Reformers, Protestant, 20–22, 39, 43, 44, 48, 50, 52, 254.
Regeneration, 237–8, 278.
Regression:
  Individual, 121–2, 214.
  Social, 13, 14, 83, 228–9, 235.
Relaxation, 49, 103, 215 f.
Relevant, relevance, 28 ff., 78, 121–2, 172, 182, 187, 189, 205, 210.
Religion, 11, 74, 171, 191, 206–7, 212–13.
  See also *Worship, Work, Mysticism, Belief in God, Vocation.*
Religious realism, see *Realism.*
Repentance, 31, 43–4, 48, 237–8, 248.
Reproduction, 96, 161.
Response, 57, 122–3, 129–130, 132, 161 f., 197, 200, 203, 206, 242, 248.
Responsible, responsibility:
  Personal, 54 ff., 80, 82, 89–90.
  Social, 70, 91, 224–5, 233–5.
Revelation, 36, 42, 135, *172–3,* 179, **238, 242–5.**

Revolution, revolutionism, 88, 173, *221–9,* 285–6.
Rigidity, 64, 67, 116, 166 f.
  Assumed, in ideal measuring rods, 152.
  Doubtful, in actual measuring rods, 156–7.
  In individual living, 83–4, 209.
  See also *Habits.*
  In social behavior, 64, 70, 210, 217, 230, 268.
  As factor in productive work, including world-making, 124–5, 193–4, 201–4.
Romantic, romanticism, 26, 81, 100, 207, 222, 225.
Ruf, 19, 254, 255.
Russia, 91, 104, 225–6, 228, 257, 266, 286.

Sagacity, 38, 122, 126, 129 f., 132, 136, 173, 238, 242 ff.
Salvation, 21, 31, 40, 46–7, 145, 248.
Satisfaction, 58, 63, 70, 100, 209, 248.
  Immediate, 104, 116–17, 121–2, 214 f.
  Remote, 58, 115, 116–17, 216.
Schizophrenia, 121–2.
Sciences, scientists, 3, 5–6, 22, 120, 173, 176, 243, 245.
Scotism, 41.
Scribes, 173.
Scriptures, 42, 43, 51, 245, 253, 255, 260.
  See also *Bible.*
Sects, sectaries, 3, 22, 23, 25, 45, 46, 47, 48.
Secularism, 22, 26–7, 31, 38, 48.
Secularization, 12, 24–7.
"Secular life" (*vs.* "spiritual life"), 21, 47.
Selection:
  Involved in attention, 120, 172–3.
  Involved in determinate nature of God, 187–192.
Self, private and public, 130–31, 138–9.
Self-commitment, 18–19, 77 f., 79, 171, 239–40.
Selfhood:
  Character of, *117–139,* 180–81.

General Index

Development of, 56–9, 63, 73, 91–3, 99, 103–4, 132–3, 180–81.
Communication of, *130–36*.
Self-indulgence, 48, 65–6, 82.
Self-transcendence, 89–90, 95.
Senescence, 84, 91–3.
Sense organs, 160, 184, 185.
Sentiency, sentient, 110, 132, 201, 281.
Separation, separateness, 12–15, 32–3, 34–6, 43 ff.
Sham, falsehood, 12, 15, 28, 47, 59, 79, 80 f., 86–7, 93, 105–6, 233.
Signals, 127–130, 133, 242 ff.
Sin, 43–4, 80–84, 181, 237–8, 248.
Original sin, 82 f., 91.
Skeptic, skepticism, 4, 6, 42, 75, 77 f., 132 f., 146, 218.
Skill, 59, 89–90, 116, 125–6, 130, 195.
Social control, 100, 136–7.
See also *Collectivism*.
Socialism, 222, 223.
Social life, see *Mind, Selfhood,* etc.
Solipsism, 133.
Soul (*psychē*), 110 f.
Sovereignty of God, 179, 186, 192, 195, 235, 236–7.
Space, spaces:
Abstract, 150–52, 275.
Actual, 149, 153, 159, 194.
Space-time, 140, 153, 154, 158, 169, 175, 182, 183, 184, 189, 191, 194, 275–6, 280.
"Specious present," 117, 120, 185.
Spinoza's thought, 93, 190 f., 240 f., 249, 279–80, 282.
Spirit:
Of men, 42, 47, 83, 190, 197.
Of God, 193, 200, 241.
"Spiritual life," 47, 50, 254.
Stable, stability, 121, 141, 158, 159, 162–5.
State, political, 32, 33, 81, 221.
Statistical:
Method, 155, 264, 270.
Laws, 155, 158.
status, 255, 262.
Stimuli, 110, 114, 122, 123, 183.
See also *Cue-stimuli.*
Stimulus-response relation, 55, 79–80, 110, 120, 122 f., 125, 126, 132–3, 161–2, 169 f., 238.

Stoic, Stoicism, 44, 93, 279 f.
Strikes, 227, 231.
Structure, 99, 157–8, 161, 167, 181, 276.
Sub-atomic events, 154, 155, 158, 175–6.
Subhuman life and behavior, 54, 83, 90 f., 96–8, 236, 262.
Subject:
Of behavior, 123–7, 198, 199.
See also *Agent.*
Of experience, 117–123, 180–81, 198, 199.
See also *Ego.*
Subjectivism, 55, 80, 95, 99, 180.
Sublime, the, 239, 286.
"Sufficient ground," 146–7.
"Sufficient reason, principle of," 145, 146, 261.
Summaries, 71–2, 74, 84, 107–8, 122–3, 126–7, 138–9.
Supply and demand, 30 f., 62, 64, 67 f.
Symbol, symbolism, 121, 190, 205, 219, 270, 281.
Symbolic behavior, 112, 115, 120, 167.
Symbols in communication, 115, 127–130, 134–5.
Symbols and apprehension of what is not immediately and actually present, 113–15, 126–7, 162, 166, 185.
Synthesis:
Integration, 111–12, 118–122.
As speculative method, 179–180, 183.

Tabus, 86, 210, 217.
Tensions, 35, 36, 38 f., 73–4, 94, 119–122, 131, 138–9, 157–9, 164–5, 169–171, 192–6, 199–200, 201–4, 231–2, 237–240, 241–9.
Terrorism, 224, 227, 228, 234.
Theology:
Task of, 11, 31, 35 f., 39, 73 f., 95 f., 105, 146–7, 174.
Traditional Christian, 17–21, 40–53, 55, 57, 107, 145–8, 174, 192 f., 240–42, 243.
See also *Augustinianism, Thomism,* etc.

General Index

Philosophical, 41-3, 51, 76, 145-8, 254, 275.
Negative, 249.
Thomism, 41-3, 51, 52, 57-8, 107, 145-8, 253-4, 255, 261, 262-3 (Antoninus of Florence).
Thought, 110 f., 119, 121, 132, 180, 183.
Time, physical, 153, 194.
"Time-cone," 183, 186, 280.
"Time-span," 185-6, 241, 280.
Transcendence:
  Radical, absolute, 139, 197-8.
  Relative, communicative, 139, 198.
Truth, 97, 99, 190, 214, 248.

Uncertainty relations, 156.
Unemployment, 30 f., 83, 104-5.
Unexpectedness, 131, 187, 199.
Unfinished universe, 54, 148, 159, 179, 240.
Unity, 34-5, 43 ff., 60, 61, 111, 117 ff., 131, 180-81.

Value, 37, 73 f., 81, 89, 96 ff., 143, 167-8, 171, 207, 210.
Variable, variability, 121, 141, 142, 156, 158, 162-5.
Variation, 159, 163, 164, 201.
via antiqua, 41, 42.
via moderna, 41, 43.
Violence, 82-3, 84, 91, 221, 223-5, 228-9, 232, 233, 235.
visio Dei, 19, 145, 254.
  See also *Mysticism*.
vocatio, 17, 18, 19, 20, 254, 255, 256.
vocation, 20, 256.
Vocation:
  Christian doctrine of, *17-24, 39-53*, 215-16, 253-260.
  Divine election, 17, 40, 46-7, 51 f.
  Earthly calling, 18 ff. 46-7, 49, 50, 74.
  Secularization of, 24-28.
  Objections to doctrine, *24-31*.
  Religious concept of, restated:
    As implied in everyday work, *53-72*, 200, 222-3, 240 242, 248.
    As constant summons to responsible, contributive liv-

ing, 54-5, 60, 61, 64-72, 163, 200, 216-17, 237-8, 246-8, 259 (*Anspruch*).
  See also *vocatio, Beruf, Ruf, Work, Calling, Vocational idealism*, etc.
Vocational idealism, *79-84*, 107.
Vocational realism, *84-107*.
War, 14, 53, 65, 72, 91, 106, 217, 225, 228-9, 234.
  Civil war, 221, 223, 227, 232-3.
Waste, 58, 91, 207, 209, 226-7.
Wave, wave bundle, 156, 158, 182, 184-5, 280.
Wholeness:
  Of individual life, 44-5.
  Of primitive life, 12, 47, 59-61, 63, 206.
  Needed in modern living, 13-15, 59-71, 74, 232, 242.
Will:
  Of man, 9, 44, 196, 245, 246.
  Of God, 20, 51 f., 190, 192, 196, 241, 242, 247, 248.
Wisdom:
  Human, 73, 125, 190, 191, 205, 245.
  Divine, 187, 189, 191, 192, 243.
Wishes, "wishful thinking," 55, 58, 88, 131, 132-3, 182, 191, 199, 205, 208, 222, 227-9.
Word, words:
  Human language, 86, 114, 125-6, 134-5, 198, 205, 219, 240 f.
  Word of God, 10, 16, 17, 31 f., 51, 242-3, 245, 248, 253, 259.
  See also *Communication, Revelation*.
Work, 54, 137, 182.
  Correlate of worship, 12, 20, 24, 206-7, 240.
  Basic to human living, 54 ff., 83.
  Ethic of, 79-84.
  Actual character of, today, 30 f., 84-96.
  Religious implications of, 12, 19, 94-96.
  As actualization of possibilities and of values, 90, 107, 116, 124-5, 171, 179, 201-4, 210-211.
  See also *Vocation, Basic pattern of work, World-making*, etc.

General Index

Workmanship, 89, 95, 212.

World-affirmation, 48–9, 213.

World-denial, 18, 48–50, 213.
    See also *Asceticism*.

World-lines, 153, 183.

World-making, 170, 179, *201–204*.
    See also *Creation, God, Work*.

World-order, 42, 71–2, 158, 172, 189, 238–9, 246–7.

World polity, 66–7.

Worship, 171, 211, 278.
    Correlate to work, 11, 20, 95, 206–7, 240.
    Separation of, from everyday life, 12–15, 74.
    Occasions of, 237–9.
    Character of, 213, 239–240.

Worth, 29, 38, 49, 76, 93, 101, 131, 213, 219.
    See also *Good, Value, "Ought to Be," Ideals*.